Louis Zukofsky
and the Transformation
of a Modern American Poetics

Louis Zukofsky

and the Transformation
of a Modern American Poetics

Sandra Kumamoto Stanley

University of California Press

Berkeley / Los Angeles / London

University of California Press
Berkeley and Los Angeles, California

University of California Press, Ltd.
London, England

Library of Congress Cataloging-in-Publication Data

Stanley, Sandra Kumamoto.
  Louis Zukofsky and the transformation of a modern American poetics / Sandra
  Kumamoto Stanley.
      p.   cm.
  Includes bibliographical references and index.
  ISBN 0-520-07357-6 (alk. paper)
    1. Zukofsky, Louis, 1904–1978—Criticism and interpretation.   2. American
  poetry—20th century—History and criticism.   3. Aesthetics, American.
  4. Poetics.   I. Title.
  PS3549.U47Z85   1994
  811'.52—dc20   93-11118
                                                                      CIP

Printed in the United States of America

9 8 7 6 5 4 3 2 1

Contents

Acknowledgments

I wish first to thank Marjorie Perloff and Jay Martin, two of my intellectual mentors who significantly influenced my thinking about American and Modern literature. My deepest gratitude goes to Marjorie Perloff, for without her steady encouragement and excellent guidance, I would never have written this work; this book is dedicated to her. I would also like to thank all my friends—especially Bob Pincus, John Tomas, Kathy Lundeen, Marilyn Moss, Wendy Furman, Eunice Howe, and Charles Adams—who kindly helped me while I was working on different stages of my book.

I would like to express my appreciation to the readers and editors from the University of California Press. My editors William Mc-Clung, Douglas Abrams Arava, and Ethan Michaels have all proven to be both patient and helpful; I would especially like to thank my project editors, Mark Pentecost and Tony Hicks, and copy editor, Dan Gunter, who provided me with helpful advice and careful assistance in the final stages of the book's publication. I am indebted to all those who have written works on Zukofsky—especially Barry Ahearn, Burton Hatlen, and Hugh Kenner. I am grateful to the librarians of the Harry Ransom Research Center at the University of Texas, and I would like to extend a special thanks to Cathy Henderson for her assistance with the Louis Zukofsky Collection. My own university, California State University at Northridge, generously provided me with a grant allowing me some release time to work on the final stages of the book's publication. I also wish to thank Paul Zukofsky not only for granting permission to use material from his father's archives but also for taking the time to read my manuscript and to give me biographical information that helped to improve the accuracy of my work. Needless to say, although many people assisted me in my endeavors, any errors in my work are solely my responsibility.

Finally, I would like to thank my family, who have steadfastly supported me. I am deeply grateful for their love and guidance; although they were often puzzled by my endeavors, they, too, had a great influence upon this book, for they helped to shape the person behind the words.

Grateful acknowledgment is also made to the following:

Harvard University Press and Faber and Faber Ltd., for permission to quote from *The Use of Poetry and the Use of Criticism*, copyright 1933, 1961, by T. S. Eliot.

Liveright Publishing Corporation and W. W. Norton and Co. Ltd., for permission to quote "of evident invisibles" from E. E. Cummings, *Complete Poems, 1904–1962*, copyright 1976 by the Trustees for the E. E. Cummings Trust.

The Johns Hopkins University Press, for permission to quote from *The Complete Short Poetry of Louis Zukofsky*, copyright 1991 by Paul Zukofsky.

New Directions Publishing Corporation, for permission to quote from *Selected Cantos*, copyright 1934, 1937, 1940, 1948, 1956, 1959, 1962, 1963, 1966, and 1968 by Ezra Pound; *Selected Poems of Ezra Pound*, copyright 1920, 1934, and 1937 by Ezra Pound; and "Old Zuk," copyright 1957 by Ezra Pound.

New Directions Publishing Corporation, for permission to quote from *The Autobiography of William Carlos Williams*, copyright 1948, 1951 by William Carlos Williams; *The Collected Poems*, volume I, *1909–1939*, copyright 1938 by New Directions, copyright 1982, 1986 by William Eric Williams and Paul H. Williams; *Paterson*, copyright 1946, 1948, 1949, 1958 by William Carlos Williams, copyright 1992 by William Eric Williams and Paul H. Williams; and *Selected Essays*, copyright 1954 by William Carlos Williams.

Sun & Moon Press, for permission to quote from pp. 50, 51, and 71 of *Content's Dream*, copyright 1986 by Charles Bernstein.

Charles Bernstein, for permission to quote from *The L=A=N=*

$G=U=A=G=E$ *Book,* copyright 1984 by Bruce Andrews and Charles Bernstein.

Paul Zukofsky, for permission to quote from Louis Zukofsky's *"A"*, published by the University of California Press, copyright 1978 by Celia Zukofsky and Louis Zukofsky, and from the Louis Zukofsky Collection located at the Harry Ransom Humanities Research Center, University of Texas at Austin. Published and unpublished Zukofsky materials appear with the permission of Paul Zukofsky; Zukofsky material may not be quoted from this book by third parties without the express permission of Paul Zukofsky.

The editor of the *Journal of Modern Literature,* for permission to reprint portions of chapter 5 that appeared as "The Link Between Williams and Zukofsky" in *JML* 17, no. 1 (Summer 1990).

September 1992
Los Angeles, California

Introduction:
Among American Friends

> In all the periods before things had been said . . . but never been explained. So they began to explain.
>
> Gertrude Stein, *What Is English Literature?*
> as quoted by Celia Zukofsky in *American Friends*

In 1988 Harry Gilonis edited a collection of poems entitled *Louis Zukofsky, or whoever someone else thought he was*. Gilonis takes his title from a letter in which Zukofsky, responding to an inquiry from John Seed, writes, "I may show some interest in 'LZ,' whoever someone else thought he was."[1] Both Zukofsky and Gilonis recognize that no unified, transcendent, unmediated "I" exists; when we seek to recover "LZ," we recover bits and pieces of Zukofsky's life and writings, all filtered through and reconstructed in our minds. Like his poetry, "LZ" is a signifier that can be deconstructed and reconstructed in multiple ways, but ultimately this signifier resists being equated with a single, determinate truth, a transcendental signified. In fact, on the cover graphic of Gilonis's book, artist Ian Robinson, in his "Portrait of Louis Zukofsky," depicts "LZ" not as an "I"—a realistic portrait of the artist—but as an "eye"—an unblinking, hawklike eye surrounded by a collage of texts. Robinson's "Portrait" seems to be a visual play on a title from one of Zukofsky's own books of poems—*I's (pronounced eyes)*—which suggests that the act of being is not only the act of seeing but also the act of linguistic free play. In Gilonis's book, subtitled a "collection of responses to Louis Zukofsky," a group of poets, including Charles Bernstein and Robert Creeley, pay homage to Zukofsky by writing poems echoing his style and subject matter. Their poems, often including fragments from Zukofsky's own poems, consist of a pastiche of their responses to the poet's identity: Zukofsky the poet-musician, Zukofsky the Objectivist, Zukofsky the translator, Zukofsky the political poet, Zukofsky the son of Russian immigrant Jews, Zukofsky the husband of Celia and father of Paul. As such, they fittingly reconstruct a collage of texts, recovering not the artist but their mediated sense of the artist, not a coherently defined self but a "plurality of other texts."[2]

I regard my own text as yet another form of a singular response to Zukofsky's works. When I first read Louis Zukofsky's poems, I had assumed that this poet and his challenging poetry occupied a peripheral place in twentieth-century American poetry. In fact, any quick survey of poetry anthologies, even today, would support such an assumption, for we would discover at best an obligatory mention of Zukofsky as an Objectivist poet, and at worst simply no mention at all of this poet who dedicated his life to his craft. In the course of my studies—which led me to the Zukofsky archives at the Harry Ransom Humanities Research Center—I came to see that this man on the margins of American literary life actually occupied a pivotal position in the development of twentieth-century American poetry.

Like his fellow poet Ezra Pound, Zukofsky self-consciously saw himself as a participant in the making of a modern American poetics; but unlike Pound, Zukofsky, the ghetto-born son of immigrant Russian Jews, was keenly aware of his marginal position in society. Born in 1904 on the Lower East Side of New York, Zukofsky witnessed the century's many political and social upheavals: the Russian revolution, the Great Depression, two world wars, and accelerated urban and technological growth. At home with the multiple voices of his age, Zukofsky could embrace both Henry Adams and Karl Marx, both Ezra Pound and Yehoash, both Einstein and Krazy Kat. Graduating from Columbia at the age of twenty, Zukofsky came away armed with the education of the elite, but he all too acutely realized that his home was the New York ghetto. In *Poem beginning "The"*, Zukofsky, aware that the university system has provided him with the tools from "the master's house," articulates an oppositional agenda:

258   The villainy they teach me I will execute
259   And it shall go hard with them,
260   For I'll better the instruction,
261   Having learned, so to speak, in their
         colleges.[3]

Zukofsky, however, would realize his oppositional stance not in a radical political life but in a radical poetics. In the 1920s he became an avid reader and student of the Modernist poets, absorbing everything he could about these "revolutionaries of the word" and developing significant relationships with Ezra Pound and William Carlos Williams. In a very short time, student Zukofsky graduated from his self-constructed school, transforming Modernist theory into a poetics of his own—a poetics that would foreground language. Championing the importance of the little words such as *a* and *the*, Zukofsky effected his own proletarian "revolution of the word" by highlighting the materiality of language and refusing to reduce language to a commodity controlled by an authorial/authoritarian self. His experimentation with the musicality and materiality of language led him to revise the relationship between sign and substance, word and prescribed meaning. Zukofsky, however, did not reduce language to a self-referential game divorcing the word from the world; Zukofsky realized that the word exists in the world and, more important, that the world exists in the word.

Focusing on a wide range of subjects, from the Marxist class struggle to his own domestic life, Zukofsky spent decades writing his epic poem *"A"*. Regarded as eccentric and difficult, Zukofsky's work was ignored by both academia and a popular audience. Increasingly, Zukofsky felt isolated; in order to see his poetry in print, he was forced to publish several of his works himself. In the latter part of his life, Zukofsky achieved a modest and belated success: in the 1960s Norton published several of his works, and the poet won an award from the Longview Foundation. Although much of Zukofsky's life had been plagued by obscurity, he did find a small and faithful audience among a number of younger poets, including Lorine Niedecker and the Black Mountain poets. Among the Black Mountain school, Robert Creeley especially recognized Zukofsky's historical importance, noting that the poet served as a link between the "poetry of the Twenties and Thirties" and the Black Mountain and Projectivist poets. In the 1970s a number of poets—under the loose designation of the Language poets—claimed Zukofsky as one of the significant precursors to their own poetics, which focuses on how language itself can constitute meaning. This new generation of poets recognized Zukofsky's historical importance as a poet who links the Modernist revolution with a postmodern aesthetics.[4]

Cary Nelson has pointed out that literary critics never engage in an "innocent process of recovery": "We recover what we are culturally and psychologically prepared to recover and what we 'recover' we necessarily rewrite, giving it meanings that are inescapably contemporary, giving it a new discursive life in the present, a life it cannot have had before."[5] At best, Zukofsky criticism has been quite spotty. Many Zukofsky critics begin their works, as I have, with a lament—now almost a convention of Zukofsky criticism—of this poet's continued obscurity. Why this obscurity? In *A History of Modern Poetry*, David Perkins honestly and earnestly describes his own dilemma in confronting Zukofsky's works. As a reader familiar with the hidden intricacies of Joyce and Mallarmé, Perkins approaches Zukofsky's own intricate work "with a more than usually vigilant, ingenious and paranoiac state of mind"; suspending judgment of Zukofsky's work, he often wonders if he has missed Zukofsky's intended meaning: "In the presence of the enormously painstaking and esoteric, we cannot easily suspect ordinary dull writing."[6] Some, like Perkins, might argue that Zukofsky's difficult work is suspect; others might argue that we are only now "culturally and psychologically prepared to recover" this man's work. In an interview with Barry Ahearn, Celia Zukofsky once commented, "Well, you know, Louis always felt, and I did too, that the artist is almost prophetic. And will put something down which seems so difficult and so impossible, and then, twenty years later, not quite that difficult or impossible to understand."[7]

With an eye to his place in "lecherery history," Zukofsky proved to be his own best literary historian. He saved a voluminous amount of letters and manuscripts, many of which can now be found in the Louis Zukofsky archives at the University of Texas at Austin. During his lifetime, fellow poets such as William Carlos Williams, Robert Creeley, and Cid Corman reviewed and commented on his work. In the 1970s Zukofsky's poetry began to attract more and more attention from academia—specifically those interested in the Pound-Williams tradition. Interest in Zukofsky has focused on two aspects:

his formalist/Objectivist innovations and his political interest in the Other, indicated by his exploration of a Marxist poetics and his interest in those disempowered by the predominant culture. For examples of these two strains, we might look at Hugh Kenner and Marcus Klein, who identify Zukofsky as a distinctly American poet either in terms of language or historical situation. Although Kenner has been a long-time advocate of Zukofsky's work and Klein mentions Zukofsky only in passing, both these authors write literary histories that adumbrate Zukofsky's significance in the context of American literature in the twentieth century. In *A Homemade World* Kenner writes of Zukofsky's lengthy epic poem *"A"*: "this life's work of a prickly Brooklyn Jew who might have been born in Russia but for *pogroms*, and spent decades teaching young engineers to manage less clumsily a language he himself learned only after he'd learned Yiddish, this long intent eccentric unread game with its homemade rules seems as intensely indigenous an artifact as American ink and paper have ever transcribed."[8] Kenner locates the "American-ness" of Zukofsky as poet in Zukofsky's language—a language born of "classroom accuracies." In *Foreigners* Marcus Klein writes that the American literature of this century has been created by "the barbarians," those Americans situated outside the elite Modernist tradition of Eliot, Pound, Stevens, Hemingway, and Fitzgerald. These Americans—writers such as Nathanael West, Richard Wright, Delmore Schwartz, and Louis Zukofsky—constructed an American literature out of the need to confront an American culture unavailable to them "for mere acceptance."[9] Klein locates the particular American sensibility of these writers in historical, social, and political constructs.

Critics who align Zukofsky with the Pound tradition have done the most work on the poet. Kenner, the author of the *Pound Era*, was the most prominent critic in the 1970s to champion Zukofsky's work. Right after the poet's death in the late 1970s, Carroll Terrell edited the first collection of essays on Zukofsky—under the auspices of *Paideuma*, a journal devoted to Pound scholarship whose editorial board includes Hugh Kenner. Moreover, Barry Ahearn, a student of Kenner, wrote the first major published book on Zukofsky: *Zukofsky's "A": An Introduction*.[10] Other scholars, such as

Marjorie Perloff and Laszlo K. Géfin, have included Zukofsky in works concerning Pound's influence on younger poets, especially through his ideogrammic style.[11] To date, *Sagetrieb*, a journal devoted to poets in the Pound–H. D.–Williams tradition, has published the most articles on Zukofsky.

In the 1980s more critics, such as Burton Hatlen and Edward Schelb, have expressed interest in Zukofsky as a political poet—an interest that parallels the critical demands of the last years.[12] As Gerald Graff has noted, "In the last decade, virtually every phase of American literature has been reinterpreted in political terms."[13] Essays on Zukofsky have appeared in such works as Eric Homberger's *American Writers and Radical Politics,* Ralph Bogardus and Fred Hobson's *Literature at the Barricades,* and Norman Finkelstein's *Utopian Moment in Contemporary American Poetry.*[14] Scholars interested in Zukofsky's political poetry focus on the poetry he wrote in the 1930s and his relationship to such politically committed Objectivist poets as George Oppen, Charles Reznikoff, and Carl Rakosi. As Homberger notes, a number of the Objectivists sympathized with left-wing politics, although many Depression-era Communist critics, valuing social realism, tended to be hostile to the Objectivist brand of avant-garde poetry. Today, some of the most interesting critical work on Zukofsky is written by poets—specifically the Language poets—who are interested in both Zukofsky's formalist innovations and his oppositional politics, in both the poet's language and his social role. Influenced by Marxist and poststructuralist theories, such Language poets as Charles Bernstein and Ron Silliman have highlighted Zukofsky's contribution to twentieth-century poetry in such works as *The L=A=N=G=U=A=G=E Book* and in non-mainstream little magazines.

The two books on Zukofsky—by Barry Ahearn and Michele Leggott—provide very helpful close readings of Zukofsky's works. Ahearn focuses on Zukofsky's epic poem *"A",* highlighting various autobiographical developments in the poet's life—tracing Zukofsky from a young poet, fascinated by Apollinaire and the collage technique, to a reclusive Ulysses figure who turns to his family as the resolution of his epic search. Leggott, focusing on Zukofsky's *80*

Flowers, engages in an exegesis (characteristic of much Pound scholarship) of Zukofsky's last book of poems.[15] Although such works are important, I want to step back and see Zukofsky from another vantage point—as a reader, writer, and innovator of twentieth-century American poetry. What contribution has Zukofsky made to American poetry? My methodology is simple: by examining how Zukofsky reads his fellow Modernists—specifically Henry Adams, T. S. Eliot, Ezra Pound, and William Carlos Williams (his American friends)—I explore how Zukofsky, working out of the vocabulary of his predecessors, created his own poetics. In part, I borrow my methodology from Celia Zukofsky, Louis Zukofsky's wife.

In 1979, a year after Louis Zukofsky's death, Celia Zukofsky published *American Friends,* a compilation of extracts from the works of seventy-five American writers and from Zukofsky's own poetry and prose responding to their works. Mrs. Zukofsky dedicated the work "to Louis on his seventy-fifth birthday":

> The following contents are a result of sorting books, faded pages and old notes. It is as Americans that Louis read most meaning into the words of these "friends."
> The L. Z. extracts are my impression of how one human being *may* have operated with such love and perfection.[16]

Mrs. Zukofsky's dedication picks up much of the cadence of her husband's language, a language that makes one stop, listen, ponder. In choosing a list of seventy-five writers to celebrate Zukofsky's seventy-fifth birthday, she echoes her own husband's love of contingent numerology that invokes both the artist's choice and a certain mathematical providence. She picks American writers, from Puritan poets to modern philosophers, who are American friends because Zukofsky had read their works. For Zukofsky, the act of reading was an act of communion: "The contingency of one poet reading another that way makes for a kind of friendship which is exempt from all the vicissitudes and changes and tempers that are involved in friendship."[17]

My work explores both Zukofsky's relationship to a select number of modern American friends who influenced his poetics and

Zukofsky's own legacy to contemporary American writers. As Mrs.
Zukofsky has stated, "It is as Americans that Louis read most
meaning into the works of these 'friends' "; I, too, would like to
perceive Zukofsky within the context of his American friendships.

In my first chapter, "Zukofsky and the Act of Reading," I concen-
trate not only on Zukofsky's poetry but also on his critical works. I
believe that the first key to Zukofsky as writer is found in an
understanding of Zukofsky as reader. The Language poet Ron Silli-
man has described Zukofsky as "the first (& for a long time the only)
to read Pound & Williams with what we wld recognize as modern
eye & ear."[18] Although the question sounds tautological, what does
it mean to read the Modernists with a "modern eye & ear"? The
question is especially interesting when one considers the importance
of the act of reading in the twentieth century; one need think only of
Pound's *ABC of Reading* or the fact that the New Criticism arose out
of readings of T. S. Eliot and James Joyce.

My second chapter, "Zukofsky and Adams: Appropriating an
American Tradition," explores Zukofsky's relationship to an Ameri-
can past and an American heritage. Adams gave Zukofsky a means
both of understanding history and locating the self within that
history. In the next three chapters, I consider Zukofsky's relation-
ship with his older contemporaries: Eliot, Pound, and Williams.
These three writers provided the young poet with the raw material of
his poetics—a raw material he would transform into his own dis-
course. Although other critics have focused on the influence of such
writers as James Joyce and Wallace Stevens on Zukofsky,[19] I selected
these three writers not only because of their influence on Zukofsky
but also because that very influence has caused some readers to
dismiss the poet as simply an imitator of these Modernist giants.
Feeling the sting of this dismissal, Zukofsky once urged a friend, and
by extension all of us, simply to look at the works and the "resem-
blances in the differences" between his work and these three pre-
decessors.[20] Focusing on the influence of these poets on Zukofsky in
the 1920s and early 1930s, I have attempted to explore these "re-
semblances in the differences." My final chapter deals with Zukof-
sky's legacy, particularly his legacy to such Language poets as Ron

Silliman and Charles Bernstein. The final question I ask is not how Zukofsky reads American writers, but how is Zukofsky read?

I would, however, like to qualify my argument. Although Kenner suggests that Zukofsky's concerns are American and "indigenous," Zukofsky is neither myopic nor provincial: Zukofsky incorporated more than one language in his epic *"A"*, and his most important critical work was his book on Shakespeare. Perhaps Zukofsky would remark that this very inclusiveness made him most American.

In fact, when Zukofsky traveled to Europe in 1933 to see Pound, he was interviewed by a *Pesti Naplo* reporter who asked him, "How do you like Europe? Don't misunderstand me, I don't mean as a tourist but as a poet?" The young Zukofsky replied: "To speak candidly, Europe does not interest me very much. In America we have grown out of this interest in Europe. We take and have taken only the best that Europe possessed. I came here chiefly to meet the master of American poetry and in a sense its father, Ezra Pound, who has now been living for several years in Rapallo." Zukofsky also noted, "Among the most important [contemporary poets] are William Carlos Williams, René Taupin, Basil Bunting, and Carl Rakosi."[21] One cannot help but smile at Zukofsky's statements. Although Zukofsky blithely states that Europe does not interest him much, he relates in the midst of his interview that Pound, a father of American poetry, lives in Italy. Moreover, the four most important modern poets that Zukofsky lists include Taupin (a Frenchman), Bunting (an Englishman), Rakosi (a Hungarian-American born in Berlin), and Williams (an American born of an English father and Puerto Rican mother). It was not only in his poetry that Zukofsky enacted his "desire for inclusiveness" (*Prepositions*, 15).

I should take a moment to clarify that my work, unfortunately, cannot enact my own "desire for inclusiveness," as I will essentially examine Zukofsky in terms of modern American poetry of the late 1920s and early 1930s rather than any broad American tradition. At the end of his essay on Henry Adams, Zukofsky admonished his readers: "Americans might do no better than to emulate the Europeans, and consider the portrait of what is at least their own Beginning—carefully" (*Prepositions*, 53). In this case, I will not be able to go back to the "Beginning," although Zukofsky's poetry invites a number of comparisons with a range of topics from the Puritan conception of the artist to the Romantic conception of the self. For instance, one could argue that Zukofsky, in his brief work "Found Objects (1962–1926)" implicitly articulates his own rejection of the antinomian heresy. The Puritan artist had to deal with the paradox that in writing he or she asserted a power that only God had—the power to create. The self was born into a world in which a transcendent God was all-powerful; in a world in which God was the primary artist, the writer's work was not so much a creation as a discovery, a discovery of God's "found objects." Of course, Zukofsky did not believe in a world of predetermined myths. Nevertheless, to some degree Zukofsky did live in a predetermined linguistic universe, for he was born into a world in which not a transcendent God but an immanent language existed before the self existed. As Kenner has stated, "Anything you can write is already somehow immanent in the language, a baffling fact that has various ways of affecting those who discern it" (*Prepositions,* vii). In such a world, language, not God, is the significant other; and poetry becomes a means of discovering language's "found objects."

But an extended discussion of Zukofsky's place in the wider American tradition would require another book. There is still much work to be done not only on Zukofsky's poetry but also on his fiction, drama, and translations. I regard my book simply as a part of an ongoing discussion; I look forward to listening to others who will participate in the conversation.

1. Zukofsky and the Act of Reading

The difficulty of poetry (and modern poetry is supposed to be difficult) . . . may be due just to novelty: we know the ridicule accorded in turn to Wordsworth, Shelley and Keats, Tennyson and Browning—but must remark that Browning was the first to be *called* difficult; hostile critics of the earlier poets found them difficult, but called them silly. Or difficulty may be caused by the reader's having been told, or having suggested to himself, that the poem is going to prove difficult. The ordinary reader, when warned against the obscurity of a poem, is apt to be thrown into a state of consternation very unfavourable to poetic receptivity. Instead of beginning, as he should, in a state of sensitivity, he obfuscates his senses by the desire to be clever and to look very hard for something, he doesn't know what—or else by the desire not to be taken in. . . . And finally, there is the difficulty caused by the author's having left out something which the reader is used to finding; so that the reader, bewildered, gropes about for what is absent, and puzzles his head for a kind of "meaning" which is not there, and is not meant to be there.

T. S. Eliot, *The Use of Poetry and the Use of Criticism*

Like the devil in the book of *Job*
Having come back from going to and fro in the earth
    I will give the world all my hushed sources
    In this poem, (maybe the world wanted them)

I will be so frank everyone
    Will be sure I am hiding—a maniac—
    And no one will speak to me.

Louis Zukofsky, "Poem 42"

To read Louis Zukofsky's poetry is to encounter Zukofsky reading—poetry, philosophy, modern advertisements, even himself. Like Ezra Pound, Zukofsky is an archaeologist of words or, as Hugh Kenner has called Pound, Eliot, and Zukofsky, a "poet of classroom accuracies." Zukofsky's multiple references, his interlayering of one text over another text, explains in part why his poetry has been described as difficult and baffling. It is not only that his poetry is allusive but that the allusions often seem elusive, and his rationale—

according to some critics—illusive. In *Little* Zukofsky writes, "I too have been charged with obscurity, tho its a case of listeners wanting to know too much about me, more than the words say."[1] Coming to terms with what "the words say" is much more than an exercise in Zukofskian hermeneutics, in discovering and interpreting all his "hushed sources"; it is also coming to terms with how "the mind constructs the world" (*Prepositions*, 18).

Commenting on *"A"*-12, William Carlos Williams once wrote, "There was always a part of this poet which would not blend. . . . I for one was baffled by him. I often did not know what he was driving at."[2] We may well remember J. Hillis Miller's words concerning readers who were baffled by William Carlos Williams's own poetry, a poetry seemingly "recalcitrant to analysis":

> Williams' presuppositions about poetry and human existence are his own. They are a unique version of a new tradition. . . . The difficulties of such interpretation may be suggested by consideration of the ways Williams' work fails to provide the reader habituated to romantic or symbolist poetry with the qualities he expects. Like a late eighteenth century reader encountering the *Lyrical Ballads,* many present-day readers of Williams' "will look round for poetry, and will be induced to inquire by what species of courtesy these attempts can be permitted to assume that title."[3]

As does T. S. Eliot in *The Use of Poetry,* Miller focuses not on the difficulty of the poetry but on the act of reading. Both Miller and Eliot recognize that we operate within the norms of our "interpretive communities," that we are shaped in part by the reading strategies and interpretive conventions of our social and cultural context.[4] For Miller, the problem that readers have confronting Williams's work is primarily epistemological; the appropriate question is not what is wrong with Williams's poetry but rather how does one break through one's preconceived notions and simply read the poet's language?

The same question is appropriate for Zukofsky's poetry. But in Zukofsky's case, readers have wanted to interpret Zukofsky's works in the context of his immediate predecessors: Eliot, Williams, and especially Pound. Moreover, critics attempt to confront Zukofsky's works against their preconceived notions of an Objectivist poetics, a term coined by Zukofsky but usually associated with Pound's Imagist and Vorticist tenets. Zukofsky, however, escapes easy classification. He doesn't quite fit. He may accept many of Pound's polemical dicta, the format of some of his earlier poems may resemble Williams's early Imagist poems, and his poetics may share Eliot's allusive quality, but these various characteristics only make it difficult to pin Zukofsky to any particular category. Part of the problem that readers have with "placing" Zukofsky comes from the multiple demands Zukofsky makes on his own poetry, demands that are inclusive rather than exclusive. In his essay "An Objective," Zukofsky articulates his desire for "what is objectively perfect." But his conception for what is objectively perfect includes both complexity of detail and the simplicity of the poetic object; both historic and contemporary particulars; both the concrete and the universal; both the poem as object in perfect rest and the poem as an object in process; and, finally, both the poem as an autonomous object and the poem as an inclusive object (*Prepositions*, 15).

Zukofsky's desire for inclusiveness creates a problem for critics who wish to subsume Zukofsky's works within their understanding of the Objectivist label. Both Tom Sharp and Michael Heller, in their works on the Objectivist poets, have convincingly argued that the Objectivists (Zukofsky, George Oppen, Carl Rakosi, and Charles Reznikoff) constituted a poetic movement based on an identifiable aesthetic: sincerity and objectification.[5] Despite the fact that Zukofsky, the group's sometimes reluctant leader, vaguely defined the Objectivist's program and felt uncomfortable about confining their poetry under the rubric of any "movement," the various members of the group did participate in joint activities: contributing to an Objectivist number of *Poetry* magazine, collaborating on *An "Objectivists" Anthology,* and founding To Publishers and the Objectivist Press. Later, however, an impatient Zukofsky would disclaim his role as leader of the group: "I don't like any of those *isms.* I mean, as soon as you do that, you start becoming a balloon instead of a person. And it swells and a lot of mad people go chasing it."[6]

To a certain degree, any label is ultimately reductive, and, as

Zukofsky feared, the Objectivist "balloon" tended to obscure rather than illuminate his poetry during his lifetime. To identify this problem, we can examine several noteworthy responses to Zukofsky's poetry: in the 1930s Basil Bunting chastises Zukofsky for straying from Objectivist dicta, while several decades later L. S. Dembo, in an interview with Zukofsky, and Charles Altieri, in his article "The Objectivist Tradition," subsume Zukofsky's poetry within their nominalistic definition of an Objectivist poetics.

In an "Open Letter to Louis Zukofsky," published in *Current Mare* on 2 October 1932, Basil Bunting writes, "It seems to me that one passage in your admirable 'Recencies' essay in the Objectivist anthology oversteps the limits of useful criticism." Bunting's choice of the word *limits* is more than appropriate, for, essentially, Bunting criticizes Zukofsky's "desire for inclusiveness": "If I am a hatmaker I seek instruction in a series of limited practical operations ending in the production of a good hat with the least possible waste of effort and expense. I NEVER want a philosophy of hats, a metaphysical idea of Hat in the abstract, nor in any case a great deal of talk about hats." "This," Bunting continues, "is what I would understand by Objectivism, if the word were mine."[7] Obviously, Bunting aligns Objectivist tenets with Pound's 1912 Imagist tenets, which he considers a model for the writing of a poem: "1. Direct treatment of the 'thing' whether subjective or objective. 2. To use absolutely no word that does not contribute to the presentation. 3. As regarding rhythm: to compose in the sequence of the musical phrase, not in sequence of a metronome." Bunting applauds Pound for developing a "pervading stress on the immediate, the particular, the concrete; distrust of abstractions; shrinking from the suspicion of verbalism; from the puns and polyvalencies in which mystics delight." For Bunting, the poem is a concrete object, an object that is not imbued with mystical abstractions.

In the chastening tones of a disappointed father, Bunting addresses Zukofsky as a prodigal son wandering away from the correct tradition: "I have always supposed you to have a greater care for facts than almost any critic now living; a greater partiality for the particular, for the 'very words.' But these paragraphs about poetry look to me like flights into darkness, away from ascertained and reascertainable fact to speculative mysticism; to a region I think void of anything permanently valuable."[8] Bunting perceives Zukofsky as wandering away from the Objectivist goals—as Bunting has defined them, not as Zukofsky has defined them. Bunting was not interested in either, as he puts it, "a metaphysical notion" or a "psychology" of poetry: "The aspirations of the hatmaker can only faintly affect the hat. The psychology of the poet is not the critic's business. Psychology has become as insidious a nuisance to our age as ethics was to the last or theology to an older one." The ontology of the poem is contained within the limits of the poem, not in "mind of the writer" or in "the unguessable intentions of an unlikely Creator." Both the "I" of the author and the "I" of God are subsumed within the text; here Bunting collapses the Platonic duality of the real and the ideal, and the Cartesian duality of subject and object. For Bunting, poetry is the "production of hats," the creation of "the thing in itself," the "direct treatment of things." He identifies Objectivist goals with Imagist and Vorticist goals.

But Zukofsky saw the Objectivists as going beyond the Imagists and the Vorticists. In a letter to Lorine Niedecker, Zukofsky writes (quoting L. C. Flint): "The Objectivists unlike the Imagists were quite contemporary, unfastidious & inclusive in their selections of images. . . . And in another respect the Obj. go beyond the Imag. Both by their choice of subjects & by the implications which are allowed to appear from the image, the Obj. suggest the direction of the streams of objects, facts, situations, incidents, the tendency in things which we call history. And by the sequences & juxtaposition of images in their poems & by the cadences of their phrases, they suggest often their own judgment on history."[9]

Zukofsky's Objectivist goals are far more inclusive than are Bunting's; Zukofsky reconciles the image with time (history) and the self (judgment). Bunting's position, however, is quite understandable, for Zukofsky and Bunting share many assumptions about poetry— assumptions that highlight concrete perception and the particularities of language. For example, in *Poem beginning "The"* Zukofsky notes a change in the modern sensibility from the Greek sensibility, a change that calls for the reevaluation of the uses of language:

> 69   How the brain forms its visions think-
>   ing incessantly of the things,
> 70 Not the old Greeks anymore,—
> 71   the things themselves a shadow world
>   scarce shifting the incessant
>   thought—
>
>   (*CSP*, 11)

Here Zukofsky alludes to Plato's allegory of the cave and suggests that modern modes of perception have been radically altered—"Not the Greeks anymore." Within the allegorical world that Plato has constructed, the systems of mediation—those avenues that lead the self to true knowledge—are faulty because the chained cave dwellers rely on faulty signifiers; they perceive only illusory shadows, not the light of *paideia*. Socrates and Glaucon, by contrast, are privileged readers; they could never be satisfied with the shadow world, the world of sight. Yet to be a privileged reader in Plato's world depends on whether or not one shares Plato's premises: a dualistic system that values the world of being over the world of becoming, the world of ideas over the world of sight. Plato's allegory, like Christ's parables, is a text that is truly discerned when both the reader and author agree: "Therefore speak I to them in parables: because they seeing see not; and hearing they hear not, neither do they understand. . . . But blessed are your eyes for they see: and your ears, for they hear" (Matt. 13:13, 16). To be among Plato's blessed constitutes an act of "correct" perception: "To endure the sight of being, and of the brightest and best of being, or in other words, of the good."

For Zukofsky, Plato's transcendent world is not our world; "the brain forms it vision think-/ing incessantly of the things," which are "themselves a shadow world." Zukofsky embraces the shadow world, the "prison-house of language." Language is not a faulty mirror of the good, the true, the beautiful, a vehicle for the author's and reader's search for paideia; rather, language itself, with all its social, political, and literary resonances, is Zukofsky's primary concern.

For Zukofsky, words do not point to transcendent certainties but embody immanent possibilities: "The poet wonders why so many today have raised up the word 'myth,' finding the loss of so-called 'myths' in our time a crisis the poet must overcome or die from, as it were having become too radioactive, when instead a case can be made out for the poet giving some of his life to the use of the words *the* and *a:* both of which are weighted with as much epos and historical destiny as one man can perhaps resolve" (*Prepositions,* 10).

Thus, we might conclude that Zukofsky's statement directs us to the language of the poem, to the "things themselves a shadow world." Yet in his presentation of the verse, Zukofsky is obviously not espousing the "direct treatment of the thing." After all, Zukofsky's allusive references tease an elaborate system of possible meaning from the reader. Indeed, the language, the things of Zukofsky's shadow world, are continually "shifting the incessant thought."

In the late 1960s L. S. Dembo, while interviewing Zukofsky, referred to one of Zukofsky's lyrics, stating what he believes is Zukofsky's Objectivist stance: "It seemed to me the poet here was seeing as an objectivist, in terms of particularities rather than wholes. He seems to be literally thinking with things as they exist and not making abstractions out of them."[10] Zukofsky quickly answers, "But the abstract idea is particular, too. Every general word is particular, *as against another*—glass, table, shoe, arm, head . . . 'reality,' if you wish. Individually they're all, apart from their sound, abstract words. I'd like to keep them so that you don't clutter them with extra adjectives, extra adverbs; the rest is just good speaking." Zukofsky does not contradict Dembo's assessment of his poem, but he demonstrates that the Objectivist dictum is not exclusive. Thus, Zukofsky need not limit his repository of poetic material to numinous things but can fill it with all the particulars of language: history, the self, society, theories—all considered objects, the words that build the poetic machine.

Charles Altieri, in his 1979 article "The Objectivist Tradition," uses Zukofsky as his primary spokesman for the Objectivist.[11] Altieri isolates what he describes as "two basic modes of lyric relatedness—the symbolist and objectivist styles," and presents valuable distinctions between these two styles. Whereas the "symbolist mode" stresses interpretation, meaning, and transcendence, the "objectivist mode" stresses perception, being, and constructions. In developing his modes, Altieri notes that Objectivists oppose the pursuit of the sublime that caused "Dante's precise vision and disciplined dream [to] give way to poetry that purchases transcendence by muddying perception with generalizations and thus cannot rest with objects until they have been transformed by metaphor into explicit analogues for the psychic life." At this point Altieri quotes Zukofsky: "In pursuit of this 'semi-allegorical gleam,' Zukofsky tells us, 'Poets put on singing robes to lose themselves in the universal.'" In confronting such a quotation, the reader should be reminded of Zukofsky's penchant not only for words such as *particulars, sounds,* and *structure* but also for words such as *concepts, ideas, contexts, allusions,* and, of course, the *inclusive object.* Neither Zukofsky's poetics nor his poetry can be easily categorized.

Zukofsky's allusions highlight the problems readers have in "placing" Zukofsky. Whereas Eliot's allusive fragments, shored against the ruins of the wasteland, are transformed into a symbolic whole, Zukofsky's allusions refuse to be transformed into any symbolic construct. Then again, for a poet who regards a poem as an object, a construction, indeed, a "machine made of words," Zukofsky uses many private and cultural allusions that escape the concreteness of such words as "red wheel barrow" or "young sycamore." Gertrude Stein can insist that a rose is a rose and in so doing clip the concrete vehicle from its abstract tenor, be it love or beauty; but an allusion, by its very definition, suggests an a priori complex of ideas. Zukofsky desires something quite different from Williams's "no ideas but in things." Zukofsky's own version of Williams's dictum is far more open to abstract possibilities: "the things themselves a shadow world." Williams demands (the imperative voice) that things themselves be the proper focus of our attention, whereas Zukofsky's ambiguous construction (objects as ideas, or ideas as objects?) allows for qualification: "No ideas but in things, as long as ideas can be considered things." Hence the universal can be transformed into the particular.

Let us examine the poetic space Zukofsky creates as he resolves "the complexity of detail into a single object." In *"A"*-3 Zukofsky situates a historic particular—the death of Christ—next to a contemporary particular—the death of Ricky.[12]

3

At eventide, cool hour
Your dead mouth singing,

  Ricky,

Automobiles speed
Past the cemetery,

No meter turns.
Sleep,

With an open gas range
Beneath for a pillow.

The cat, paw brought back
Over her seat, velvet,

Puss—.

"Who smelt gas?"
"—Would I lie."

"No crossin' bridges,
Rick'—
No bridges, not after midnight!"

"—God's gift to woman!"

Out of memory
A little boy,
It's rai-ai-nin',

Ricky,
Coeur de Lion.

Lion-heart,
A horse bridled—

Trappings rise,
Princelet
Out of history.

Trappings
Rise and surround

Two dark heads,
Dead, straight foreheads,

The beautiful
Almost sexual

Brothers.

I, Arimathaea,
His mirror,
Lights either side—

   Go,
   Beg His corpse

—Wish I had been broken!

In another world
We will not motor.

Dead mouth
(Cemetery rounded
By a gastank)

The song reaches home
'Here are your dead,

Not yours—
A broken stanchion,

Of leaves,

Lion-heart, my dove,
Pansy over the heart, dicky-bird.'
               ("*A*"-3, 9–11)

Zukofsky's elegy on Ricky draws on two "songs": Bach's *Saint Matthew Passion* and Ricky's own song. "*A*"-3 begins with the first line of the first recitative sung after Jesus's death: "*At eventide, cool hour.*" Here the line from Bach's text serves as the beginning line of a meditation (three is the number for meditation in the Pythagorean system) on Ricky's death. Thus, the line from Bach's *Passion* acts as a particular that reminds the narrator of another particular—the suicide of a young man.

Still, the reader is left with a series of questions. Who is Ricky? How did he die? What has his death to do with Christ's death? How does one read the poem? Initially, we attempt to find a familiar context for this poem. For instance, we may first look at literary contexts: is Zukofsky drawing on conventions of either meditation or elegy in unconventional ways? Typically, in the schema of the traditional Ignatian meditation, the speaker, through the senses and memory, vividly recalls a scene, reflects on the subject, and then engages the will and affection in a colloquy with God. Zukofsky's speaker does indeed recall the scene of death ("With open gas range / Beneath for a pillow") and the scene of the dead ("past the cemetery"); but the speaker, in his clipped syntactic units, hardly engages in a colloquy with God. Moreover, Zukofsky's poem strangely echoes traditional pastoral elegy, for, like Milton's *Lycidas*, *"A"*-3 commemorates a young individual and a dying god. But the sparse pastoral images—flower (granted, the pansy is hardly the immortal hyacinth) and leaves—are overwhelmed by urban images: automobiles, meters, gas, cemetery "rounded by a gastank." Furthermore, there is no promise of renewal for Ricky, nature, or the dying god. In this world of *a*'s and *the*'s, there is no hope for resurrection: "In another world / We will not motor."

In Zukofsky's poetry, resolution of meaning in familiar contexts is forever just eluding us. Thus, as Zukofsky suggests, we must move from possible contexts to the actual text itself—"just read the words." But first just listen to the music of the poem:

> I'll tell you.
> About my *poetics*—
>
> $\int$ music
>   speech
>
> An integral
> Lower limit speech
> Upper limit music
>   (*"A"*-12, 138)

Like Christ's broken body, like the broken stanchion, the poem's rhythm is also broken—by commas, periods, dashes, and the clipped units of one- and two-syllable words. Language itself is caught in the "trappings" that "rise and surround."

Over and over again the words resonate with suggestions of sex, death, and entrapment:

No meter turns.
Sleep,

With an open gas range
Beneath for a pillow.

The cat, paw brought back
Over her seat, velvet,

Puss—.

"Who smelt gas?"
"—Would I lie!"

Here Zukofsky's puns suggest a variety of referential possibilities:
meter (gas meter? taxi meter? the poem's meter?); range (stove?
frontier?); seat (car seat? rear end?); lie (dishonesty? a prone posi-
tion?). Zukofsky freely employs the pun for the purposes of art.
Indeed, the pun is as significant to Zukofsky as the allegory is to
Plato or Bunyan, as the parable is to Christ, or as the symbol is to
Eliot and Yeats. Each word is allowed a whole play of referential
possibilities; thus, each word is *significant* even though the word
may not *signify* a given meaning: "Poets measure by means of
words, whose effect as offshoot of nature may (or should) be that
their strength of suggestion can never be accounted for completely"
(*Prepositions*, 7). Zukofsky recognizes that the power of language
does not reside simply in an extralinguistic referent, so that language
transparently mirrors reality; language's power is also intralinguis-
tic, with the potential to subvert any authorial attempt to circum-
scribe it. As such, to invoke Derrida, because signifier and signified,
sign and substance are never fully joined, meaning is continually
deferred; language also becomes the site of production for meaning.

Here we encounter another problem that readers have in con-
fronting Zukofsky's poetry. In a poetics in which each word is
significant, we then have a poetry in which all language is fore-
grounded, a poetry in which, as Hugh Kenner states, "all is atten-
tion" (*Prepositions*, vii). Yet Zukofsky also writes that the poet
resolves "words and their ideation into structure" (*Prepositions*,
13): "the isolation of each noun so that in itself it is an image, the
grouping of nouns so that they partake of the quality of things

being together without violence to their individual intact natures" (*Prepositions,* 13). Thus, in the passage above, "sleep," "pillow," "back," and "lie" suggest a matrix of references aligned to a bed— also the scene of sexual intercourse ("seat," "velvet," "puss"). "Meter," "range," and "gas" suggest a stove—also the scene of Ricky's death. Both groups of images reify death and sexuality.

Even the free play of words is caught in the restraint of death; there is no transcendence. Ricky's song finally "reaches home," and, although his dead mouth sings of a broken stanchion (does it refer to a support or a harness?), the last line of the song—"Pansy over the heart, dicky-bird"—suggests, through wordplay, both a graveyard and a dicky, or diseased, heart.

Thus, we may, as Zukofsky suggests, simply "read the words," but Zukofsky's two major allusions—Bach's *Saint Matthew Passion* and Ricky—continue to intrigue us. While the first allusion springs "out of history" and the second allusion springs "out of memory," both allusions lead us to texts beneath Zukofsky's own text. This example of intertexuality reminds us that Zukofsky's text is set against, to use Barthes's term, "the already written." The first lines of the poem refer to a point in the Passion narrative in which Pilate has agreed to deliver Christ's body to Joseph of Arimathaea:

> At evening, hour of calm and peace,
> Was Adam's fall made manifest:
> At evening, too, the Lord's redeeming love;
> At evening homeward turned the dove
> And bore the olive-leaf as token.
> O beauteous time! O evening hour!
> Our lasting peace is now with God made sure,
> For Jesus hath His Cross endured.
> His body sinks to rest.
> Go, loving servant, ask thou it—
> Go, be it thine, the lifeless Saviour's Body.
> O, wond'rous Gift! A precious, holy burden.

Bach's recitative tells the whole of biblical history: Adam's fall and Christ's redemption. The speaker celebrates the evening hour because in this moment of time, time itself was both fractured by the fall and fulfilled in Christ's act: "Our lasting peace is now with God

made sure." Out of the gift of Christ's broken body, the entire
community is redeemed.

The second allusion to which Zukofsky refers is the text of mem-
ory. Ricky was Whittaker Chambers's younger brother, who died in
1926. Zukofsky knew both brothers and was aware of the young
man's self-destructive behavior. Barry Ahearn cites a chapter in
Chambers's *Witness* that recounts a story he is sure Zukofsky knew:

> He is standing on our front porch, dressed in one of those shapeless
> wraps children used to be disfigured with. It is raining softly. I am in the
> house. He wants me to come out to him. I do not want to go. In a voice
> whose only reproach is a plaintiveness so gentle that it has sounded in the
> cells of my mind through all the years, he calls: "Bro (for brother), it's
> mainin (raining), Bro." He calls it over and over without ever raising his
> voice.[13]

Reading the references to these allusions, we realize that we have
encountered not one but two sacred texts. In reading Zukofsky's
poem, we are engaged in a study of hermeneutics, but we move from
significant text to significant text, not from text to a precise matrix
of meaning. "*At eventide, cool hour*" Adam falls, Christ redeems,
and Ricky sings. The structure intrinsic to each allusion stands side
by side in the poem. As the speaker, adopting the persona of Joseph
of Arimathaea, states:

> I, Arimathaea,
> His mirror,
> Lights either side—
>
> > Go,
> > *Beg His corpse*

In Zukofsky's poem, both brothers are begging his corpse, and they
stand side by side in a contingent poetic space. Thus, Zukofsky is
not, on the one hand, glorifying Ricky as a Christ figure, nor is he, on
the other hand, devaluing the mythic structure implicit in Chris-
tianity. As Zukofsky writes, "Linguistic usage has somehow pre-
served these acts which were poems in other times and have trans-
ferred structures now. The good poems of today are not far from the
good poems of yesterday" (*Prepositions*, 18).

In his poetry Zukofsky creates a poetic space that might best be described as a contingent space—not an ideogram, not a symbolic construct, not a rendering of numinous objects. Indeed, Bunting is correct when he chastises Zukofsky for not writing about "the production of hats," for Zukofsky allows both history and judgment into his contingent space. Moreover, in terms of Altieri's categories, which divide Symbolist and Objectivist modes, Zukofsky's poetry allows for both meaning and being, both interpretation and perception. Like a multilevel puzzle, Zukofsky's words push themselves into the foreground, allow for a background of references, and break into various patterns that are always significant, even though they do not signify a specific meaning.

In a talk on Wallace Stevens, Zukofsky describes "the contingency of one poet reading another":

> It is not a temporal thing, may be felt only an instant, but that instant call it love, eternity, infinity: whatever you *want*—that's it. Stevens describes that feeling. It *dures* Stevens might be saying. . . . But what *dures* or endures as impersonal friendship when one poet reads another is a reading removed from yet out of time, without actual mutual influence or conscious awareness of tradition, literary handbooks or chronometers. Both poets may not be contemporaries, only one of them actually alive—the other legend like Shakespeare or Homer. (*Prepositions*, 25)

Zukofsky creates both in the act of reading and in the construction of his poems a contingent poetic space, one that allows text and reader to *dure*.

2. Zukofsky and Adams: Appropriating an American Tradition

> The effort must begin at once, for time pressed. The old formulas had failed, and a new one had to be made, but, after all, the object was not extravagant or eccentric. One sought no absolute truth. One sought only a spool on which to wind the thread of history without breaking it.
>
> Henry Adams, *The Education of Henry Adams*

In "About the Gas Age" Zukofsky wrote, "The man who taught me the most about history . . . was Henry Adams."[1] Zukofsky's statement, written in 1970, might seem surprising to those individuals aware of Zukofsky's admiration for Lenin and of his desire to write a politically committed poetry in the 1930s. Why doesn't Zukofsky give this place of honor to Karl Marx, father of modern socialism, rather than Adams, a representative of a defunct American aristocracy? First, Zukofsky's interaction with Adams's works had been a lifelong enterprise. In an essay on Wallace Stevens, Zukofsky recalled his activities in the early 1920s: "Remembering what was happening to me at that time, I imagine he [Wallace Stevens] was reading a good deal of philosophy. I was reading Henry Adams, and had heard of Wittgenstein" (*Prepositions,* 29). For Zukofsky, Adams was a significant text in the library of his memory. While at Columbia University, Zukofsky wrote his master's thesis on Henry Adams, who would later be regarded by many as the father of American Modernism. Alfred Kazin notes that Adams's autobiography became a "primer in history" for the "Younger Generation" when the Massachusetts Historical Society released it in 1918, the year of Adams's death.[2] In 1924, before he would write his first critical essay on Ezra Pound or any other American poet, Zukofsky composed "Henry Adams: A Criticism in Autobiography," which he later sent to Pound for publication. In the 1930s Zukofsky incorporated Adams's works into his own poetry, especially "A"-8. As student, critic, and poet, Zukofsky merged Adams's texts into his own texts, Adams's life into his own life.

Still, one may wonder why Zukofsky was preoccupied with Adams. Certainly not all of his fellow poets shared Zukofsky's perceptions of Adams. Pound passed over Henry Adams's letters in favor of John Adams's letters. Cid Corman politely wrote to Zukofsky, "The Adams are too much of a clan for my blood, I'm afraid, but they are intelligent, fiercely so, and they serve remarkably well as a concentration of America in its ideal history."[3] Although T. S. Eliot respected Adams's works, in "Gerontion" he perceived Adams as a figure not of ideal history but of cultural decline. Basil Bunting railed against Zukofsky for choosing Adams as a "god": "He [Adams] remembered the past of what had survived, but not the future of what had perished."[4]

Most significantly, Zukofsky—descendant of immigrant Russian Jews and child of twentieth-century multiplicity—stands in stark contrast to Adams, the inheritor of an extended American dynasty and child of eighteenth-century unity. In fact, observing that the Adamses were far closer to being protofascists than protosocialists, Burton Hatlen has argued that Zukofsky, in his poem "A"-8, ultimately opts for Marx over Adams, "rejecting conservatism in favor of socialism, aristocratic despair in favor of revolutionary action."[5] Zukofsky's own comments, however, have complicated Hatlen's view of Adams. When Zukofsky published his article on Henry Adams in the *Hound & Horn* in 1930, he stated in a footnote that Adams "knew all there was to know about Marx": "To treat Henry Adams as the usual fin-de-siècle, slowly dying scion of a defunct American dynasty, à la 'Marxian' interpretation of literature, is obviously a mistake. The great regret is that Adams did not live ten years more than eighty to write down such a force as Lenin."[6] Rather than choosing one man over the other, Zukofsky synthesizes their dialectical visions. For Zukofsky, Adams early became a useful vehicle of appropriation, for through Adams's heritage Zukofsky appropriated an American past; through Adams's theory of history Zukofsky appropriated a means for shaping his poetic form; and through Adams's use of the autobiographical self Zukofsky appropriated a means for incorporating the self into an Objectivist poetry. Before Zukofsky encountered Eliot's philosophy of the surrender of the self or Pound's theory of personae, Zukofsky was learning from Adams how to construct an objective persona as a means of confronting history.

A Usable Past

Born on 16 February 1838 "under the shadow of Boston State House," Adams was a descendant of a long line of makers—of the American Revolution, of the American republic, of American history. Fixed in Bostonian space—"under the shadow of Boston State House"—in the fullness of time—16 February 1838—"a child was born," writes Adams, and started a "twentieth-century career from a nest of associations so colonial—so troglodytic—as the First Church, the Boston State House, Beacon Hill, John Hancock and John Adams, Mount Vernon Street and Quincy."[7] Thus begins Adams's autobiographical *Education of Henry Adams*. Adams had a whole series of family and social associations that firmly anchored him. in time and space. But even so he wondered: "What could become of such a child of the seventeenth and eighteenth centuries, when he should wake up to find himself required to play the game of the twentieth? . . . Whether life was an honest game of chance, or whether the cards were marked and forced, he could not refuse to play his excellent hand" (*Education,* 4).

Born in January 1904 in New York's teeming Lower East Side, Zukofsky, son of a Russian immigrant, owned no such marked cards. In his *Autobiography* Zukofsky sums up much of his life in a single paragraph:

> But the bare facts are: I was born in Manhattan, January 23, 1904, the year Henry James returned to the American scene to look at the Lower East Side. The contingency appeals to me as a forecast of the first-generation American infusion into twentieth-century literature. At one time or another I have lived in all of the boroughs of New York City—for over thirty years in Brooklyn Heights not far from the house on Cranberry Street where Whitman's *Leaves of Grass* was first printed.[8]

Zukofsky's landmarks are literary landmarks: time is dictated by James's return to the American scene; place is dictated by the house where Whitman's *Leaves of Grass* was first printed. Unlike Adams, Zukofsky's associations are not bequeathed to him but rather claimed by him. Bearing no "troglodytic" or "colonial" associations, Zukofsky connects himself to a past precisely so that he might project himself into a future: "a forecast of the first-generation American infusion into twentieth-century literature." For Zukofsky, both James and Whitman became an extension of his cultural self, and in turn Zukofsky transformed his cultural self into a literary self; as he stated, he wished to perceive himself as "an infusion into twentieth century literature": the self becomes a text.

But while Zukofsky concentrated on a literary infusion, both Adams and James worried about cultural infusions. Zukofsky's elliptical reference to James's visit to the Lower East Side in *The American Scene* eliminates James's impression of the teeming masses of the New Jerusalem: "There is no swarming like that of Israel when once Israel has got a start, and the scene here bristled, at every step, with the signs and sounds, immitigable, unmistakable, of a Jewry that had burst all bounds."[9] He dubiously notes the East-side cafes filled with the sound of Yiddish—the "torture-rooms of the living idiom; the piteous gasp of which at the portent of lacerations to come could reach me in my drop of the surrounding Accent of the Future."[10]

Although Zukofsky, in his critical essay, quotes Adams quite extensively, one quotation, which could have been addressed to Zukofsky himself, is absent:

> His world was dead. Not a Polish Jew fresh from Warsaw or Cracow— not a furtive Yacoob or Ysaac still reeking of the Ghetto, snarling a weird Yiddish to the officers of the customs—but had a keener instinct, an intenser energy, and a freer hand than he—American of Americans, with Heaven knew how many Puritans and Patriots behind him, and an education that had cost a civil war. He made no complaint and found no fault with his time; he was no worse off than the Indians and the buffalo who had been ejected from their heritage by his own people; but he vehemently insisted that he was not himself at fault. (*Education*, 238)

One must read Adams's statement carefully. The passage may appear to be a literal translation from Arnold's "Stanzas from the Grande Chartreuse"; Arnold's "gypsy-scholar" wanders "between two worlds, one dead, / The other powerless to be born."[11] Adams did not actually exist between two such worlds. Indeed, one world might have been dead, but the other world was being born with relentless profusion—with "a keener instinct, an intenser energy, and a freer hand than he." The world of the Puritans and the Patriots was being overwhelmed by the world of the "Yacoob or Ysaac still reeking of the Ghetto"—that is, Zukofsky's world.

Although the original version of the above quotation does not appear in Zukofsky's critical article on Adams, a truncated version of it does appear in *American Friends*: ". . . wandering between two worlds, one dead, the other powerless to be born . . . not a furtive Yacoob . . . but had a keener instinct, and intenser energy than he . . . ejected from their heritage by his own people . . . forced out of the track . . . his energies exhausted in the effort to see his own length."[12] By the use of ellipsis, Celia Zukofsky has created a text of mediation, a text that reflects her husband's appropriation of Adams's text. What was once a passage about division now becomes a passage about unity, even a shared identity. One is not sure who is "wandering between two worlds"—Adams or the "furtive Yacoob." In fact, the two seem to share a similar tragedy—"ejected from their heritage by his own people." Not only through texts but in his life, Zukofsky would learn how to mediate between the world of Adams and James and the world of Yacoob and Ysaac. But in order to do so, he would need to select, to use Van Wyck Brooks's term, a usable past.

In *Foreigners* Marcus Klein describes Zukofsky's Lower East Side, especially the world of the Russian Jew at the turn of the century, during the influx of the Great Immigration.[13] This world did have a tradition of its own, but it was an immigrant's tradition alien to the homegrown myth and romance of America, a tradition that emphasized the immediate past and the cultural perimeters of the home. Our knowledge of Zukofsky's family history is very sketchy. In an interview with Zukofsky's wife, Celia, Carroll Terrell notes, "As for Zukofsky's own heritage and parentage facts are hard to come by. His parents were from obscure backgrounds in Russia and as was traditional among immigrants they did not talk about it. . . . As Celia put it, 'You didn't talk about coming to the new world by steerage. Now if you came by first class it would have been something to talk about.' "[14]

Thus in his personal memory, Zukofsky could reach back only a few generations, into the immediate past. In fact, what would threaten the immigrant tradition of such young Americans as Zukofsky would be the overriding cultural memory of America itself. The war cry on the unsuspecting immigrants was "Americanization." It would be in school—in the education of Louis Zukofsky—that the son of a Russian immigrant would find another cultural past available to him. Although Adams saw his world threatened by the "snarling Yiddish," the world of the immigrant orthodox Russian Jew— the world of Zukofsky's father—was threatened by the sounds of American English supplanting the sounds of Yiddish, an American cultural myth displacing the orthodox faith of the Russian Jew. In "*A*"-4 Zukofsky writes:

> Our beards' familiars; His
> Stars of Deuteronomy are with us,
> Always with us,
> We had a Speech, our children have
> > evolved a jargon.
> > > ("*A*"-4, 12)

Both first-generation Puritan descendant and first-generation Russian immigrant feared the "Accent of the Future." But for Zukofsky that "Accent of the Future"—language itself—represented power. In a letter to Cid Corman, Zukofsky recalled an incident from childhood: "As a kid, I used to get all A's but since my parents couldn't read English, it didn't make much difference, and I'd sign my own card for them, often wishing I had gotten poor marks instead."[15] Zukofsky easily mediated between two social systems— the home and the school. Although he chose to accommodate and succeed within both systems, Zukofsky acknowledged that his understanding of English actually allowed him a modicum of control over both systems—through the card and the signatures.

Mediating between the voices of home and the voices of school, Zukofsky selected his own usable past, but it was a past he forged together through the sounds and words of language—from what he heard, from what he read. In his *Autobiography* Zukofsky writes, "My first exposure to letters at the age of four was thru the Yiddish theater, most memorably the Thalia on the Bowery. By the age of nine I had seen a good deal of Shakespeare, Ibsen, Strindberg and Tolstoy performed—all in Yiddish." But in school he learned another voice, another language: "My first exposure to English was, to be exact, P.S. 7 on Chrystie and Hester Streets. By eleven I was writing poetry in English, as yet not 'American English,' tho I found Keats rather difficult as compared with Shelley's 'Men of England' and Burns' 'Scots, wha hae.' "[16]

Zukofsky mastered the language of the school system, enough so that he would enter Columbia University at the age of sixteen. Zukofsky, however, stood on the margins of American education; he understood that he was not merely accepting but actually appropriating the cultural tradition offered by academic institutions. In *Poem beginning "The"* Zukofsky adopts the voice of Shakespeare's Shylock and writes of his own experience:

251   Assimilation is not hard,
252   And once the Faith's askew
253   I might as well look Shagetz just as much
          as Jew.
254   I'll read their Donne as mine,
255   And leopard in their spots
256   I'll do what says their Coleridge,
257   Twist red hot pokers into knots.
258   The villainy they teach me I will execute
259   And it shall go hard with them,
260   For I'll better the instruction,
261   Having learned, so to speak, in their
          colleges.

                          (*CSP,* 17–18)

In *The Merchant of Venice* Shylock's villainy is chastened with forced assimilation; not only is he deprived of his "pound of flesh," but he is forced, by the Duke's decree, to become a Christian himself and leave his legacy to his daughter and Christian son-in-law. Shylock's demand for inexorable justice clashes with the inexorable demands of Shakespeare's play—the generic structure of comedy and the Christian superstructure of the Duke's Venice. The very institutions, economic and legal, that Shylock thinks he can control in the end defeat him.

Unlike Shylock's forced assimilation, Zukofsky's cultural assimilation does not end in defeat. Indeed, by mastering the language of academia, Zukofsky "will better the instruction / Having learned, so to speak, in their colleges." Here Zukofsky asserts his own authority over institutional authority, his own identity over a cultural identity; Zukofsky would actively appropriate rather than passively be assimilated into the predominant culture. Selecting from both the tradition of the homegrown "Shagetz" and the tradition of the foreigner Jew, Zukofsky would construct the boundaries of his own American tradition.

A Theory of History

Like Adams, Zukofsky "sought for a spool on which to wind the thread of history without breaking it," a spool that would help shape his poetic form. As Zukofsky had explained to Lorine Niedecker, the Objectivists "go beyond the Imagists" by "the tendency in things which we call history" and "their own judgment on history."[17] What distinguishes the Imagist from the Objectivist is history itself. But the question still remains: how would Zukofsky choose to manifest history in his poetry and to reconcile the temporal demands of history with the spatial demands of the image?

In his 1924 essay on Henry Adams, Zukofsky quotes an excerpt from *The Education of Henry Adams:*

> Any schoolboy could see that man as a force must be measured by motion, from a fixed point. Psychology helped here by suggesting a unit—the point of history when man held the highest idea of himself as a unit in a unified universe. Eight or ten years of study had led Adams to think he might use the century 1150–1250, expressed in Amiens Cathedral and the works of Thomas Aquinas, as the unit from which he might measure motion down to his own time, without assuming anything as

true or untrue, except relation. The movement might be studied at once in philosophy and mechanics. Setting himself to the task, he began a volume which he mentally knew as "Mont-Saint-Michel and Chartres: A Study of Thirteenth-Century Unity." From that point he proposed to fix a position for himself, which he could label: "The Education of Henry Adams: A Study of Twentieth-Century Multiplicity." With the help of these two points of relation, he hoped to project his lines forward and backward indefinitely, subject to correction from any one who should know better. (*Education,* 434–35)

Here Adams describes not only his exigency to write but also a dialectical conception of history, which is defined as neither linear nor sequential. History is not a teleological chain of events; rather, the human mind chooses to give significance to a point in time: "Eight or ten years of study had led Adams to think he might use the century 1150–1250 expressed in Amiens Cathedral and the works of Thomas Aquinas, as the unit from which he might measure motion down to his own time, without assuming anything as true or untrue, except relation." One point of reference is an architectural space—Mont-Saint-Michel and Chartres—and another point of reference is the self; and out of these two historical reference points Adams creates a framework in which to explore the relationship between unity and multiplicity, "to project his lines forward and backward indefinitely."

Zukofsky learned much from Adams's conception of history—at least as Adams articulates his conception in *The Education.* At one time Adams had also written that "historians undertake to arrange sequences—called stories, or histories—assuming in silence a relation of cause and effect." But for Adams these "old formulas had failed." Thus, Adams creates another paradigm, wherein language—not historical telos—orders the chaotic universe. Adams's historical points of reference offer Zukofsky a historical paradigm and, more important, a possible poetic framework on which he could shape his own autobiographical poem, *"A":* he would choose a fixed point of unity "as the unit from which he might measure motion down to his own time, without assuming anything as true or untrue, except relation."

In a letter to Niedecker, Zukofsky explains one of his conceptions of *"A"*: "Point is, tho, I start from a sitooation—the performance at Carnegie & lead to a world back—forward."[18] Like Adams, Zukofsky creates a work in which he projects "his lines forward and backward indefinitely," a work, in Zukofsky's case, in which relationships between images often collapse linear time. Zukofsky typically organizes history synchronically rather than diachronically, in terms of structured relationships rather than sequential events.

In the first portions of *"A"*, we can see how Zukofsky constructs his own historical reference points of unity and multiplicity. In *"A"*-1 Zukofsky would pick Bach's *Saint Matthew Passion* as both his entrance into the poem and as his historical point of departure:

> A
>   Round of fiddles playing Bach.
>   *Come, ye daughters, share my anguish—*
>   Bare arms, black dresses,
>   *See Him! Whom?*
>   Bediamond the passion of our Lord,
>   *See Him! How?*
>   His legs blue, tendons bleeding,
>   *O Lamb of God most holy!*
>   Black full dress of the audience.
>
>   (*"A"*-1, 1)

In the notes of a 1931 Objectivist issue of Harriet Monroe's *Poetry*, Zukofsky writes that Bach's *Passion* is related to two central themes of *"A"*: "I.—desire for the poetically perfect finding its direction inextricably the direction of historic and contemporary particulars; and II.—approximate attainment of this perfection in the feeling of the contrapuntal design of the fugue transferred to poetry."[19]

Through the first lines of the poem, we simultaneously enter a world of music, history, and poetry. Zukofsky's allusion to Bach's *Passion* brings the eighteenth-century past into the duration of the poem's present, thus serving as both a historic and contemporary particular. The historic particular does not, however, simply merge into the present moment at Carnegie Hall but maintains a historic integrity of its own. Zukofsky specifically places Bach's *Passion* within the space and time of Leipzig in the Easter of a "dead century." The reader is very aware that the country people—with their "matronly flounces"—heard the *Passion* in a Leipzig church nearly two centuries before the sophisticated secular audience—"black full dress"—would hear it in Carnegie Hall.

Like Adams's Mont-Saint-Michel, Bach's *Saint Matthew Passion* functions as a point of origin, a "unit in a unified universe." In a 1928 article on William Carlos Williams's *A Voyage to Pagany,* Zukofsky compares Adams's and Williams's need to return to an origin. Both men, he writes, were impelled to voyage "towards a Beginning . . . toward what might be termed the European unchanging—in the words of Williams, 'the ancient springs of purity and plenty' " (*Prepositions,* 51). Whereas Adams's voyage to pagany results in his *Mont-Saint-Michel and Chartres*—which "attains an imaginative completeness, a clarity originally foreign and resolves into unity"—Williams's novel, his animated itinerary, never lingers "for what is final, for what resolves into unity." In discussing Williams's "animated itinerary," Zukofsky lists a number of the thoughts of the principal character, Dev; one of these thoughts, significantly enough, is "of Bach's *St. Matthew Passion*—'I heard him agonizing, I saw him *inside,* not cold but he *lived* and I was possessed by his passion' " (*Prepositions,* 53). In *"A"* Zukofsky makes his own voyage to pagany—not by seeing Mont-Saint-Michel and Chartres but by hearing the *Saint Matthew Passion,* permeated with its own Baroque vision. Like Williams's Dev caught in an aesthetic moment, Zukofsky, too, "heard him agonizing . . . saw him *inside.*"

It is important to note, however, that Bach's Christian myth does not offer Zukofsky a teleological view of history; contemporary man cannot reside in a "dead century." Like Adams, Zukofsky "sought no absolutes." The Logos of Bach's Baroque music is caught in the logos of a concert program, where historic and contemporary particulars are intertwined:

The Passion According to Matthew,
Composed seventeen twenty-nine,
Rendered at Carnegie Hall,

Nineteen twenty-eight,
Thursday evening, the fifth of April.
(*"A"*-1, 1)

On Good Friday of 1729, Bach first presented his *Passion* to a
Leipzig audience, and on Maundy Thursday of 1928, the narrator
sits among his own "black full dress of the audience," listening to
"liveforever" music. Outside, however, are "the autos parked, honk-
ing." As the speaker leaves Carnegie Hall, moving from the music of
the concert to the discordant sound of the street, he ostensibly
reenacts—through a series of wordplays—the fall.

A German lady there said:
  (*Heart turned to Thee*)
"I, too, was born in Arcadia."

The lights dim, and the brain when the flesh dims.
Hats picked up from under seats.
Galleries darkening.
"Not that exit, Sir!"
Ecdysis: the serpent coming out, molting,
As tho blood stained the floor as the foot stepped,
Bleeding chamfer for shoulder:
"Not that exit!"
"Devil! Which?"—
. . . .
I lit a cigarette, and stepped free
Beyond the red light of the exit.
(*"A"*-1, 2)

The seemingly random remarks—" 'I, too, was born in Arcadia' ";
"Ecdysis: the serpent coming out, molting"; " 'Devil! Which?' ";
"stepped free / Beyond the red light of the exit"—form a loose
pattern of associations: Arcadia/pastoral Eden; serpent/Devil; exit/
expulsion. It is the play of language, however, not the motif of the
fall, that dictates the speaker's movements; the series of wordplays
offers us referential possibilities, not allegorical certainties. After all,
the speaker steps *free* of the harmony of the liveforever music into
the cacophany of the crowd. The speaker realizes he lives not in an
idealized, prelapsarian Eden but in the flux of history and in often
dire social conditions where people do not have enough to eat:
"Existence not even subsistence."

The poet has traversed time—nearly two centuries—and in so doing has radically altered contexts. The Passion text remains intact, but as the context changes, the paradox of the passion—God/man, death/life, sacrificial love/judgment—transforms into irony and puns: the passion of Johann Sebastian, with twenty-two children; of the artist's "desire longing for perfection"; of the Classics' "women raped by horses"; of memory's "love in a taxi"; of the Wobblies "hollering reply"; of nature's "hell-fire." The unity of Bach's Easter Passion breaks into the multiplicity of the twentieth century. "Thus," writes Zukofsky, "one modernizes / His lute" (*"A"*-6, 24). But for Zukofsky, playing on a modern lute does not mean accepting the Modernist's conception of Art as a quasi religion. Although Modernists such as T. S. Eliot and James Joyce would attempt to transcend the chaos of history through art, Zukofsky realizes that he must confront that chaos.

When played on a modern lute, Zukofsky's beginning becomes much more complex:

A
    Round of fiddles playing Bach

Zukofsky's first syntactic unit demands more pondering. Why is the "A" separated from the second line? Answers are easily enough posited: "A," after all, is the title of the work, a title that could signify anything from an indefinite article to the first thematic subject of a fugue. Furthermore, poised as it is on the top edge of the second line, "A" gives the word "round" an initial sense of ambiguity—"around" or "a round"? The reader must momentarily adjust his or her lenses to see "the rays of the object brought to a focus." As Zukofsky stated in his 1946 article "Poetry," the poet should focus on the historical destiny of little words such as *a* and *the* rather than the word *myth* (*Prepositions*, 10).

But this answer invites another question: Why are the fiddles playing Bach's *Passion*, a work that retells the essential Christian myth? On reexamining the line, the reader notes that the fiddles (synecdoche focuses attention on the playing objects rather than subjects) are not only playing Bach, so to speak, but also the notes B-A-C-H.

Known for his complex system of symbols and numerology, Bach often signed his works only in the notes of his piece. But as musicologists have noted, his signature is more than a means of identification: "If one draws lines between the middle notes A and C, and outer ones B and H, the sign of the cross appear."[20] But for Zukofsky the notes remain a signature without the cruciform; the structure has been stripped of its myth—but the structure remains. The indeterminate *a,* not a determinate myth, shall inherit the earth, for it carries "as much epos and historic destiny as one man can perhaps resolve." In one line man has indeed fallen—from unity into multiplicity, from transcendent eternity into time and history, from myth into language. Perceptions are radically altered: *"See Him! Whom? / See Him! How?"* The answer is no longer simple; for on Easter and Passover week of 1928, the text—*"O Lamb of God most holy!* (dying God and paschal lamb)"—set against altered contexts, reverberates with multiple ironies. Instead of fearing Adams's dynamo of multiplicity, Zukofsky harnesses the dynamo into poetic form.

Although Zukofsky celebrates the relationship between unity and multiplicity, between the past and the present, he does not celebrate the past over the present. Unlike Adams, Zukofsky embraces both the Virgin of unity and the dynamo of multiplicity. In *"A"*-8 Zukofsky writes:

> What is music which does not
> In any sense progress?
> Great improvement of the sense
>   of hearing.
> Concordant old as good as good
>   Discordant new:
>   (*"A"*-8, 103)

Moreover, unlike Eliot, Zukofsky is not searching for a transhistorical narrative. Instead, Zukofsky, like Adams, is interested in relationships, in projecting "his lines backward and forward indefinitely." Finally, in *"A"* the controlling and shaping force of the poem is the poet himself, the creator of relationships, the observer of history. Both Adams and Zukofsky discover that, in the end, the "spool on which to wind the thread of history" would be the self.

The Self and History

In the essay "For Wallace Stevens," Zukofsky asserts, "I balk at speaking about *an identity*. I don't think there is any such thing or state of things, but sometimes a word impels, well, an impersonal thing—a feeling of duration, best defined I think as Spinoza defined it, an indefinite continuance of existence" (*Prepositions*, 24–25). Yet in a 1935 letter to Lorine Niedecker, Zukofsky had excitedly written, "Yessum you've guessed at the fact that A 1–7 is perhaps finally justified by A-8. Not '*all* history in me'—I'm not that good—but yes, always coming in A 1–7 'to where I am now.' Swell how you see it— for me for you to see."[21] Apparently, Zukofsky distinguishes between "*an identity*" and a self that contains history—"to where I am now."

Adams, like Zukofsky, also balked at the word *identity,* or more specifically what, in the preface to *The Education,* he calls the Ego: "As educator, Jean Jacques [Rousseau] was, in one respect, easily first; he erected a monument of warning against the Ego. Since his time, and largely thanks to him, the Ego has steadily tended to efface itself, and, for purposes of model, to become a manikin on which the toilet of education is to be draped in order to show the fit or misfit of the clothes. The object of study is the garment, not the figure" (*Education,* xxiii–xxiv). Adams shifts the focus away from any central identity to a matrix of ideas that constitutes the self, to garments draped on the manikin.

Yet both men write autobiographical works: *"A"* is Zukofsky's lifelong poem, and *The Education* is Henry Adams's labeled "position for himself." Interestingly enough, although both men would never adopt the transcendental "I" of either Emerson or Whitman—the "I" that attempts to bridge the chasm between the self and the world by transforming that world into an expression of the self—Adams and Zukofsky do write, in essence, an Emersonian history of the self. In "History" Emerson writes, "All history becomes subjective; in other words, there is properly no history, only biography."[22] How, then, do Adams and Zukofsky resolve the tension of writing autobiographical works that deny the existence of a central "identity"? What is the function of the self in Adams's "self-effacing" autobiography and in Zukofsky's Objectivist poetics?

In "Henry Adams: A Criticism in Autobiography," Zukofsky isolates what he terms "two actuating forces of his [Adams's] nature: poetic intellect is its continual undertow, and detached mind the strong surface current in the contrary direction" (*Prepositions,* 86). Obviously, Zukofsky is noting from the outset a tension between the "poetic intellect" and the "detached mind." Neither thinking intellect nor detached mind smacks of emotional subjectivity, yet Zukofsky depicts the poetic intellect as an "undertow" set against the "detached mind," a "strong surface current." Apparently, Zukofsky sees a tension between the poetic intellect—the creative subject—and the detached mind—the subject that distances the mind from the self and, in so doing, perceives that self as an object. How might we reconcile such a tension, especially as that tension relates to the self's relation to history? We might well posit that the self plays a dual role: the self is both the form that holds history and, at the same time, an object in that history.

To better understand the dual role of the self, we might simply examine the following passages. In his essay "Poetry: For My Son When He Can Read," Zukofsky comments, "Writing this, Paul, for a time when you can read, I do not presume that you will read 'me.' That 'me' will be lost today when he says good night on your third birthday, and not missed tomorrow when he says good morning as you begin your fourth year" (*Prepositions,* 11). In a letter to Elizabeth Cameron, Adams writes, "Really I think I do not much care, for I feel that the History is not what I care now to write, or want to say, if I say anything. It belongs to the *me* of 1870; a strangely different being from the *me* of 1890. There are not nine pages in nine volumes that now express any of my interests or feelings."[23] In these passages both Zukofsky and Adams express a tension between the subject "I" and the object "me." The "I" exists in a moment of perception, while the "me" is bound in historical time—of today or tomorrow, of 1870 or 1890. Moreover, from moment to moment that perceiving "I" continually transforms into a perceived "me."

The self is both a creator of history—a signifying subject—and a partaker in that history—a signified object.

In *The Education* Adams articulates this tension by being both the author of the work and the major character in the work—one Henry Adams. Although his character is continually being acted on by forces of either chance or fate, Adams still acknowledges that "man's function as a force of nature was to assimilate other forces as he assimilated food": "Long before history began, his education was complete, for the record could not have been started until he had been taught to record. The universe that had formed him took shape in his mind as a reflection of his own unity, containing all forces except himself" (*Education*, 475). Adams is caught in an Augustinian paradox: at the same time that he asserts power as a recording and thinking mind, he also denies himself power, relinquishing that power to the "universe." The self both contains the universe and is contained by that universe.

In *"A"*-8 Zukofsky specifically uses the self as "a spool on which to wind the threads of history," for Zukofsky writes a poem that, as suggested in his letter to Niedecker, is not "all history in me" but all history "to where I am now." In *"A"*-8 more than any of the other movements in *"A"*, we can see Zukofsky's concern with history and the self's role in that history. Moreover, it is in *"A"*-8 that Zukofsky most clearly appropriates Henry Adams's past as a cultural past.

Zukofsky begins *"A"*-8 by reformulating Spinoza's paradox "Natura Naturans— / Nature as creator, / Natura Naturata— / Nature as created" into "Labor as creator, / Labor as creature." Here Zukofsky is again suggesting the dual role of the self, but in this case he delineates not an individual, authorial self but a social self—Labor as creator or creature. Clearly, the question of labor as creator or creature raises questions not only about identity but also about revolution (will labor act or continue to be acted on?). In this movement Zukofsky intertwines a number of themes, from Bach's music to Marx's economics. But rather than focusing on the Christ of Bach's *Saint Matthew Passion*, he focuses on "the poor" who have been "betrayed and sold," who have agonized "inside all their lives." Zukofsky realizes that culture is tied to the historical conditions in which human beings create their material lives. Invoking Marx's labor theory of value, Zukofsky indicts the capitalists who would rob the poor of even their subsistence; the history of exploitation and revolution has been a long one.

One of the threads in this complex movement is that of American history embodied in the Adamses—a history that tells of America's own struggle with centralized unity and destabilizing revolution. In *The Education* Henry Adams notes that Karl Marx was one of the most important thinkers of his age, one of the few to foresee radical change. Speaking of himself, Adams writes, "By rights, he should have been also a Marxist, but some narrow trait of the New England nature seemed to blight socialism, and he tried in vain to make himself a convert" (*Education,* 225). Like Marx, Adams was also a critic of capitalism and its alienating economic system, but he shied away from a final Marxist critique not only because of his "New England nature" but also because of his fear of the overwhelming forces of revolutionary change. Later in his famous chapter "The Dynamo and the Virgin," Adams relates that although "he had studied Karl Marx and his doctrines of history with profound attention," he found it difficult to apply those doctrines to the chaos of the twentieth century (*Education,* 379). Zukofsky, however, perceived a continuity between Marx's dialectic vision and Adams's own version of history.[24]

Zukofsky first introduces Adams passing the baton of history to Marx:

> Phase, the pit, Marx waiting, time to go, said Adams.
>
> Thought eighty years—a void in which nothing was
> dead—
> And if he could come back—Henry Adams—to see
> The mistakes plain in light of the new—one had seen:
> ("A"-8, 51)

Zukofsky calls Adams forth from the grave to be not a Lazarus but a Tiresias, "to see / The mistakes plain in light of the new." Actually, Zukofsky is alluding to two sections from *The Education*. Recounting the impact that a journey through Birmingham and the Black

District had on him, Adams recalls, "The revelation of an unknown society of the pit—made a boy uncomfortable, though he had no idea that Karl Marx was standing there waiting for him, and that sooner or later the process of education would have to deal with Karl Marx much more than with Professor Bowen of Harvard College or his Satanic free-trade majesty John Stuart Mill" (*Education*, 72). Then, in the final lines of his autobiography, Adams states, "Perhaps some day—say 1938, their centenary—they might be allowed to return together for a holiday, to see the mistakes of their own lives made clear in the light of the mistakes of their successors; and perhaps then, for the first time since man began his education among the carnivores, they would find a world that sensitive and timid natures could regard without a shudder" (*Education*, 505).

In Zukofsky's poem Adams returns not only to see history in the making but to hear the various voices of history—from Washington and Jefferson to Marx and Engels, to Lenin and Stalin. Zukofsky depicts the history of Adams's own family as moving from John Quincy Adams's desire for "constructive centralization" to Henry Adams's fear of the "movement of disintegration":

> Were we on the edge of a . . last great
>   centralization,
> Or a first great movement of disintegration?
> These are the facts on both sides . .
> And this is what satiates my instinct for life . .
> That our . . civilization . . has failed to
>   concentrate further.
> Its next effort may succeed . .
> With Russia . . the eccentric on one side and
>   America on the other . .
>   (*"A"*-8, 80)

At the same time that Adams, in halting language, mourns over the possible disintegration of his civilization, he also foretells a possible success—"With Russia . . the eccentric on one side and / America on the other." As Adams envisions a possible future outlined by Russia and America, Zukofsky juxtaposes images of Russian immigrants against the Russian environment, "Ice-cap of Russian inertia." He then funnels history down into his own family history:

> Arrived mostly with bedding in a sheet
> Samovar, with tall pitcher of pink glass,
> With copper mugs, with a beard,
> Without shaving mug—
> To America's land of the pilgrim Jews?
>
> ("*A*"-8, 83)

Finally, history funnels down into himself: "And the youngest being born / here (in New York)." "*A*"-8 continues as Zukofsky then funnels the voices of history out of himself, listening to the confused sound of his own contemporary history. In the language of his poem, Zukofsky is both creator and creature of history. Like Adams, he is a recorder and shaper of history—standing outside the forces of the universe—while at the same time he is part of the history, part of the "universe that had formed him." Choosing the garments to drape on his own manikin, Zukofsky selects his own cultural past. History is a means of defining his own poetics—how the Objectivists "go beyond the Imagists"—and history is a means of defining himself. And as Zukofsky has noted, Adams was the man who taught him most about history. In the inside front cover of a manuscript for "*A*"-12, Barry Ahearn discovered a list of themes for "*A*", several of which are circled.[25] Zukofsky had depicted one of the themes in the following manner:

This diagram encircles an American cultural past as envisioned by Adams but also infused with the hopes of a Russian Marxist revolution. Zukofsky claims Adams's troubled vision of history and transforms that vision into a working aesthetic for his own poetry—"a forecast of the first-generation American infusion into twentieth-century literature."

3. Wut Wuz in the Air of a Time: Eliot, Pound, Williams

In a letter dated 25 December 1930, Pound wrote to Zukofsky, "Your problem coming after T. S. E. me an' Bill is very dif. from what ours was coming after Yeats and Bliss Carman. Praps best for you not to worry about it at all, and cease considering it as a problem."[1] Zukofsky, however, did consider his literary lineage a problem, one that would plague him for a good part of his life. Whereas Pound takes a polemical stance, defining himself against what preceded him—Yeats and Bliss Carman—Zukofsky must define himself against the backdrop of a stronger tradition. Throughout his career Zukofsky would be compared to, and at times dismissed as an imitator of, these three giants of modern poetry: Eliot, Pound, and Williams. Zukofsky felt the sting, a sting—as indicated in Pound's statement—that Zukofsky anticipated from the outset of his career as a poet.

Zukofsky was very conscious of his place in what he called "lecherery history." In a letter to Lorine Niedecker, Zukofsky defends his contribution, documenting—with almost scholarly care—the dates of his own composition of "A":

> Chronology etc since you ask. I started to think about "A" as soon as I finished The in 1926. Wrote A 1–7 so it wuz complete . . . in summer of 1930. Earliest A i.e. 1–4 done by 1928. I had not seen any of Cantos at that time, tho the first 16 had been pubd. in expensive folio edtn. in Paris in 1925, & 17–27 same way, same place in 1927. It was these copies I saw in 1930 . . . certainly not before 1929, when I wrote the Criterion essay on E. P. finished, I see on M.S., Sept. 7/30. The first collected XXX

which I reviewed briefly when E. P. sent me a copy appeared in 1930. First letter E. P. sent me wuz in Aug. 1927 about *The* & no mention of *Cantos* ever for years.[2]

Although Zukofsky's explanation is directly addressed to Niedecker, his audience really includes posterity. Zukofsky is not merely chronicling dates but establishing the poetic self within the greater framework of literary history. At this moment he is both poet and scholar/critic viewing the poems as dated artifacts, documented evidence that Zukofsky is a peer rather than an heir to the great moderns:

> So that there's no direct influence except wut wuz in [the] air of a time that affects young & elder alike to make the same shapes. But that's what influence is? Yes. And who gets affected first gets patent rights. . . . Wuts interesting: *after* A-8 had appeared, E. P.'s later Cantos started to include references to *St. Matthew Passion* & other L. Z. notions. I told him so when he became nasty about my impatience with his "economics," politics etc. And Bill's Paterson I re—*particulars* etc. comes *long after* A-1, as do other motives in him that were in A. But then there's Bill's letter saying he's reading me—& that lots wd. come out of it for him, while working on Paterson.

Despite the fact that the style of the above paragraph, with its many Poundian echoes (slang, spelling, syntax), is a testimony to Pound's presence, Zukofsky deemphasizes Pound's influence on him. Instead, he emphasizes his own influence on Williams: "young and elder" have changed places. Zukofsky stresses that influence is more collective than personal for influence is not merely a private act in which one individual affects another but is grounded in culture: "wut wuz in [the] air of a time." Influence becomes an impersonal act of history and society, a force of time and relationships that uses the self as a vehicle for creation. But at the same time, the creative self is not a passive subject merely absorbed "in the air of a time," yielding to a literary Zeitgeist. Zukofsky finds his own authoritative voice within this collective experience; for Zukofsky the reader is also read, and Zukofsky is able to recognize his own marked language—his "patent rights"—in the texts of Pound and Williams.

Although Zukofsky cultivated lifelong friendships with Pound and Williams, his relationship with Eliot was formal; he knew Eliot primarily as the editor of the *Criterion* and later as the editor and director of the publishing firm of Faber and Faber. But early in his career as a poet, Zukofsky was influenced by Eliot, or, more precisely, by Eliot's *The Waste Land*. In 1926 he modeled his significant early poem, *Poem beginning "The,"* after Eliot's most famous work. In fact, it was this very poem that excited Pound's interest in the young Zukofsky, an interest that led him to urge Williams to befriend the young poet.

"Out of olde bokes in good feith": Zukofsky's *Poem beginning "The"* and Eliot's *The Waste Land*

Poem beginning "The" serves as a fascinating example of, in Zukofsky's words, "the contigency of one poet reading another," for in this poem Zukofsky both appropriates and challenges the Modernist tradition evident in Eliot's *The Waste Land*. Zukofsky, a child of the Great Immigration, appropriates Eliot, a child of the "Genteel Tradition," as a literary father whom, in the process of cultural and linguistic individuation, he inevitably kills. In reviewing Eliot's oeuvre, some critics have regarded *The Waste Land* as a transitional work, a work that suggests that Eliot, after surveying his wasteland, would eventually move from accepting the incarnation of the word as symbol to accepting the incarnation of the Word as religious symbol. Zukofsky, however, as one of the members—one of the "Bleisteins"—of Eliot's "unreal cities," appropriates Eliot's poem in order to reject Eliot's solutions. For Zukofsky the answer would not lie in the symbolic word and the certainties of transcendent structures; rather, Zukofsky would look for his answers by embracing the linguistic word and the possibilities of history.

Before examining the works, I would like to discuss some of the underlying assumptions of the use of quotations for these two writers. For the Modernists, the use of quotations—the issue of how one poet reads another—involves a number of complex social and political ramifications. Eliot once said that Pound "is often most 'original' in the right sense, when he is most 'archeological.' "[3] Eliot is highlighting Pound's, as well as his own, penchant for digging into cultural history, transforming allusions to the past into cultural artifacts. Pound and Eliot's—as well as other Modernists'—excavation of the multiple voices of the past (from Provençal poetry to the *Upanishad*) indicates not only a desire to recover the artifacts of Civilization, Kulcher, and Tradition but also a desire to define the cultural authority of Modernism. Thus, in his act of appropriating quotations from the past, Eliot is, on the one hand, shoring his fragments against the ruins, but, on the other hand, codifying, out of those ruins, the materials of Tradition.

In *The World, the Text, and the Critic,* Edward Said, who has aligned a hegemonic culture with a hegemonic State, points out that texts are "facts of power": "Words and texts are so much of the world that their effectiveness, in some cases even their use, are matters having to do with ownership, authority, power, and the imposition of force."[4] Attesting to the significance of tradition as an "operative in the process of social and cultural definition and identification," Raymond Williams has recognized that tradition is not merely an "inert historicized segment" but "the most powerful practical means of incorporation."[5] Despite the fact that these Modernists were revolutionaries of the word, they were, in many ways, also reactionaries, preferring the authority of Tradition and Kulchur— Eliot's changeless past, "existing monuments and the ideal order"— to the chaos of the present, preferring mythic order to an open-ended history.

The use of quotations, however, suggests a number of different implications for Zukofsky than it does for Eliot—not only as artists but also as social and political beings. These two poets inhabit distinct social and political camps: the royalist, Anglican Eliot is a member of the elite Modernist tradition, while the Jewish Zukofsky resides in, to use Klein's term, the camp of the "barbarians." Zukofsky is very aware that he is an outsider to the predominant culture, and his dilemma reflects the one that Adrienne Rich, nearly a half century later, outlines in her poem "Burning Paper Instead of Children": "This is the oppressor's language / yet I need it to talk to you." In using his quotations, Eliot will attempt to codify cultural authority, whereas Zukofsky will attempt to decenter that authority.

When Eliot's *The Waste Land* appeared in the *Criterion* (London) and the *Dial* (New York) in 1922, public and critical reaction was decidedly mixed but passionate, signaling the controversial nature of the work. Eliot's poem had a few immediate supporters; among them were his friends Ezra Pound and Conrad Aiken. Years later Aiken recalled that his 7 February 1923 review of *The Waste Land* was one of the first full-length favorable reviews the poem had then received.[6] But Pound and Aiken did not represent the opinions of the literary establishment. Many reviewers, even when tentatively praising the poem, seemed confused. Elinor Wylie of the *Literary Review* wrote, "If this is a trick, it is an inspired one."[7] But F. L. Lucas of the *New Statesman* was neither tentative nor confused in his heated reaction: "In brief, in The Waste Land Mr. Eliot has shown that he can at moments write real blank verse; but that is all. For the rest he has quoted a great deal, he has parodied and imitated. But the parodies are cheap and the imitations inferior."[8]

While Lucas damned Eliot's poem by dismissing it, William Carlos Williams damned the poem precisely because it was a significant work—indeed, a "great catastrophe." In the now well-known passage from his *Autobiography,* Williams recalls, "I felt at once that it [*The Waste Land*] had set me back twenty years, and I'm sure it did. Critically Eliot returned us to the classroom just at the moment when I felt that we were on the point of an escape to matters much closer to the essence of a new art form itself—rooted in the locality which should give it fruit."[9] Williams felt that Eliot, in giving "the poem back to the academics," thwarted the immediacy of experience, privileging, as Kenneth Burke has noted, society's culture rather than the "culture of the ground," preferring abstractions rather than the fulfillment of individual desires.[10]

In 1922 Zukofsky was getting an education in his own academic classroom: Columbia University. In four years (1920–1924) he digested John Erskine's Great Books class and John Dewey's and Frederick Woodbridge's philosophy classes, receiving a master's degree in 1924. At the same time, he was also reading such little

magazines as the *Dial,* which awarded Eliot's *The Waste Land* its
1922 poetry prize. In 1926 he wrote *Poem beginning "The",* which
Barry Ahearn has identified as significant for a number of reasons:
first, *The,* along with a small group of other poems, marked a
departure from Zukofsky's college juvenilia; second, the poem was
his calling card to Pound, who published the poem in *Exile;* third,
The became a preliminary plan for his long poem *"A".*[11] Here, I
would also argue, the young Zukofsky articulates an oppositional
agenda—demonstrating his ambivalent relationship to the materials
of a patriarchal Western tradition and its social claims to cultural
authority.

By the time Zukofsky wrote *The,* Eliot was enjoying a measure of
success as editor for the publishing firm of Faber and Gwyer. Still a
controversial poem, *The Waste Land* had become a cause célèbre,
famous enough to be a familiar target for both parody and praise.
Indeed, in a 1925 letter to Harriet Shaw Weaver, James Joyce could
casually jot down a parody of *The Waste Land*—replete with a one-
armed host, interspersed with "Hurry up Joyce, it's time," and con-
cluded with a benedictory "Shan't we? Shan't we? Shan't we?"—
without any need to explain his reference.[12] Moreover, Eliot's poem
became quite a popular model for young writers, who subjected the
poem to their highest form of flattery—endless imitation. As Brian
Howard writes, "It became such a plague that the moment the eye
encountered, in a newly arrived poem, the words 'stone,' 'dust,' or
'dry' one reached for the waste-paper basket."[13] *The Waste Land*—
with its montage of myths, its cinematic dissolves, its images of
contemporary urban life, its Jazz Age rhythms, its *entre deux guerres*
sensibility—was a grand experiment of language and form that
attracted a whole generation of would-be poets.

Zukofsky's poem, however, was hardly "yet another imitation of
The Waste Land" of the sort that drove such editors as Brian How-
ard to reach for the wastepaper basket. When Zukofsky submitted
Poem beginning "The" to Pound in 1926, Pound—this proponent of
"make it new"—did not reach for the wastepaper basket but instead
published the poem in the *Exile.*

At first glance, *The* simply seems to parody *The Waste Land.*

While Eliot appends explanatory notes to the end of his poem, Zukofsky introduces his poem with a series of playful dedications, including one to "Anyone and Anything I have unjustifiably forgotten." While Eliot numbers every tenth line, Zukofsky numbers all his lines; while Eliot divides his poem into five movements, Zukofsky divides his poem into six. Unlike Joyce's parody, however, *The* is not a lighthearted poke at a famous work; Zukofsky is taking a much more iconoclastic swipe at the monumental poem, challenging several of Eliot's assumptions. We must be careful in assessing how Zukofsky challenges the poem, for if we look at the reasons reviewers criticized Eliot's poem—charges that the poem is idiosyncratic and obscure—we notice that these same charges have been repeatedly leveled at Zukofsky's poetry. In fact, Lucas's remark that Eliot has "quoted a lot, he has parodied and imitated," could also apply to Zukofsky's *The* as well as his later allusive works. Moreover, rather than sharing Williams's lament that Eliot has given "poetry back to the academics," Zukofsky is himself a "poet of classroom accuracies." Thus, how Zukofsky models his poem on Eliot's poem bears close examination.

In a footnote to his article "American Poetry 1920–1930," Zukofsky discusses the relationship between the two poems:

> Zukofsky's *Poem Beginning "The"* (1926) written as a reply to people concerned with the end of the world, the dedication and attendant numbers intended as a kind of hors d'oeuvre not as an aid to digestion, is obviously more of a thought sequence than *The Waste Land* is from movement to movement. The images in *The* are incidental and its intention is hardly an atmosphere. The result is certainly not an improvement on *The Waste Land* but something different—something perhaps nearer to an intellectual control (one doubts its value), to statement than to pointilism.[14]

Here Zukofsky cites *The Waste Land* as the catalyst for his poem; at the same time, he distinguishes his poem from Eliot's. First, *The* differs from *The Waste Land* thematically, for Zukofsky's poem is a reply to the apocalyptic tone of Eliot's poem, "a reply to people concerned with the end of the world." Zukofsky echoes common assumptions about Eliot's poem—that it is a poem about contemporary despair, with a pervasive, fin de siècle foreboding. Zukofsky regarded with impatience what many perceived to be Eliot's disaffection with an entire generation; as one writer bluntly, if facilely, stated: "I don't know why Eliot should feel so badly about things. There is no reason why he should have to write in that 'I-cannot-be-gay' manner. He did not have to go through the war."[15] Later, Eliot himself disavowed any intention of being a spokesman for a generation's disillusionment: "To me it was only the relief of a personal and wholly insignificant grouse against life; it is just a piece of rhythmical grumbling."[16]

But this "piece of rhythmical grumbling" projected an epic sensibility that suggested the impending crisis of a civilization: the Fisher King sits against the backdrop of an arid plain, and London Bridge is falling down. Like many of his contemporaries, Zukofsky did not read *The Waste Land* as Eliot's "insignificant grouse against life" but as a piece of social criticism whose hope for the future of the world was limited and provisional.

As his main point in the paragraph, Zukofsky states that *The* "is obviously more of a thought sequence than *The Waste Land* is from movement to movement." Now, Zukofsky's initial references to *The Waste Land*—its apocalyptic tone and appended notes—deal with common assumptions shared by many contemporary readers of the poem. But his main point gives us an insight into a young Zukofsky experimenting with a poetics that leads the reader away from the poetic image to a sequence of ideas. Stressing the propositional rather than imagistic nature of his poem, Zukofsky concludes that his poem has greater intellectual control.

Zukofsky makes a revealing distinction between his poem and Eliot's. The words Zukofsky chooses to describe his poem—"thought sequence," "intellectual control," and "statement"—are all words much more akin to abstract ideas than to concrete images. In fact, Zukofsky suggests that Eliot's poem—not his own poem—inheres more in particulars. Elaborating on this idea, Zukofsky places his poem nearer to statement than pointillism, nearer to, say, philosophy than the visual arts. Late in his life Zukofsky wrote, "I wish that instead of studying philosophy I had studied some botany."[17] His friend and fellow poet Basil Bunting would gladly have agreed with him. After reading Zukofsky's *"Mantis," An Interpretation,* Bunting wrote to his friend, "But concerning the philosophy, I don't know whether I will be really grateful for a commentary. I take my poetry neat as a rule: finding Dante has a lot more kick without St. Thomas. Which is just the difference, I thought, between us and Eliot, and gives us a better chance, for all our less slick technique, of outstaying him."[18]

A believer in Pound's precepts for poetry that is immediate, particular, and concrete, Bunting could just have well added a series of other "slick techniques" that distinguished the "Eliot camp" from the "us camp": abstractions, verbalism, and "the puns and polyvalencies in which mystics delight." Bunting ignores the fact that Eliot, like Pound, was also a soldier in the "revolution of the word." Both Eliot and Pound—along with a whole generation of Modernists such as Joyce, Ford, and Conrad—were inheritors of Flaubert's precept of "le mot juste." These inheritors of the prophet's mantle, however, took on the quest to purify the language in their respective ways. Indeed, Bunting could chastise not only Eliot but also Joyce and Conrad for their use of "puns and polyvalencies in which mystics delight"—these "slick techniques." Unlike Bunting, Zukofsky was not unduly concerned about these slick techniques, which he used in *Poem beginning "The"*.

Although Zukofsky would come to be impatient with the academic hegemony associated with Eliot in the decades ahead, he never really shared Bunting's or Williams's perception that Eliot was the leader of the enemy camp. In his article "Program: 'Objectivists' 1931," Zukofsky included Eliot's *The Waste Land* along with Pound's *XXX Cantos* and Williams's *Spring and All* among a "list of works absolutely necessary to students of poetry." For Zukofsky, all three of these poems seem "to have been written in accordance with the principles heading this note," that is, Objectivist principles. In his 1936 *An "Objectivists" Anthology,* Zukofsky included Eliot's *Marina,* which he considered Eliot's "most fruitful product to date." Essentially, Zukofsky felt that Eliot, too, was on an Objectivist quest: the "desire for what is objectively perfect, inextricably the direction of historic and contemporary particulars."[19] Finally, though, Eliot went one step further, and this was what bothered both Bunting and Zukofsky; for Eliot transformed the historic and contemporary particulars into a symbolic mode—synthesizing the past and present into a transhistorical myth.

In *The* Zukofsky challenges not only Eliot's apocalyptic sense but also his "historical sense" as manifested in both *The Waste Land* and Eliot's literary criticism. As Eliot explains in "Tradition and the Individual Talent," "The historical sense involves a perception, not only of the pastness of the past, but of its presence." Both the past and tradition give shape to the present: "The existing monuments form an ideal order among themselves, which is modified by the introduction of the new (the really new) work of art among them." The present is carefully initiated into the "ideal order" of the past, and the poet "must inevitably be judged by the standards of the past."[20] Eliot asserts the power of the past and tradition upon the present. In *The* Zukofsky's only direct reference to Eliot challenges such a hegemony of the past:

24   Kerith is long dry, and the ravens that
        brought the prophet bread
25   Are dust in the waste land of a raven-
        winged evening.
26   And why if the waste land has been explored,
        traveled over, circumscribed,
27   Are there only wrathless skeletons exhumed
        new planted in its sacred wood
                     (*CSP*, 10)

In essence, Zukofsky asks, "Why, after exploring the waste land, can you offer us only the 'ideal order,' the tradition inscribed in *The Sacred Wood?* Is this the lesson of history, to plant the past anew? After such knowledge, what forgiveness?"

Of course, Eliot did not merely dismiss the present and celebrate the past. Indeed, as critics since F. O. Matthiessen have pointed out, Eliot links the past and present in a circular pattern of history.[21] Eliot was looking primarily for a means of ordering the present, giving shape to its chaos. He looked to the authority of the past and to a method that incorporated, but transcended history: the mythic method. Although both Eliot and Zukofsky juxtaposed the past and present, Zukofsky looked to the "direction of historic and contemporary particulars," whereas Eliot attempted to synthesize his historic and contemporary particulars into a central myth.

The differences between the methodology of the two works are suggested from the outset: in their titles. In his notes on *The Waste Land*, Eliot cites Jessie Weston's *From Ritual to Romance* as the source for his title. Influenced by both Weston's book and James Frazer's *The Golden Bough*, Eliot intertwines the pagan fertility myth of the Fisher King and the Christian myth of the Holy Grail into one of the fundamental layers of this polysemous poem. The Fisher King's impotence or death renders his own land into a wasteland—hence the title of Eliot's poem. A series of ritual acts—a knight, undergoing a number of ordeals, travels to the Chapel Perilous and asks the correct questions about the grail and the lance—must be accomplished before physical and spiritual regeneration is possible in the wasteland. Eliot shores various allusions, both ancient and contemporary, pagan and Christian, against the framework of the myth signified in the title—*The Waste Land*.

In "Ulysses, Order, and Myth," Eliot maintains that Joyce—"in manipulating a continuous parallel between contemporaneity and antiquity"—has implemented the revolutionary mythic method, which "is a step toward making the modern world possible for art."[22] In essence, myth replaces narrative, for the mythic method alters linear concepts of time and history. In "manipulating a continuous parallel" between the past and the present, in controlling and shaping the "immense panorama of futility and anarchy which is contemporary history," the mythic method subverts time and history by transcending both. As Joseph Frank suggests, Eliot transforms the temporal into the spatial, a temporal narrative into a timeless order.[23] The mythic method, as already noted, is closely linked to Eliot's definition of the historic sense in "Tradition and the Individual Talent"; both the past and present no longer exist in a continuum of events but are enmeshed in a simultaneous existence and simultaneous order. Thus, Eliot's historical sense is based on an ahistorical sensibility.

In Zukofsky's title—*Poem beginning "The"*—the relationship between the signifier and signified is not as clear as it is in Eliot's title. On the one hand, Zukofsky's title is a literal fact, for his poem does begin with the word *the*. On the other hand, the title also has a parodic intent, for *The Waste Land* is also a poem whose title begins with the word *the;* thus, the relationship between signifier and signified is delineated in the relationship of one text to another. But what is clear in Zukofsky's choice of a title is that Zukofsky is making a linguistic choice; unlike Eliot, Zukofsky foregrounds the article, not the noun. In making this choice, Zukofsky suggests here what would later become one of his most significant poetic statements: "The poet wonders why so many today have raised up the word 'myth,' finding the loss of so-called 'myths' in our time a crisis the poet must overcome or die from, as it were, having become too radioactive, when instead a case can be made out for the poet giving some of his life to the use of the words *the* and *a:* both of which are weighted with as much epos and historical destiny as one man can perhaps resolve" (*Prepositions,* 10). Zukofsky is not as interested in the superstructures of myth suggested in such words as *waste land* as he is the epos and historical destiny held in such words as *the* and *a*.

In fact, it is noteworthy that whereas Eliot places myth and narrative in an antithetical position—"instead of the narrative method, we now use the mythical method"—Zukofsky perceives a linguistic antithesis—the word *myth* is set in opposition to the word *the*. For Eliot, the mythic method allows the contemporary and historical particulars to be subsumed in the universal. For Zukofsky, particulars need not define themselves against the universals of authoritative myth; the noun *myth* need not be valued over the word *the*. Zukofsky writes, "Those who do not believe this are too sure that the little words mean nothing among so many other words" (*Prepositions,* 10). Zukofsky's statement carries not only linguistic but also political and sociological implications. Zukofsky's linguistic intent is egalitarian in spirit—transforming "all men are equal in the sight of God" into "all words are equal in the eye of the poet." Even at this early stage in his career, Zukofsky aligns words with social entities: articles and prepositions should not be ghettoized, alienated by labor without value; by the same token, nouns should not be endowed with the authorial power of transhistorical significance.

Inasmuch as Zukofsky is interested in myth, he is interested not in a myth that makes the present a function of the past but in what he calls a "sociological myth"—essentially the power of history—that propels the present toward the future. For the same issue of *Exile* in which his poem *The* was published, Zukofsky wrote a piece entitled "Preface" in which he stated:

> Mr. T. S. Eliot has told us that "Poets in our civilization, as it exists at present, must be difficult." But they must be more that that if they are to outlive their experience—a refined sensibility for appreciating love, war, death, El Greco, Krazy Kat, Negro Spirituals and relativity,—and mean anything to the future. Especially if the future will find it necessary to subordinate the cries and twists of our present to the creation of a singular sociological myth as great in its way, and as binding on peoples, as the solar myths of the ancients in their times.[24]

Influenced in this passage by the revolutionary fervor of George Sorel's *Reflection on Violence,* the young Zukofsky suggests that if one must succumb to a myth, why not choose a sociological myth that has the potential to transform society? Both Eliot and Zukofsky hear the "cries and twists of our present," but Zukofsky subordinates the present not to the monuments of the past but to the dynamics of the future. Of course, Zukofsky in no way dismisses tradition. In "Poetry" Zukofsky, articulating his own version of "Tradition and the Individual Talent," writes that the poet "secretly measures himself against each word of poetry ever written. Furthermore, if he is of constant depth, he thinks of others who have lived, live, and will live to say the things he cannot say for the time being" (*Prepositions,* 3). The poet himself is a vehicle for all of language— past, present, and future. But in *The* Zukofsky addresses the problem that tradition can pose, especially if our response to the past dictates our response to the present. The title of the first movement of *The,* "And out of olde bokes, in good feith," suggests that Zukofsky, like Eliot, will work with the materials of the "ideal order." But for the young Zukofsky, tradition offers not so much a resolution as a dilemma.

Zukofsky begins his poem by referring to characters of two fundamental cornerstones of Western civilization, the Judeo-Christian and Greek tradition:

1   The
2   Voice of Jesus I. Rush singing
3   in the wilderness
4   A boy's best friend is his mother,
5   It's your mother all the time.
6   Residue of Oedipus-faced wrecks
7   Creating out of the dead,—
8   From the candle flames of the souls of dead mothers
9   Vide the legend of thin Christ sending her
                   out of the temple,—
10 Books from the stony heart, flames rapping
                   the stone,
11 Residue of self-exiled men
12 By the Tyrrhenian.

                                              (*CSP*, 9)

What are we to make of the voice of Jesus (or is that Jesus I. Rush?) and the residue of Oedipus (or, rather, "Oedipus-faced wrecks")? We hear a number of resonances—from the colloquial saying "A boy's best friend is his mother" to the Freudian implications of the Oedipus complex. But we must admit that Zukofsky's Jesus certainly bears no resemblance to the mythic Hanged God of Eliot's *The Waste Land*—a symbol suggesting a framework of references to life, death, and possible regeneration. In *The Waste Land* Eliot creates a symbolic construct in which the Christ figure—the Son of Man, the red rock, the hooded figure on the road to Emmaus—is closely linked to the central symbol of the poem, the maimed Fisher King. Moreover, Eliot provides the reader with a cast of characters—from Mr. Eugenides to the young man carbuncular—who as representative wastelanders, symbols of modern decadence, all reinforce the symbolic motif of the poem.

Zukofsky, in contrast, does not replicate Eliot's complex sym-

bolic construct. He does, however, announce one clear symbol in
his prefatory dedications. "Wherever the reference is to the word
mother," writes Zukofsky, that is a "Symbol of our Relatively Most
Permanent Self, Origin, and Destiny." Zukofsky's reference to this
proclaimed symbol points, on the one hand, to a self-conscious
mockery—the capital letters call attention to the symbol's height-
ened grandiosity. On the other hand, Zukofsky's symbol—with a
capital S—stands in direct contrast to *The Waste Land*'s own Sym-
bol: the procreative mother has replaced the impotent Fisher King.

But it is important to note that Zukofsky's "mother" is not so
much part of a symbolic construct as she is a thematic referent point.
Throughout his poem Zukofsky uses the figure of the mother to
represent the "other"—as a challenge to Eliot's Fisher King and, ul-
timately, the privileged patrilineal culture of Western society. Aware
of his own Jewish matrilineal culture, Zukofsky tells his readers, "A
boy's best friend is his mother." Both Jesus and Oedipus, however,
have violated this motto: Jesus denies his mother, and the Oedipus-
faced wrecks (referring both to Oedipus's self-inflicted blindness and
the pun on Oedipus Rex) commits incest with her. Have Jesus and
Oedipus violated the "Symbol of our Relatively Most Permanent
Self, Origin, and Destiny"? Yes and no. When Christ is told that
"Your mother and Your brothers are standing outside to speak to
you," he replied, "Who is My mother and who are My brothers?"
For Christ, "Whoever shall do the will of My Father who is in
heaven, he is My brother and sister and mother" (Matt. 12:46–50).
In affirming the universal family over his specific family, Christ is
affirming his universal role and affirming his proclaimed destiny.
When Oedipus discovers his origin—that Jocasta his wife is his
mother—at that selfsame moment he fulfills his destiny and dis-
covers his identity. But for both men there is a corresponding human
loss in the fulfillment of their mythic story—the dissolution of the
specific human family, suffering, and alienation. The reader will not
comprehend the full significance of the "mother" until the fifth
movement of *The,* when Zukofsky focuses on his own family and
addresses his own mother. Nevertheless, in this first movement
Zukofsky juxtaposes the "flames of the souls of dead mothers"

against "books from the stony heart," and, as we shall see, he chooses to link himself with (m)others and a culture of otherness rather than "Paters" and a culture of "olde bokes."

Zukofsky then lists a number of literary allusions referring to texts ("books from the stony heart" or "out of olde bokes, in good feith") written, for the most part, by Modern writers, including Pound, Joyce, Eliot, Lawrence, Cummings, and Woolf. If Jesus and Oedipus—these "residue of self-exiled men"—offer us "books from the stony heart," will these Modern writers successfully resurrect motifs "out of olde bokes, in good feith"? Zukofsky's series of literary allusions, however, are often phrased in questions that lead not to the resurrected but to the dead:

15 The broken Earth-face, the age demands an
            image of its life and contacts,
16 Lord, lord, not that we pray, are sure of
            the question,
17 But why are our finest always dead?
18 And why, Lord, this time, is it Mauberly's
            Luini in porcelain, why is it Chelifer,
19 Why is it Lovat who killed Kangaroo,
20 Why Stephen Daedalus with the cane of
            ash,
21 But why les neiges?

                                                    (CSP, 9)

In line fifteen Zukofsky alludes to Pound's *Hugh Selwyn Mauberley*, by simply stating, "the age demands an image of its life and contacts."[25] But when the speaker of Pound's *Mauberley* states "the age demanded," he first renders a judgment on the age:

The age demanded an image
Of its accelerated grimace,
Something for the modern stage,
Not, at any rate, an Attic grace;
. . . .
The "age demanded" chiefly a mould in plaster,
Made with no loss of time,
A prose kinema, not, not assuredly, alabaster
Or the "sculpture" of rhyme.

Later, in "The Age Demanded" section of *Mauberley,* the speaker
also renders a judgment on the poet who is committed only to the
"inward gaze." For Pound, the demands of the age offer the poet two
dangers, the poet's Scylla and Charybdis. On the one hand, the age
demands that poets compromise their ideals and accommodate their
art to public taste, "an image / Of its accelerated grimace." On the
other hand, if artists are unable to conform in any way to the age,
they are in danger of becoming passive aesthetes: "Invitation, mere
invitation to perceptivity / Gradually led him to the isolation."

Pound associated the age with artificial "plaster" and "prose
kinema"; Zukofsky, by contrast, associates the age with the elemen-
tal "Earth-face," which demands an image not of "accelerated gri-
mace" but a revitalized version of Mauberley's "life and contacts."
Zukofsky discovers that if the age demands an image of its life and
contacts, artists have responded with images of death and aliena-
tion. Referring not only to the soldiers who died in the War to End
All Wars but also to a Modernist wasteland vision, the poet queries,
"Why are our finest always dead?" The exiled Mauberley's legacy is
not the living book of the "Envoi" but the intractable "Luini in
porcelain"; the aesthete Daedalus carries a cane of ash to test out
experience; snow, "les neiges," falls on the land of "The Dead."

Moreover, in line nineteen Zukofsky, alluding to D. H. Law-
rence's *Kangaroo,* has the speaker ask, "Why is it Lovat who killed
Kangaroo?" Zukofsky is intentionally pitting the writer Richard
Lovat Somers against the radical Jewish barrister, "Kangaroo" Ben
Cooley. In actuality, Lovat does not kill Cooley, who is killed in a
violent Labour meeting. But in transforming the exact facts, Zukof-
sky does make his point, for Cooley is never able to win support
from the writer Lovat for his radical political program. What is
the response of the writer who hears the "cries and twists of the
present"? After Kangaroo's death Lovat leaves Australia, retreating
from Kangaroo's world.

What has the speaker learned "out of olde bokes in good feith"?
Although Zukofsky understands that he, both as reader and artist, is
a product of these books, he is also aware of the danger of that
world, as he learns all too well from the aesthetes Mauberley and

Daedalus. Such a world can be a retreat from, rather than the fulfillment of, the age's demands. What should be the reaction of writers like Lovat to Kangaroo's radical politics, to the "cries and twists of the present"? Are writers caught in the world of "olde bokes," as "wrathless skeletons exhumed / new planted in its sacred wood"? Is such a world a dream world from which one needs to awake? The speaker states, "And the dream ending—Dalloway! Dalloway— / The blind portals opening, and I awoke!"

After waking out of his dream, the speaker concludes:

54 Let me be
55 Not by art have we lived,
56 Nor by graven images forbidden to us
57 Not by letters I fancy,
58 Do we dare say
59 With Spinoza grinding lenses, Rabbaisi,
60 After living on Cathedral Parkway?

(*CSP*, 11)

Zukofsky juxtaposes existence—"Let me be"—against art. In a triad of negatives, the speaker states it is "not by art" (secular or religious), "nor by graven images forbidden to us" (religious images forbidden to us because we are Jews, or because we are Jews, we must not replace religion with art?), nor by "letter I fancy" (Joyce, Eliot, Pound, et al.) that we live. Rather, existence is contingent on the everyday earning of one's bread. The poet remembers that the philosopher Spinoza earned his living by grinding and polishing lenses. And Zukofsky knows that his own impoverished "place" is New York's Cathedral Parkway—a name suggesting both his economic and cultural displacement. Zukofsky uses Spinoza—who, like Zukofsky, is a Jewish intellectual whose unorthodox ideas alienated him from traditional Judaism—as a point of reference, a point of identification. A free thinker, Spinoza was ostracized by both Jewish and Christian communities. Although Spinoza could not give the age what it demanded, he nevertheless committed himself to that age, advocating liberalism in politics and tolerance in religion.

Zukofsky uses *The* as an arena to voice various responses to art, civilization, and tradition. What can art give to those who work on

Cathedral Parkway and live in cemetery-tenements? What should be
the artist's political commitment? Should the artist subsume himself
to the authority of any system? Ultimately, what alternative to
Eliot's wasteland can Zukofsky offer? Zukofsky looks for his an-
swer not among wasteland characters but among the displaced of his
own Jewish culture. At the end of the first movement, he turns to
Spinoza, his Rabbaisi. For Zukofsky's entire life, Spinoza would
remain an important teacher to him. Like Pound's Confucius, Spi-
noza, a philosopher concerned with truth and clarity, provides Zu-
kofsky with important precepts for his poetry: the need to "apply
names rightly to things"; *natura naturans, natura naturata* (nature
as creator, nature as created); and "hatred should be overcome by
love." In the second movement Zukofsky aludes to the poetry of the
Yiddish writer Yehoash, and in the final movements he cites a series
of examples, including his own family. Even as Zukofsky challenges
the apocalyptic tone of Eliot's poem, he also attempts to enlarge the
aesthetic and sociopolitical framework of the poem to include the
impoverished and despised—to recode the social relations of the
predominant culture.

In his second movement, "International Episode," Zukofsky cre-
ates a type of Prufrockian subject, a dual self. Instead of "Let us go
then, you and I" on a journey to ask that "overwhelming question,"
the characters Zukofsky and Peter Out take their constitutional and
discuss the theater:

61   This is the aftermath
62   When Peter Out and I discuss the theatre.
63   Evenings, our constitutional.
64   We both strike matches, both in unison,
65   to light one pipe, my own.
66   'Tis, 'tis love, that makes the world go
             round and love is what I dream.
                    (*CSP*, 11)

Peter Out and Zukofsky's immediate decision is hardly an over-
whelming one: "Eh, what show do we see tonight, Peter?" We soon
discover, however, that the issues of the second movement deal with
the overwhelming questions of life-death and love-sexuality, set in

international, private, and literary contexts. They may dream of life and " 'Tis, 'tis love," but the allusion to the nightingale's cry reminds us of Philomela's rape, undercutting their Dantesque vision of idealized love "that makes the world go round." Suggesting both death and sexuality, Peter Out's name refers to both Cartesian matter—Yeats's dying animal, the body that peters out—as well as the phallus. And the backdrop of the second movement consists not of "talk of Michelangelo" but references to the burgeoning anti-Semitism in Europe ("Time, time the goat were an offering. . . . Black shirts—black shirts—some power / is so funereal"), Richard Chamber's suicide ("Hours, days, months, past from us and gone, / Lion-heart not looked upon, walk with the / stars"), and life in death ("And so quickly grown old that we on earth like / stems raised dark / Feel only the lull, heave, phosphor / change, death, the / One follow, the other, the end?"). The speaker wonders how he may cheat death: "What in revenge, can dead flesh and bone / make capital?" For his answer the speaker looks to Yehoash's story of the Bedouin, Sa-idi, who seizes the Desert-Night: "Big his heart and young with life / younger yet his gay, wild wife / The Desert-Night." The answer is actually Marvell's answer to his coy mistress—"Thus, though we cannot make our sun / Stand still, yet we will make him run." Before time can devour us, we must devour time; or, as Prufrock fails to do, we must squeeze the universe into a ball.

But Zukofsky and Peter Out are not Bedouins: "I've changed my mind, Zukofsky, / How about some other show." A more pressing concern than the wild Desert-Night is Peter's hoped-for if mundane position at the post office; but Peter Out is handicapped by his weight: "less than one hundred twenty-five pounds, / One half of a disabled veteran, and / probably / the whole of an unknown soldier." Prufrock might be trapped in the social futilities of a life "measured out in coffee spoons," but Zukofsky and Peter Out are constrained by social necessities—the sheer endeavor to earn a living and to survive the crippling disabilities of the "War to End All Wars." Alluding to Horace, Zukofsky ironically states, "That's indomitaeque morti for you"—the wild and the dead. The final shows that Peter Out and Zukofsky consider reflect the wild and the dead: "Tear the Codpiece Off, A Musical Comedy," "Panting for Pants," and "The Dream That Knows No Waking."

In the third movement, "In Cat Minor," Zukofsky's voice merges into the wild, elemental cat world: "Hard, hard the cat-world. / On the stream Vicissitude / Our milk flows lewd." In such a world, cats cry, "wet the floor," and prowl. Such a world takes Marvell's edict quite to heart: "—And r-r-run—the Sun!" Here Zukofsky sets the wild, animal world against the social world of life-denying constraints. Ultimately, however, human beings live in society, and they must find their answers in a cultural rather than a natural setting. For Zukofsky, an artist articulating an aesthetic and social agenda, the answer must come from a literature that does not exclude the displaced and dispossessed. John Tomas, in his reading of *The,* suggests that Zukofsky is protesting not only the limitations of society (poverty, anti-Semitism, war, repressed sexuality) but also the canonical limitations of a Western culture; thus, Zukofsky intends to expand the boundaries of Tradition by "empower[ing] alternate cultures . . . suppressed by the dominant West."[26]

In this poem, which Barry Ahearn has described as "an introspective house of mirrors,"[27] we see Zukofsky both as a created object and a speaking subject. The multiple voices of the poem reverberate with echoes—alternating tones of irony, self-reflection, anger, and celebration. What holds all these voices together is the central voice of Zukofsky himself, for Zukofsky is both the creator and product of the language. In the last three movements, Zukofsky steps forward out of his shapeshifting self to speak, drawing heavily on autobiographical material. Here he defines the self through conflict, especially conflict with institutional authorities. His voice is the angry and demanding voice of the dispossesed living in cemetery-tenements: "Angry against things' iron I ring / Recalcitrant prod and kick." Zukofsky gives Eliot's Bleisteins and Sweeneys a voice.

Zukofsky embraces his anger, for without it he could easily and unthinkingly be assimilated into Eliot's cultural tradition. He could forget that he lives on the margins of that tradition, that he comes from a ghetto wasteland that needs to be transformed, not denigrated. Zukofsky especially focuses his anger on the educational system which gave him access to that tradition—which processed him through "Askforaclassic, Inc." He understands all too well that he has not been "merely accepting" but actually appropriating the cultural tradition offered him.

In the fifth and sixth movements, Zukofsky finally clarifies why "books from the stony heart" can be an oppressive force. Here he directly addresses his mother, "who could never sing Bach, never read Shakespeare." His mother stands in direct contrast to such institutions of assimilation as Askforaclassic, Inc. She never learned English; she never read the "olde bokes, in good feith" or the "books from the stony heart." We now understand why Zukofsky refuses to be absorbed fully by the authoritative institutions, for complete assimilation into the culture, into the tradition of existing monuments, could very well mean a form of annihilation of the self and alienation from his familial and cultural origins. Adopting the voice of Shakespeare's Shylock, he tells his mother that he will both use and "kick and prod" the tools of assimilation:

250   If I am like them in the rest, I should
              resemble them in that, mother,
251   Assimilation is not hard,
252   And once the Faith's askew
253   I might as well look Shagetz just as much
              as Jew.
254   I'll read their Donne as mine,
255   And leopard in their spots
256   I'll do what says their Coleridge,
257   Twist red hot pokers into knots.
                              (*CSP*, 17–18)

Zukofsky will not simply be absorbed by the cultural and religious institutions of his day. Instead, he will master their tools far more successfully than did Shakespeare's Shylock: "The villainy they teach me I will execute / And it shall go hard with them, / For I'll better the instruction, / Having learned, so to speak, in their colleges." Zukofsky's poem *The* is proof of this mastery. The multiple voices of the poem—its literary allusions, the Yiddish verses, the biblical references, the popular songs—all converge into the voice of the speaker. In the end the recalcitrant poet is not assimilated into the "ideal order"; rather, his poem becomes a collage of assimilated material. In *The* Zukofsky, quoting Max Stirner, asks whether or not an "egoist" can embrace or "take up with a party"; he answers, "Oh yes, only he cannot let himself / Be embraced or taken up by the party" (*CSP*, 16). The poet can embrace the existing monuments, but he cannot let himself be absorbed by those existing monuments.

In "Tradition and the Individual Talent," Eliot posits his own argument for the relation of the self to cultural authority: "The progress of the artist is a continual self-sacrifice, a continual extinction of personality." Not only must the poet "develop or procure the consciousness of the past," but he must continually surrender himself "as he is at the moment to something which is more valuable."[28] For Eliot the artistic process demands a surrender of the self to the authority of tradition. Zukofsky's search for an epic form, however, will not lead him to Eliot's surrender to cultural authority; but neither will it lead him to Whitman's self-expressive lyric epic. In his quest for poetic form, Zukofsky will turn neither to the authority of tradition nor to the authority of the self; rather, as he continues to develop his own poetics, he will make a third choice and choose language as his mediating expression of authority—the "epos and destiny" inherent in words. Such a choice allows Zukofsky to use the structures of both tradition and the self within his language, without subsuming the self into Eliot's tradition or insisting that tradition simply become an expression of a "Whitmanesque" self. The materials of tradition, history, and the self are all merged into the language of the poem. We hear the voice of the poet thinking, but the poem is far more than the sum of the poet's personality. Indeed, the poet is the creator of the poem, but the focus of the poem is its language; Zukofsky's multiple voices resist being subsumed—in a Bakhtinian sense—within a monologic voice.

Although Zukofsky perceives the limitations of a Modernist apocalyptic vision of death and alienation, he develops his poetics against the framework of a Modernist tradition that he mirrors through his use of fragmentation, juxtapositions, multiple voices, and ironic interplays. Nevertheless, Zukofsky is interested in displacing the Modernist vision of alienation with a socially conscious vision of hope, one that will incorporate aspects of "otherness"— allowing the silent and repressed of the culture to have a voice, moving them from the margins to the center of aesthetic and social discourse. In foregrounding the article *the* in his title, Zukofsky, I believe, also begins to see the displacement of individuals mirrored in the displacement of language: articles and prepositions, too, have a central place within language, this socially constructed sign system. Whereas Eliot, through his wasteland poem, searches for a utopian world of transcendent myth, Zukofsky, through *The*, begins his search for a utopian world free of commodification—reinstating value for both individuals and language.

Zukofsky's final movement is appropriately entitled "Finale, and After." Eliot's *Waste Land* only suggests a possible regeneration; Zukofsky's *The* unabashedly declares hope for the future. Indeed, both poets are interested in "the direction of historic and contemporary particulars," but Eliot looks back to the authority of the past and the superstructure of myth, whereas Zukofsky looks forward to an open-ended history and to the epos and destiny of little words. If the present is to be subordinated, it would be subordinated not to a past but to a future. Once again, grafting Yehoash's words into his poem, Zukofsky writes:

    319   Under our feet will crawl
    320   The shadows of dead worlds,
    321   We shall open our arms wide,
    322   Call out of pure might—
    323   Sun, you great Sun, our Comrade,
    324   From eternity to eternity we remain true to you,
    325   A myriad years we have been,
    326   Myriad upon myriad shall be.

                                        (*CSP*, 20)

For Zukofsky, life is an ongoing process that was, and is, and is to come. The process of history and the voice of the poet transform the materials of existence into art: "Speaking about epics, mother— /

Down here among the gastanks, ruts, / cemetery-tenements." With-
out the promise of history, epics among cemetery-tenements seem
little more than an ironic or escapist gesture, "the dream that knows
no waking." For Zukofsky, unlike Stephen Daedalus, history is not a
nightmare from which he is trying to wake; history is the dream he
wishes to realize.

4. Pound: The Vicissitudes of Friendship

In a September 1978 interview with Carroll Terrell, Celia Zukofsky stated that her husband "felt that Pound was probably the greatest literary mind in the 20th century and the finest writer in English." According to Mrs. Zukofsky, when Pound died in 1972, Zukofsky felt he had lost a father: "Louie [Louis], the only thing Louie did was go back and read some of his stuff. Louie could not respect the dead by going to a church or a synagogue. I mean Louie didn't respond that way. . . . No, his only response was to pick up a Pound book and read it. He thought that was the only way he could pay his respect or commune with Pound."[1] Appropriately, Zukofsky mourned for his dead friend through the communal act of reading. After all, for more than half a century Zukofsky and Pound's relationship had been governed by the reading of each other's letters and poetry: the two men had praised, criticized, and argued with each other since the 1920s. For Zukofsky, Pound was not only the father of modern American poetry but his own literary father as well.

The father-son relationship between Pound and Zukofsky has puzzled many—and not only because of Pound's Fascist and anti-Semitic beliefs. Although Zukofsky and Pound both dreamed of a revitalized culture, Pound desired to preserve heroic and aristocratic values as the basis of his ideal culture, reserving political authority for a chosen elite; Zukofsky, however, desired to include the displaced and dispossessed within the framework of a transformed sociopolitical and aesthetic structure.

Significantly, the two men became acquainted during the late 1920s, a formative period in both their lives: Zukofsky had not yet articulated his Objectivist vision; Pound had not yet finished shaping his ideological vision. Learning much from Pound, Zukofsky incorporated Pound's Imagist techniques and his ambition to write a "poem including history" into his own poetics. During these formative years, however, Zukofsky was less concerned about Pound's capitulation to a totalizing ideology and more concerned about his own capitulation to Pound's totalizing influence. Although Zukofsky considered Pound a master craftsman, Zukofsky was an independent and often recalcitrant apprentice.

Years later, from the grounds of Saint Elizabeth, Pound would read Zukofsky's poetry and comment, "I now divide poetry into what I CAN read and what I cannot. I hv/read thus far and expect to read to the end. I note that you got OUT of influence of E. P. and Possum/NO longer the trace of linguistic parisitism that I noted with surprise on rereading some early Zuk." He concludes, "Damn all I think yu have got yr/own idiom."[2] In these few words Pound attests to Zukofsky's evolutionary development as a poet—a development that arises out of Pound's own and Eliot's influences. Pound's comments reflect what he perceived to be his own development from his literary fathers, a process that included both an absorption and a cleansing. Pound's model suggests a reverse baptism, in which the poet is first filled with the holy speech of the poet's literary gods and then is born into a linguistic world in which the poet adamantly states "Non serviam" and creates his or her own artistic style. Zukofsky, like Pound before him, escaped this "trace of linguistic parisitism" and created his own "idiom." Like Athena leaping out of Zeus's head, the young Zukofsky leapt out of the legacy of Eliot and Pound into "wut wuz in [the] air of a time."

I feel that it is necessary to make this distinction about the nature of influence in order to clarify Zukofsky's role as either an inventor/master, to use Pound's categories, or a diluter—that is, a man who came after the inventor/master and "couldn't do the job quite as well."[3] For a good part of his career, Zukofsky had to struggle with the second label, although, as Pound acknowledged, Zukofsky was a master/inventor of his own idiom. As early as 1928 Zukofsky reported to a friend of his that he was mentioned in an article as an imitator of Eliot. Of course, in subsequent years—because of his close relationship with Williams and, especially, Pound—Zukofsky would be called their imitators. Such a label could be quite galling for the young poet. In a 1937 letter to Lorine Niedecker, Zukofsky commented on the resemblance between his *Test of Poetry* and Pound's *ABC of Reading:* "My debt to him [Pound] really goes back to How to Read. . . . I wuz about thru with my test when A.B.C. of reading wuz pub'd. Funny thing iz he shd be working along same line at same time. Like 'A' of course, the critics will say I take it all from Ezra—but—you know & I & Ezra knows."[4]

As early as 1930 Zukofsky attempted to come to terms with the nature of his literary debt to his predecessors. In a short excerpt he categorizes three types of influence:

> 1. its presence in the air: sometimes the proximity of a poet's edified literary acquaintances, however conscious or unconscious a poet may be of the almost literal drafts around him; 2. coincidence of the temperament affected and the temperament only apparently, not actually affecting; since the modality of events of a period of fifty or seventy-five years may show, at any time of their calendar, two similar individuals, different as to locale, and contemporary or anachronistic as to their birth and mortuary dates; 3. conscious choice or rejection of a literary tradition. (*Prepositions,* 135)

In his need to clarify his own literary debt, Zukofsky suffers his own anxiety of influence; yet here Zukofsky also affirms his influences. Influence can consist of the interaction of a poet and his "edified literary acquaintances," like Pound and Williams; of a shared temperament, not bounded by time, like Dante and Shakespeare; or, finally, of a choice or rejection of a literary tradition, such as the Modernist tradition. In each of these cases, Zukofsky affirms his influence much the same way as he affirms friendships: influence, too, can be regarded as a contingent act. In raising the issue of literary influence, Zukofsky is essentially foregrounding the issue of both origin and originality. For Zukofsky, influence does not lead to a single pure origin; rather, it consists of a labyrinth of contingent discourses: there is no prediscursive origin. And as a corollary, originality can also be a contingent act; for writers from Shakespeare to Pound find that originality can be defined not by invention but by assimilation—recasting the materials of the culture into a new form.

Zukofsky's long relationship with Pound began when Zukofsky first read Pound's poetry. In a 1941 letter to Lorine Niedecker, Zukofsky describes his initial impression of Pound's work, which he had first read in 1919: "Knew some of Pound, The Return etc Cathay (Crazy about Exile's Letter in Cathay) since I wuz 15—but on whole thought he wuz precious & suspected him, till I read some of the Prose & Dials 1925 (?) & then sent him 'The' written end of 1926."[5] Pound might very well have agreed with Zukofsky's response to his work, for at times he suspected it himself. In 1911 he had seen Ford Madox Ford roll on the floor laughing as he listened to the "stilted language" of Pound's third volume of poetry, *Canzoni;* a few years later he had seen his imitators turn Imagism into Amygism; and in *Hugh Selwyn Mauberley* he had written of the danger of a poet equipped with technical skill but without vision.

More than likely, in reading Pound's early poetry, Zukofsky was responding to Pound's residue of "precious" nineteenth-century mannerisms, what Pound called "the crust of dead English, the sediment present in my own available vocabulary." "It takes six or eight years to get educated in one's art," writes Pound, "and another ten to get rid of that education."[6] In 1930, after reading a portion of *"A"*, Pound would give very similar advise to the young Zukofsky: "eliminate top dressing inherited. You'll have to work at that, just as hard as I did to get Roberto de Brownening's chic vocablary outer my system."[7]

Zukofsky, however, is "crazy about Exile's Letter in Cathay." Pound based *Cathay,* published in 1915, on Ernest Fenollosa's material, which contributed much to the development of his ideogrammic method. In these poems, which stood in stark contrast to often overelaborate nineteenth-century translations of Chinese poetry, Pound uses "luminous details" and precise diction to convey highly charged moments of human experience.

Like Zukofsky, Pound, too, favored "Exile's Letter." In an inscription in one of the two copies of *Cathay* he sent to John Quinn,

Pound indicated his fondness for the poem.[8] In the elegiac "Exile's Letter," the famous Chinese poet Li Po writes his friend a letter filled with memories of drink, "song and laughter," and "vermillioned girls." The poem conveys a moment of loss and separation; Li Po's memories are punctured by absence, the longed-for past pierced by the empty present: "And all this comes to an end. / And is not again to be met with." Zukofsky, with his love of internal rhymes and half rhymes and repetitions, no doubt admired Pound's manipulation of sound and rhythm: the repetition of the two *and*s compounds the speaker's resignation, the ineluctable *end* resonates against the hollow *again,* and the finality of the two end stops cuts off any hope for the speaker (note the stressed "end" set against the unstressed "with"). Both Zukofsky and Pound, as artists who worked on the margins of society, identified with the image of the exile.

For Pound, the "Exile's Letter" communicated his own sense that he was an exile, separated not from "vermillioned girls" and "laughter and song" but from the British and American culture. At the end of his 1915 edition of *Cathay,* Pound indicated his sense of alienation, his sense that the audience for his book might not be an "audience of goodwill." Thus, he needed to be particularly selective in the translations he included in *Cathay,* for "it is quite certain that the personal hatred in which I am held by many, and the *invidia* which is directed against me because I have dared openly to declare my belief in certain young artists, will be brought to bear first on the flaws of such translations, and will then be merged into depreciation of the whole book of translations."[9] And a few years hence, in *Hugh Selwyn Mauberley,* Pound would relate his attempt to "resuscitate the dead art / Of poetry" in a world of lies, plaster, and "prose kinema."

Of course, Pound was not alone in his sense of alienation. The exile was a crucial symbol for such European writers as James Joyce, who used "silence, exile and cunning" as his weapons; and as Malcolm Cowley documents in *Exile's Return,* a whole generation of American expatriated writers shared Pound's sense of alienation— an inability to communicate with their own culture. But Pound, the perennial "village explainer," was never one to give up. From the outset of his career, he had taken on a didactic role to reform the sensibilities of a whole generation—especially an American generation—whether they desired to be reformed or not. To that end Pound had maintained a close relationship with America through such magazines as *Poetry* and the *Dial*. But eventually Pound desired to send his own little magazine, *The Exile,* back to America; like Li Po, Pound sent his own letter "a thousand miles, thinking." In 1926 Zukofsky was one of the young writers to answer Pound's "letter" with his *Poem beginning "The"*. In submitting his poem, Zukofsky (the Jew as historical exile) wrote to Pound (the self-exiled American), "I don't suppose anybody dares print this, but if anybody does, it will be you."[10]

Pound published Zukofsky's poem in the third issue of *The Exile*. A short-lived venture, this little magazine provided an appropriate meeting ground, for it reflected both Pound's and Zukofsky's commitment to art as a social and cultural force, as a means of communal survival. As Zukofsky once commented in a poetry discussion in the 1930s, "It's obvious a poet lives in his time . . . obviously he can't escape to the so-called ivory tower, for he's likely to find it's in the Chrysler Bldg."[11] In *The Exile* Pound stated he would present a forum for the social and economic revolutions—both Fascist and Communist—that were occurring in the 1920s. In the first issue of *Exile,* Pound outlined an editorial program to which the young Zukofsky would not have objected:

> At present, in that distressed country [the United States], it would seem that neither side ever answers the other; such ignoring, leading, in both cases, to ignorance. I should like a small open forum in which the virtues or faults of either side might be mentioned without excessive animus.
> Both Fascio and the Russian revolution are interesting phenomena; beyond which there in the historic perspective Herein and Passaic are also phenomena, and indictments.[12]

Pound, an admirer of Mussolini, and Zukofsky, an admirer of Lenin (see Zukofsky's poem "Constellation"), might well have found themselves debating on the opposite sides of that forum. But in actuality, Pound, who admired both these "men of action," felt comfortable about pairing Mussolini and Lenin: "Practical men like

Lenin and Mussolini differ from inefficients like Otto Bauer in that they have a sense of time."[13] In fact, Pound praised Lenin's desire to eliminate bureaucracy, a problem that he felt the English and Americans had failed to eliminate.

Some—looking ahead to the 1930s—might feel that Pound's viewpoint was contradictory; Zukofsky, however, felt that Pound was eclectic, for Pound often blurred the distinctions between Left and Right. In fact, during these years Pound had not yet committed himself to any party, except for his own "Party of Intelligence." In the 1920s Pound, developing his own "revolutionary credo," would listen to the multiple political voices of his time. For example, Peter Nicholls has noted that Pound's interest in the American left-wing periodical *New Masses* in 1926 "coincided with his first declaration of enthusiasm for Mussolini."[14] Burton Hatlen has argued that Pound's Fascism, a Fascism Hatlen considers a blend of conservative/authoritarian and socialist/populist ideologies, was created out of a mixture of the Right's desire for order and authority and the Left's aspirations for an egalitarian community.[15] And, as any number of scholars have observed, Pound's own desire for a totalizing vision was continually disrupted by his own text: his polyphonic voices, fragmentation, and ideogrammic method continually freed his poems from "hardening into a univocal . . . cultural summa."[16]

During *The Exile*'s publication in the late 1920s, Pound was as vociferous about politics—in the style of *Patria Mia*—as he had always been, but he emphasized art over politics. His increasing political preoccupations in the 1930s distressed many of Pound's friends and admirers, including Zukofsky. After the 1920s the issue of politics and especially economics would become a sore point between the two poets. When Pound traveled to America in 1939, Zukofsky visited with him, only to find his time with Pound marred by arguments about Father Coughlin, Major Douglas, and paper money. Zukofsky was simply bewildered by Pound's anti-Semitic and pro-Fascist stance. Years later, Zukofsky, in referring to Pound, would comment, "I hope he isn't crazy devoting so much time to the idea that they charged six-percent interest in Pisa, and how wonderful it was. No—rather 'Imperial power is / and to us what is it? /

The fourth; the dimension of stillness.' That's the great Pound."[17]
Zukofsky was interested in the poetry, not the dogma, of Pound's
economics.

But in *The Exile* Zukofsky had encountered a Pound he could
more readily understand, for as William Chace has noted, "Pound,
on the eve both of his most active years as a political spokesman and
of a great economic depression, was still toying with being a politi-
cian of the arts, not of society at large."[18] As Pound stated in the
first issue of *The Exile:* "The artist, the maker is always too far ahead
of any revolution, or reaction, or counter-revolution or counter-
reaction for his vote to have any immediate result."[19] Neither Pound
nor Zukofsky felt that the artist should be an ivory-tower aesthete
disengaged from political activity, but at the same time, the artist
must not become a tool of a political party. Politics should serve as a
handmaiden to culture.

Although the two writers ultimately would hold irreconcilable
economic and political beliefs, their shared commitment to poetry
made Zukofsky an ideal candidate as one of Pound's "*les jeunes.*"
Indicating Pound's special interest in mentoring American writers,
Eliot once noted, "Though young English writers, and young writers
of any nationality, could count on his support if they excited his
interest, the future of American letters was what concerned him
most."[20] And for Pound, in his search for intelligent life among H. L.
Menken's "booboisie," poets like Zukofsky represented "the future
of American letters." In 1912 Pound had written Harriet Monroe
about her magazine *Poetry* and the state of American poetry: "Can
you teach the American poet that poetry *is* an *art,* an art with a
technique, with media, an art that must be in constant flux, a
constant change of manner, if it is to live? Can you teach him that it
is not a pentametric echo of the sociological dogma printed in last
year's magazines? Maybe. Anyhow you have work before you."[21]
The "work" he outlined for Harriet Monroe was the work he had
outlined for himself. Eliot commented that "Pound's great contribu-
tion to the work of other poets (if they choose to accept what he
offers) is his insistence upon the immensity of the amount of *con-
scious* labour to be performed by the poet; and his invaluable sug-

gestions for the kind of training the poet should give himself—study of form, metric and vocabulary in the poetry of diverse literatures, and study of good prose."[22] Pound advocated that the poet be a trained craftsman; in Zukofsky, Pound had found another skilled poet who proved to be an exception to Pound's opinion that "apart from Mr. Mencken and the New Masses, American thought is entirely covered by the Harding memorial stamp."[23] Several years later Zukofsky would receive a note from a young Italian poet desiring to meet Zukofsky because, as the young man stated, "My dear friend Ezra Pound told me that you were the only intelligent man in America."[24]

Through Pound's urgings, Zukofsky met such poets as William Carlos Williams and Basil Bunting. Moreover, Pound encouraged Zukofsky to generate his own artistic activity in New York. In a letter of 12 August 1928, Pound writes:

> I further suggest that you make an effort toward restarting some sort of life in N.Y.; sfar as I know there has been none in this sense since old [Alfred] Steiglitz [sic] organized (mainly foreign group) to start art. . . .
> I suggest that you form some sort of gang to INSIST on interesting stuff (books) ⟨1.⟩ being pubd. promptly, and distributed properly.
> 2. simultaneous attacks in as many papers as poss. on abuses definitely damaging la vie intellectuelle.[25]

Eventually, Zukofsky did organize "some sort of gang" when he developed an Objectivist poetics with his friends William Carlos Williams, George Oppen, Charles Reznikoff, and Carl Rakosi. Affirming his support of Zukofsky, Pound persuaded Harriet Monroe to let Zukofsky edit an Objectivist edition of *Poetry*. And in the early 1930s, Pound sent Zukofsky passage money to visit him in Italy. During his trip in Europe, Zukofsky was asked by a reporter for *Pesti Naplo* how he liked Europe; Zukofsky answered that he had come to Europe "chiefly to meet the master of American poetry and in a sense its father, Ezra Pound."[26] If Pound was the master and father of American poetry, he was also Zukofsky's artistic father during these years, influencing Zukofsky at several key moments of his life. Carroll Terrell once asked Celia Zukofsky when she thought her husband realized that *"A"* would be his magnum opus. She answered, "As soon as Pound used some of the movements in his anthology. Pound apparently saw some of the value of the 'A' movements immediately; otherwise he wouldn't have printed them. There I feel was Pound's judgment: he did that right away."[27]

Zukofsky also offered his own judgment of Pound's work. In *The Exile* Zukofsky demonstrated that from the first, he, like Pound, was both a practitioner and a critic, using prose as an extension of his poetry—both of which "are but an extension of language." In his prefatory note to his collection of critical essays in *Prepositions,* Zukofsky writes that his collected essays "may be viewed as steps in the excursion of a poet who wished to imbue criticism with something of the worth and method of his craft" (*Prepositions,* xi). Blurring the demarcation between poetry and prose, Zukofsky's essays often share the elliptical nature, the collage technique, and the use of quotations found in his poetry. In 1929 Zukofsky turned his critical acumen on his mentor and wrote an essay on Pound's poetry, demonstrating that he was a perceptive reader of Pound's work.

Pound not only approved of Zukofsky's essay but desired to have it translated into French. In a letter dated 31 October 1929, Pound writes: "Ten years too soon to print the thing in England or America. So far as I know no one else has writ. a crit of me AFTER reading the work. This method has advantages. Also so far as I know you are the first writer to credit me with an occasional gleam of intelligence or to postulate the bounds or possibility of an underlying coherence."[28] Appreciating Zukofsky's insight into his work and feeling that literary criticism should be left to "blokes like us," Pound encouraged his young colleague to accept the mantle of the artist's dual roles—that of poet and educator of a culture.

Zukofsky's 1929 essay, entitled simply "Ezra Pound: The Cantos," would be significant if only because Pound believed Zukofsky to be the first writer "to postulate the bounds or possibility of an underlying coherence" to his works—especially the *Cantos.* Zukofsky's essay is also interesting in terms of critical hindsight, for Zukofsky makes a number of assertions about Pound on such issues as the coherence of his work and the relationship of his ideas to his language—issues over which critics years hence would continue to debate. Moreover, Zukofsky's essay on Pound enumerates the lessons the young poet learned from the master poet—lessons that emphasize the primacy of language. In a few pages Zukofsky outlined what he perceived to be the central concerns in Pound's oeuvre, dividing his essay into three sections: "Ta Hio," "Translation," and "Cantos 1–27."

Essentially, Zukofsky begins his essay with an Aristotelian premise—that the purpose of art is closely tied to the good of society. After quoting two stanzas from *Hugh Selwyn Mauberley* that highlighted Pound's search for "the expression of an idea of beauty (or order)," Zukofsky comments, "This classifying of values shows Pound sufficiently moral" (*Prepositions*, 67). Admittedly, Zukofsky's pronouncement is an odd opening line on an essay about a poet who is famous for his controversial political beliefs. But, as Zukofsky notes, Pound's moral vision provides the basis for Pound's need to transform language and, in so doing, to transform society—an underlying purpose to Pound's work. Zukofsky draws the title of his first section, "Ta Hio," from Pound's American version of the Confucian *Ta Hio* (Great Learning), which Pound first published in 1928. The *Ta Hio*, which Pound described as "what I believe," states that if men want good government, if they want order in their homes, if they wish to discipline themselves, and if they wish to rectify their hearts, they must first seek "the precise verbal definitions of their inarticulate thoughts"—a precision they could attain when they "set to extend their knowledge to the utmost."[29] In essence, the basis for good government, families, and character is linked with the precise use of language: Flaubert's "le mot juste." Seeing a fundamental connection between Pound's "poetry of music, image and logopoeia" and Pound's personal "humanity," Zukofsky states that Pound "has treated the arts as a science so that their morality and immorality become a matter of accuracy and inaccuracy" (*Prepositions*, 68). As such, through his own sincerity Pound can objectify in language his moral claims. In Pound, Zukofsky sees the marriage of the "isolated creator" and "worldly pamphleteer," the artist who synthesizes textual aesthetics with social ethics. In his use of examples, Zukofsky, reflecting his own political sympathies, links

Pound's Confucian ideals with Lenin and the "Soviet Idea" rather than, as Pound would do in the 1930s, with Mussolini and Fascism.

In this first section Zukofsky looks for the rationale that gives birth to Pound's concrete use of language. In his second section Zukofsky raises the issue of whether or not Pound's translations are a mimetic or creative act. First, an inherent problem exists within the nature of translations: that is, how can one contribute something original when repeating something that has already been said? Zukofsky asks, "What, then is his contribution? Briefly, the distinction of rendering into English unexplored poetic forms, and of translating himself through personae" (*Prepositions,* 71). Here, then, Pound can follow his dicta and even make the old new by rediscovering forms and translating, not so much one text into another text, as himself into various personae; thus, Pound himself is inscribed in a poetic palimpsest—with his utterances interwoven with past utterances. In using translations and highlighting the role of the translator Divius in *Canto* 1, Pound acknowledges the fact that texts are linked, to use Barthes's term, to the "already written."

Next, Zukofsky analyzes the dynamic relationship of the poet to the cited text. In translating, the poet does not adopt the role of a passive medium but rather actively communicates his or her judgment within the text. Quoting from Pound's essay on Henry James, Zukofsky notes Pound's distinction between poetry ("the assertion of a positive, i.e. of desire") and poetic satire ("an assertion of this positive, inversely, i.e. of an opposite hatred"): "Most good poetry asserts something to be worthwhile, or damns a contrary; at any rate asserts emotional value . . . Poetry = Emotional Synthesis" (*Prepositions,* 71). Thus, the act of translation can be an "homage, though this appears mostly between the lines, to the poets themselves," or in poetic satire, it can be an act of criticism.

For Pound, the persona is not an extension, a mere expression, of his own ego but rather a role he uses to investigate principles of culture and history. Still, Zukofsky queries, "What construction can be considered truth about the past?" How does Pound gain access to historical truth through his imaginative construction of an objective persona? After all, Zukofsky states, "Try as a poet may for objectivity, for the past to relive itself, not for his living the historical data, he can do only one of two things: get up a most brief catalog of antiquities (people become dates, epitaphs), or use this catalog and breathe upon it, so that it lives as his music" (*Prepositions,* 73). Here Zukofsky privileges what he considers objectivity—"for the past to relive itself"—over subjectivity—"not for his living the historical data." One may strive for the historian's objectivity—a catalog of antiquities—or the poet's objectivity—"use this catalog and breathe upon it, so that it lives as his music." Pound, through the music of his poetry, achieves the poet's objectivity, the poet's way of knowing truth.

In his third and final section, Zukofsky focuses on the *Cantos,* which "'have invented a whole world of persons' (said W. C. Williams) and given this world oneness, notwithstanding a multiplicity of speech" (*Prepositions,* 73). He further asserts that Pound's definition of poetry—as a positive—and poetic satire—as an assertion of this positive by way of an opposite hatred—are also enacted in the *Cantos.* Moreover, Zukofsky states, "The immediacy of Pound's epic matter, the form of the *Cantos,* the complete passage through, in and around objects, historical events, the living them at once and not merely as approximation of their statistical historical points of contact is as much a fact as those facts which historians have labelled and disassociated" (*Prepositions,* 77).

In these statements Zukofsky expands some of the central ideas he has already explored. First, Zukofsky asserts that there is a coherence in the *Cantos;* the work's "multiplicity of speech" and a "whole world of personae" does not preclude, but can confer, oneness to this world. In fact, Zukofsky perceives that the same coherence that governed Dante's *Divine Comedy* governs Pound's *Cantos*—that is, the conception "directed towards inclusiveness, setting down one's extant world and other existing worlds, interrelated in a general scheme of people speaking in accord with the musical measure, or spoken about in song." Nevertheless, "the poet and his personae in the *Cantos* are not present in sharp, mediaeval outline. Dante wore robes and had a theology to accompany him on his journey" (*Prepositions,* 75). Whereas Dante dons his "Dantesque persona," Pound wears the masks of various personae; whereas Dante relies on the "religious geometry" of the inferno, purgatorio, and paradiso, Pound relies on the three loci of his world, "which are present as hate, comprehension and worship." And whereas Dante relies on narrative time in his journey to paradiso, Pound relies on juxtaposition and simultaneity.

Second, Zukofsky feels that Pound controls the direction of his *Cantos* by a process of assertion and criticism, or poetry and poetic satire. In essence, Zukofsky is raising an issue concerning voice: can we identify Pound's authorial voice in a polyphonic text? Does the fact that the poet's "I" has been transformed into a persona preclude the poet's power to act as judge in these poems? For instance, in "My Last Duchess," although Browning adopts the voice of the duke, he relies on dramatic irony in order to direct the reader. Thus, at the same time that we hear the duke's voice, we also hear the authorial voice that condemns the duke for his overreaching arrogance. But the *Cantos*, as Zukofsky notes, are not the "meditative, egocentric poetic-drama and dramatic monologue evolved in the nineteenth century" (*Prepositions*, 75). If the *Cantos* are molded by juxtaposition and simultaneity, where, then, is the guiding voice? Zukofsky locates that voice in the poet's use of contrast; thus Pound, without using a didactic "I," is able to demonstrate his judgment through contrast: that is "the narrator as contrasted with the obstructors of knowledge and distribution (Canto 14); T. E. H. who read Kant in a war hospital, and the hospital staff who didn't like it (Canto 16)." Still, as Jean-Michel Rabaté has noted, Pound's voice, expressing his "volitional aim," often falls between the gap of utterance and enunciation, of "typographical fragmentation and ideological assertion."[30] As Zukofsky discovers with his own poetry, language does not obediently remain within the confines of the dominant authorial voice; rather, Pound's process of enunciation tends to disrupt the authorial voice, liberating alternative voices.

Finally, Zukofsky turns to the issue of history, the raw material of Pound's epic, and states that the poet's facts are as valid as the historian's facts—"as those facts which historians have labelled and disassociated." We can't help but hear Zukofsky invoking Eliot's phrase "dissociation of sensibility." Eliot used this now-famous expression in his essay "Metaphysical Poets" to suggest a time when thought became separated from feeling: "A thought to Donne was an experience; it modified his sensibility . . . in the seventeenth century a dissociation of sensibility set in, from which we have never recovered."[31] Zukofsky is not using the word *disassociated* to affirm Eliot's historical analysis; rather, he is suggesting that Pound has recovered that world of feeling, experience, and thought—a world that the historian could only label. No doubt Zukofsky is also invoking Aristotle's remark that poetry can be "a more philosophical and higher thing than history: for poetry tends to express the universal, history the particular"; history focuses on specific details as they happened, whereas the artist, enacting a selective process, shapes and develops the concrete into a unified form. Aristotle, however, would be quite perplexed by the shaping process of Pound's ideogrammic method, a method that Pound contrasted with Aristotelian logic.

Zukofsky concludes his essay on Pound by listing Pound's three divisions of poetry: (1) *melopoeia*, "to wit, poetry which moves by its music"; (2) *imagism*, "or poetry wherein the feelings of painting and sculpture are predominant"; (3) *logopoeia*, "or poetry that is akin to nothing but language which is a dance of the intelligence among words and ideas and modifications of ideas and characters" (*Prepositions*, 77–78). In this section Zukofsky is especially interested in the music of the *Cantos*—how Pound controls vers libre by focusing on the "quantitative element in metre." But for all his love of the music of the *Cantos*, Zukofsky realizes that the image is the basic unit of Pound's poetry. Zukofsky, however, does not clearly make this observation until he writes his next critical piece, "American Poetry 1920–1930."

When Zukofsky wrote "American Poetry 1920–1930," he subtitled the work "A Sequel to M. Taupin's Books, 1910–1920." Zukofsky perceived his own article to be a sequel to René Taupin's *L'influence du symbolisme français sur la poésie américaine (de 1910 à 1920)*, portions of which Zukofsky had translated for Taupin in such journals as *Poetry* and *Symposium*. Taupin outlined distinctions between Eliot and Pound: "Pound deals with poetic diction, Eliot deals with style; Pound defines the image, Eliot defines the synthesis of image, their complications thus always adding to a complete description of these particular problems." Taupin saw Eliot as a link between imagism—the "defining of the image"—and symbolism—"the synthesis of images." In fact, Zukofsky begins his original version of "American Poetry" with a quotation from Taupin stating that very assertion: "Eliot should be considered as forming the transition between pure imagism and the new symbolism which is more complex; between a first generation which sought sincerity of expression and of rhythm, and a new generation of poets taking from the world of their conscience forms and sound to combine them according to the laws of harmony and sensibility and to express the movements of their brain."[32] Zukofsky, however, is quick to clarify that such a statement does not suggest that Eliot is higher on any evolutionary scale of poetry than is Pound: "his [Taupin's] word 'complex,'" writes Zukofsky, "does not necessarily suggest improvement."[33]

Years later, when he revised "American Poetry," Zukofsky would eliminate this discussion about Eliot and Pound, in a sense revoking Taupin's observation as a necessary literary development in the 1920s. In reference to Pound, however, he would retain his statement that "the image is at the basis of poetic form": "His *Cantos* are, in this sense, one extended image. . . . [T]hey are an image of his world, 'an intellectual and emotional complex in an instant of time'" (*Prepositions,* 142–43). For Pound, "pure imagism" did not transform into "new symbolism"; Zukofsky realized that the image was the building block of Pound's ideogrammic method.

These two essays suggest much about Zukofsky's understanding of the fundamental purview of Pound's poetry. Moreover, they indicate that Pound influenced Zukofsky in a number of ways: in his interest in history as material for poetry—"both contemporary and historic particulars"; in embedding texts within the poem—in effect, language refers to language rather than to a cohesive self or a transcendent entity; in the musical play of vers libre—"the melody, the rest are accessory"; in privileging the language of the objective poem over the voice of the subjective self—"desire for what is objectively perfect"; and in the juxtaposition of fragments against fragments. Of course, the question of influence can be quite fuzzy: what does one attribute to Pound or, according to Zukofsky, to "what wuz in the air of a time"? After all, Zukofsky was also very familiar with the works of Eliot, E. E. Cummings, Gertrude Stein, James Joyce, William Carlos Williams, as well as a number of other Modernists.

Furthermore, it is quite clear that Zukofsky was an independent thinker; he and Pound had a number of disagreements about poetry throughout their lifetime. Although Pound respected Zukofsky, he did not always understand Zukofsky's poetry; at times it seemed incomprehensible to him. And although Zukofsky revered Pound, he remained at best a recalcitrant disciple. We may well say that both men spoke, to use Pound's terms, two different "idioms" of the same language. To locate the fundamental differences between the two poets, we need only look at Pound's criticism of Zukofsky's work.

Let us focus on two specific critical statements that Pound wrote about Zukofsky for a public audience. The first statement Pound wrote in his introduction to his *Active Anthology,* in which he included Zukofsky's works. He writes, "A whole school or shoal of young American writers seems to me to have lost contact with language as language. . . . In particular Mr. Zukofsky's Objectivists seem prone to this error." Again, referring to Zukofsky, Pound notes, "One of my colleagues says he 'likes that mathematical use.' I think the good poem ought probably to include that dimension without destroying the feel of actual speech."[34] In 1957 Pound published in the *European* a limerick entitled "Old Zuk":

> This is the grave of old Zuk
> who wasn't really a crook
> but who died of persistence
> in that non-existence
>   which consists in refusing to LOOK.[35]

In these two excerpts Pound challenges Zukofsky's mode of poetic perception and execution. Pound states that Zukofsky is prone to two errors: (1) "destroying the feel of actual speech" and (2) relying on abstract thought rather than concrete images ("that nonexistence / which consists in refusing to LOOK"). Moreover, Pound indicates that Zukofsky has done this by choice, for Zukofsky *refuses* to look. In a 1935 letter Pound wrote to Zukofsky, "Most Americans miss the boat/but it is more irritatin' to see 'em catch it; and then step off."[36] Pound's statement could apply to any number of disagreements the two were having at that time, but Pound suggests that Zukofsky was deviating from a common purpose, perhaps even a common language.

To understand Pound's criticism of Zukofsky's poetry, let us first look at the basic construction of Pound's own poetics—the image. It is now a critical commonplace to trace Pound's poetic lineage from Imagism to Vorticism to his ideogrammic epic *The Cantos*. Throughout Pound's artistic development, the image continued to be his fundamental building block, the cornerstone of his vortex and ideogram. As Zukofsky recognizes in "American Poetry," for Pound, "the image is at the basis of poetic form."

As Pound himself has stated, however, his Imagist poems are far too restrictive to represent his entire poetics, most notably his "poems which include history": but, allowing for this statement, let us briefly examine his most representative Imagist poem in order to establish his basic credo. "In a Station of the Metro"—a once revolutionary poem that now rings with a comfortable familiarity—is Pound's most famous Imagist poem, a poem that Hugh Witemeyer has called the "program poem for Imagism":

> The apparition of these faces in the crowd;
> Petals on a wet, black bough.[37]

In these two lines Pound records a precise moment of perception: "the precise instant when a thing outward and objective transforms itself, or darts into a thing inward and subjective." First, the reader processes the words of the poem; then perceives distinct images— "faces in a crowd" and "petals on a wet, black bough"; and, finally, in a moment of cognition, synthesizes the two images into one. Pound has achieved his equation: "Poetry = Emotional Synthesis."

Moreover, "Metro" fulfills the three "tenets of the Imagiste faith": "1. Direct treatment of the 'thing,' 2. To use absolutely no word that does not contribute to the presentation, 3. As regarding rhythm: to compose in sequence of the musical phrase, not in sequence of the metronome."[38] Although Pound has aligned Imagism with the superimposed planes of Cubism, not the "cinematograph" of Impressionism, "Metro" is like an Impressionist painting in that it highlights a flickering moment of perception.

In "Poem 21" Zukofsky, has also created a brief poem dealing with a moment of perception. But there is a distinct difference between Zukofsky's "Poem 21" and Pound's "Metro," for Zukofsky renders not so much that moment of perception as a statement *about* that moment of perception:

> Can a mote of sunlight defeat its purpose
> When thought shows it to be deep or dark?
>
> See sun, and think shadow.
>
> (*CSP*, 88)

Zukofsky is not attempting to present a locus of images; rather, Zukofsky is, more or less, stating a theoretical problem: the conflict between perception and cognition. Very simply put, the poet is asking what happens when one sees sunlight but thinks shadow? In these three lines Zukofsky succinctly encapsulates what he explored in his book *Bottom*. "I wrote 500 pages about Shakespeare," notes Zukofsky, "just to say one thing, the natural human eye is OK, but it's that erring brain that's no good" (*Prepositions*, 170). Keeping such a statement in mind, one might conclude that the most crucial word in "Poem 21" is "mote." Although one should *see* the mote of sunlight, the "erring brain" has become the "mote in one's eye"; the "I" defeats the "eye." Thus, the mote of sunlight is defeated by the mote of the erring brain, for one is simply projecting human thought onto the natural landscape; the thinking subject usurps the external object. Zukofsky's statement is hardly new; one can trace the roots of his premise to numerous sources—to the conflict between Platonic idealism and Aristotelian realism in the fifth century B.C. to John Ruskin's criticism of Romantic poets in the nineteenth century A.D. to Pound's own emancipation proclamation, demanding freedom from "emotional slither." In essence, Zukofsky is emphasizing the fallacy in the concept of the pathetic fallacy, which Ruskin has stated is a "falseness in all our impressions of external things."

Pound would hardly disagree with Zukofsky's premise, but in this poem, Pound would say, Zukofsky commits his own fallacy; for Zukofsky has rendered an idea, not an image. In discussing the development of his own poem "Metro," Pound described the "one image poem" as "a form of super-position, that is to say, it is one idea set on top of another."[39] One could argue that the pun "mote" effects its own form of "super-position," for that one word suggests an inherent paradox: that opposing ideas—both the victorious and the defeated mote—are contained in the same word, even as opposing forces—both the I and the eye—are contained in the same individual. In his own way Zukofsky has superimposed two ideas in one word. In "Metro," however, Pound is not concerned with the double meaning of any single word—that *bough,* for instance, could also suggest *bow.* Rather, Pound superimposes one image on another; and Pound is quite specific by what he means by the resulting synthesis of the "super-position" of an image. "By the 'image' I mean such an equation [one which causes form to come into being]; not an equation of mathematics, not something about *a, b,* and *c,* having something to do with form, but about *sea, cliffs, night,* having something to do with mood."[40] Pound is interested in the *presentation* of the image, not "yatter about" the image; he is interested in experiencing the image, not theorizing about the image. As Pound writes, "No impression, however carefully articulated, can, recorded, convey the feeling of sudden light which the work of art should and must convey."

In juxtaposing these two lyric pieces, we can easily see Pound's argument that Zukofsky fails to "LOOK," or to put it another way, that in this instance Zukofsky emphasizes *logopoeia* over *phanopoeia.* But we'd be hard put to understand how "Poem 21" violates speech. Indeed, the poem states an almost straightforward premise. Zukofsky's poems ostensibly oscillate between two extremes: either the poem's language seems propositional and set within familiar frames of references, or the poem's language seems to move beyond familiar frames of reference—so that one may appropriately wonder if Zukofsky is transforming language into an essentially nonreferential framework, like music, or is replacing a social speech system with a private idiolect. It is this second type of poem in which language can literally "break down."

In "Two Dedications" ("Poem 28" and "Poem 29"), for instance, Zukofsky writes one poem for his friend Tibor Serly, a composer and violist, and another poem for the Mexican muralist Diego Rivera. In his poem dedicated to Serly, Zukofsky, in focusing on the musicality—the sound patterning—of words, disrupts a clear system of referentiality; clearly, Pound would regard such a poem as "destroying the feel of actual speech." In Zukofsky's second poem dedicated to Rivera, however, the "peasants and / Workers," addressing "Comrade D. R." and "Executives of industry," speak from Rivera's murals in predominantly propositional statements. Here the peasants articulate the exploitive relations that govern the social and economic order ("Our biceps, unspared") and speak of their enduring strength: "Marshal to say: / We are the / Heads over industry." But to conclude that one poem is more referential than the other, or that one poem reflects the machinations of social forces, while the other foregrounds the "literariness" of language is ultimately reductive, for implicit in both poems is the enactment of the struggle for power. In fact, these two poems—the first emphasizing the musicality and materiality of language, and the second highlighting the social reality of Rivera's murals—foreground some of the early theoretical Marxist debates concerning the language of formalism/Modernism and social realism. Both poems question a monologic authority, but whereas the dedicatory poem to Rivera challenges the authority of the ruling class ("executives of industry"), the dedicatory poem to Serly subverts the authorial/authoritarian power of the poet by highlighting the dynamic and unstable referentiality of words. In the poem dedicated to Serly ("Poem 28"), we can specifically see how Zukofsky breaks the "sequence of the metronome" and, in so doing, violates "the feel of actual speech":

Red varnish
Warm flitch

Of cello,
They play

Scroll before
Them—Sound

Breaks the
Sunset!—Kiss

With wide
Eyes—With

Their music
The (no?)
        (*CSP*, 37)

Zukofsky writes a series of twenty-two unrhymed couplets with his own tightly controlled prosody—two or three syllables and not more than two stress counts, often in spondee form, to a line. Moreover, Zukofsky finds intricate means of working with sound patterns, often echoing assonant or consonant sounds in adjoining words. In the fifth couplet, for example, he links the consonant sound of *w* in "with" and "wide," then connects the long sound of "wide" with the similar assonant sound in "eyes," and ends the couplet with the preposition "with," repeating his initial word. In this couplet Zukofsky also relies on the pitch of quantitative meter, pairing the short and long *i* sound in each line of the couplet. The staccato beats and sound effects of each word are interrelated to the adjoining word or line.

"Poem 28" is very much a poem about music—Pound's melopoeia. Carefully appropriating Pound's dicta about the music of poetry, Zukofsky has taken the lessons of the master to their logical conclusion. In his 1929 article on Pound, Zukofsky enumerates a number of Poundian music lessons: (1) In a 1928 *Dial* article, Pound warns against the "mere 'runnin' dahn th' road'" effect of vers libre and encourages the use of classical quantitative meter; (2) in his essay on Arnaut Daniel, Pound notes that a poet/singer such as Arnaut demonstrates a care of "clear sound and opaque sound . . . a clear sound with staccato, and of heavy beats and of running and light beats"; (3) in an essay on vers libre and Arnold Dolmetch, Pound cites Mace's "Musick's Monuments," in which Mace urges poets to strive first "for the most Exact Habit of *Time-keeping*," and once poets become masters to "then *take Liberty* . . . to *Break Time; sometimes Faster, and sometimes Slower*, as we perceive the *Nature of the Thing* Requires, which often adds, much grace, and luster, to the Performance" (*Prepositions, 79*).

In the poem dedicated to Serly, Zukofsky is creating his own musical performance by disciplining the libre of the vers with his own type of quantitative meter, by duplicating heavy and light staccato beats, and by taking the master's prerogative, as suggested by Mace, to "Break Time": "Sound / Breaks the / Sunset!—Kiss." Here Zukofsky has taken the lessons of melopoeia to the extreme and has transformed language into sound. But, as Zukofsky is well aware, words are not notes, for they "cannot escape having a reference." Zukofsky is breaking not only the sequence of the metronome but also the sequence of language and clichéd thought.

From the first two lines of the poem, Zukofsky inverts conventional expectations and, in cubist fashion, continually shifts perspectives and dissolves form. One might expect a poem dedicated to a string musician to begin with a melodic line—the typical lyric impulse of string instruments—not the harsh, almost ugly, sounds of "Red varnish / Warm flitch." But Tibor Serly, a student of Bartok, was not a traditional string musician, and "Poem 28" is not a conventional lyric poem. Zukofsky pairs "red varnish," which suggests a hard, polished surface, with "warm flitch," which connotes a soft, warm piece of pork or bacon, and associates both these images with the cello. We can quickly associate "red varnish" with an image of a cello's surface, but what are we to do with "warm flitch"? To make sense of "flitch" in this particular syntactical sequence, we can either transform the "side of pork" into a metaphor (the side of the cello resembles a bacon strip); or we can look for an alternate definition for "flitch" (a strip from a tree trunk or a beam or layers of veneer?); or we can consider the word's Old English base (to tear, to flay). Or, relying on sound associations, we can contrast the red, varnished surface of the cello with either the musician's "warm flesh" or the "flick" of the musician's wrist as he plays the cello. In any case, meaning alters according to context; one word can have myriad possibilities.

In a 1933 interview Zukofsky was asked to describe the intention of his Objectivist group; he replied, "We tend to write an expressive and musical verse rather than a magniloquent one. We seek the plasticity of words and their interrelations and musical connections rather than denotations."[41] Indeed, in the lines of this poem Zukofsky works with the plasticity of his words; in this way meaning becomes unstable or, at the very least, unpredictable. Even when a syntactical unit seems fairly straightforward, language can still be fractured. For instance, in the next line our attention shifts from the object to the agent: "They play / Scroll before / Them." If we assume that "scroll" functions as a synecdoche for cello (referring to the end of the cello's neck), we could read the first three words as a subject–verb–object sequence—a very simple and basic sentence pattern. But "scroll" could also refer to the parchment of music set before the players; then we would read "They play" the music or "They play" with the music before them—"play" would be transformed into an intransitive verb, and "scroll" would be the object of an implied preposition such as "with."

Meaning can also be altered not only by a word's various connotations but by the sheer placement of a word. For instance, the word "kiss" pivots on the end of the eighth line and changes its meaning according to its relationship to the surrounding words: "Sound / Breaks the / Sunset!—Kiss / With wide / Eyes—With / Their music / The (no?)." Zukofsky enacts a number of possible connections: "Kiss / With wide / Eyes" suggests a physical and sensual act (between two individuals? between the musician and his cello?); "Kiss . . . With / Their music" suggests a metaphorical relationship between the musicians and their audience; and the two words "The (no?)" sound like not only an aborted attempt to say "note" but an attempt to abort either the physical or metaphorical kiss.[42] Moreover, "kiss" is also a navigational term meaning "to touch in tangency as limb of sun to the horizon"; hence, "kiss" is appropriately paired with "sunset," a time when the sun "kisses" the horizon.

In the end, what are we to make of Zukofsky's musical and linguistic wordplay in his poem? Indeed, Zukofsky has taken very familiar words and defamiliarized them, unmooring us from any anchor of complacent preconceptions. But to further understand Zukofsky's rationale behind his play of language and sound, we might consider two contentions of Charles Sanders Peirce, an American philosopher whom Zukofsky respected. Peirce rejected Descartes's individual and intuitive epistemology, suggesting that the test of truth is both social and contextual. We do not understand ideas in isolation; rather, we understand something in terms of how we relate it to other things. Moreover, Peirce challenged the Cartesian view that intuition is the ultimate source of self-evident truth. Peirce questioned the assertion that our intuition allows us to distinguish between what seems to be true and what really is true; after all, we may assume that something is self-evident only because it agrees with our own presuppositions: "Merely to have such an acquaintance with the idea as to have become familiar with it, and to have lost all hesitancy in recognizing it in ordinary cases, hardly seems to deserve the name of clearness of apprehension, since after all it only amounts to a subjective feeling of mastery which may be entirely mistaken."[43] In his own way Peirce is asking the reader to examine the production of meaning.

These two assertions—that knowledge is contextual and that an idea may be considered true when in reality it is only familiar or conventional—are implicitly conveyed in Zukofsky's poem. By defamiliarizing and foregrounding language, Zukofsky is forcing his readers to think about the medium we so casually use. Let us now reexamine the lines "Sound / Breaks the / Sunset!—Kiss / With wide / Eyes—With / Their music / The (no?)." We've already noted in these lines that the word "kiss" must be perceived in context with other words; it is not an autonomous sign. But we are still left with the primary question, what do these lines mean? So far in the poem, despite the varied connotations of words, our primary images have been that of the cello and the player in the concert hall. What does the phrase "Sunset!—Kiss" have to do with cellos and musicians? Perhaps we are in an outdoor concert, or the red varnish resembles a sunset? But most likely we can assume we have moved from physical images to metaphorical associations: the music reminds the poet of sunsets and kisses. Nature and romance, after all, are conventional topics associated with, for instance, nineteenth-century tone poems, the lyric songs from Provençal poets, and twentieth-century popular songwriters. But in Zukofsky's poem, "Sound / Breaks the / Sunset!—Kiss"; the dissonant music breaks into the harmony of the spheres, upsetting conventional associations. Furthermore, the music—"With / Their music / The (no?)"—becomes a means to voice a challenge. Like Pound's translations of the Noh—"(no?)"—plays, the poem's music revitalizes familiar forms.

In the following lines of the poem, Zukofsky continues to expand semantic codes as each word collects a series of references:

Pit, weather
Of tears

Which plagues
Us—Bodies

Of waves
Whose crests
    (*CSP*, 37)

Although the associations seem prolific, the poem's language actually suggests select categories of associations—music/musical/instruments/musicians; sunset/light/dark; human bodies/flesh/sensuality; water/waves/sea. One word is usually associated with more than one category: for instance, "pit" suggests the orchestra pit, the dark pit of hell, the pit of the stomach, and even the armpit; "tears" suggests the tearing (the Old English origin of "flitch") sound across the cello, rain ("weather/Of tears), tear stains ("tears / Which plagues Us—Bodies"), and water ("Bodies / Of waves"); "bodies" suggests human bodies, bodies of water, and the sensual contact between the cello's and the musician's body (the cello is "plagued" by the "tears" of the bow and the musician is "plagued" by "emotional tears"). The words have the freedom and ambiguity of numerous connotations while at the same time they are caught within arranged semantic categories. Like musical notes ranging "over / Bars," the words resonate freely yet are caught within patterns.

Finally, Zukofsky concludes both the musical and poetic perfor-
mances of the poem:

> An assumed
> Poise among
>
> Crowds! Blue—
> Withdraws sunset—
>
> Tones sound—
> Pluck—dissonant—
>
> Stops sing
> The welter
>   (*CSP*, 38)

The soft sibilants and the hard consonants enact their own play of
harmony and dissonance. Zukofsky informs his reader that the
poem will end as he plays on yet one more pun; "stops sing" suggests
both a cellist's finger position—holding down a string in order to
alter pitch—and the end of the musical piece. Finally, both musical
and natural images find a resting point in the last word, "welter."
Taking a quick inventory of the meaning of *welter*, we discover
a number of previously established associations: to wallow like a
pig (flitch); a tossing and tumbling like waves ("of waves / Whose
crests / Spear air"); to be soaked, stained, or bathed ("Pit, weather /
Of tears); tumult or confusion (dissonant sounds). We can well
imagine that after the moment of silence at the conclusion of the
musical and poetic performance, the audience, too, responds with
their own welter—the clapping of hands. Thus, Zukofsky brings his
numerous semantic codes to rest in the single word.

    Although Zukofsky appropriates much of Pound's Imagist credo,
Zukofsky's poetics is fundamentally different from Pound's—for
whereas Pound focuses on the image, Zukofsky focuses on the word.
Pound wishes to use language primarily to convey experience; Zu-
kofsky is interested in the experience of language. Thus, even though
Zukofsky seems to concentrate on logopoeia in "Poem 21" and
melopoeia in "Poem 28," in the first poem we inevitably focus on the
word "mote," and in the second poem all the patterns of association
come to a point of "rested totality" in the word "welter" (the poem
as "object in perfect rest," attaining a "rested totality").

Perhaps this divergence between Zukofsky and Pound is no more evident than in the comparison of the two men's epic works. In *The Cantos* Pound has taken the "luminous detail" of the image and set it in the complex cultural patterns articulated in the ideogrammic method. In his juxtapositions of economic, social, political, artistic, and personal particulars, he still aims for the sudden moment of insight, that revelation which comes from emotional and intellectual synthesis. Pound began writing *The Cantos* in 1915, and by the late 1920s he had completed his first thirty *Cantos*. Zukofsky began writing *"A"* in 1927, and by the early 1930s, he had completed the first seven movements. In examining his development from *"A"*-1 to *"A"*-7, we can see how Zukofsky took his lessons from Pound about the primacy of language to their logical conclusion.

In a letter dated 12 December 1930, Zukofsky wrote to Pound about the relationship of *"A"* to *The Cantos*. The young poet seemed especially distressed at the thought that *"A"* might be considered a pale imitation of the older poet's work:

> You remember that I had read *Cantos* 4, 5 and 6 as separate poems, or poems dealing with the histories of several periods—I still had no inkling of the main intention of *The Cantos*. Had I seen Cantos XIV, XV, and XVI and the later American ones before I wrote A 1 & 2, the poem would never have been written—certainly not the invectives in the first movement or the instinctively beautiful(!) 2nd.[44]

Later in his letter, Zukofsky (whom Pound had once addressed as "Our beloved son") gave Pound (whom Zukofsky had once addressed as "Our Favver who art on Earth") the power to kill his creation:

> Be hard on the damn thing—slash it—if you think it's a dilution of *The Cantos*—and no one ought to feel that better than you—and that it's dead to begin with say so—I won't be hurt. I don't think there's Bill [Williams] in it—& I don't think there's anyone else in particular—but I wonner if you can pick it up and say diction, that ictus, is Z—if you can't say so—and maybe I'll start a new procedure in consequence.[45]

Like God staying the hand of Abraham, Pound replied, "Re/yrs/ re/'A' I concurrrrr. I see no reason fer yr/being discouraged. No pale regrets."[46] Zukofsky had appropriated much from Pound, but he desired to invent a language of his own:

> The only things that might possibly save me would be the objective evaluation of my own experience, an indigenous emotion controlling a versification which would (possibly) be my own and a natural ability (or perverseness) for wrenching English so that (again, *possibly*) it might attain a diction of distinction not you, or Eliot, or Bill, or anyone before me. Of course, that's no mean program.[47]

In the first seven movements of his epic, Zukofsky would seek to "attain a diction of distinction"; if Zukofsky would dance a dance of the intellect, it would be to a music of his own making.

Barry Ahearn has described *"A"* 1–7 as poems in which Zukofsky placed himself, separated from family and culture, under inspection. Although these poems, notes Ahearn, catalogue loss and death, they also enact resurrection. Indeed, they measure the growth of a poet in search of a revitalized language. Unlike Pound's failed poet Hugh Selwyn Mauberley, Zukofsky succeeds in finding his language, a language epitomized in his seventh movement. Ron Silliman has noted that although the "open-ended interconnectedness in *1–6* marks the debt to *The Cantos*," it is from *"A"*-7 forward that "a new conceptualization as to the function of part-to-whole relations in the formation of a longpoem starts to emerge: each moment is a totalization, complete to itself, capable of entering into larger structures as a relational fact."[48] Zukofsky, too, perceived *"A"*-7 to be a breakthrough poem. While he was still working on the poem, he wrote to Pound, "Think if I may humbly say so, that A-7 performs the revolution in the sonnet I hinted at elsewhere. May be . . ."[49]

After first reading *"A"*-7 at Zukofsky's request, Pound, with discernment, wrote the young poet, "Wot you want me to tell you about it that you can't find out for yourself?" Although Zukofsky would ask Pound for advice, he could be quite stubborn and independent in his reaction to Pound's suggestions. Nevertheless, Pound did comment, "Recd. one development or fugue or fuagal etc. produced by Ludwig von Zuk und Sohn, on not always digested meat of his forebears but with a ditional and final contortion or fugal (quasi) termination in form of canzone."[50] Pound advised Zukofsky to be careful of the influence of his forebears and of his own "perfessorial" leanings. Zukofsky, Pound's "Sohn" not withstanding, did challenge Papa's advice.

Of course, it was quite natural for Pound to see a reflection of himself ("not always digested meat of his forebears") in Zukofsky's epic. What he constructed as a revolutionary method of poetry—the Imagist credo, the collage form, the epic as a "poem including history"—had now become part of a common vocabulary for poets such as Zukofsky. Moreover, Pound could identify a number of additional elements in Zukofsky's "A" that he had explored in his work. In the Objectivist issue of *Poetry*, Zukofsky stated that "A", his poem in process, included two themes: the "desire for the poetically perfect finding its direction inextricably the direction of historic and contemporary particulars" and the "approximate attainment of this perfection in the feeling of the contrapuntal design of the fugue transferred to poetry."[51] Zukofsky's "historical and contemporary particulars" have an obvious kinship to Pound's luminous and concrete details; and his "contrapuntal design of the fugue" also is related to the form of *The Cantos*. Of course, the problem of form in Pound's epic has been a long-argued question— with Pound, at various times, arguing for or against the idea of a coherent framework in his epic. But in the late 1920s, Pound, both in a letter to his father and in a conversation with Yeats, compared the form of *The Cantos* to a fugue. In *A Vision* Yeats reports that Pound relayed to him that his "immense poem" will, "when the hundredth canto is finished, display a structure like that of a Bach Fugue."[52] Years later, however, Pound would grumble about Yeats's statement, noting that Yeats's remarks had "done more to prevent people reading Cantos for what is *on the page* than any other one smoke screen."[53] But, clearly, in the late 1920s Pound was thinking of Bach's fugues as a means to describe *The Cantos*'s structure.

Of course, Pound perceived Zukofsky's need to free himself from the influence of his predecessors to be similar to his own need to exorcise any evidence of Browning's influence in his own poem. In his introduction to his *Selected Cantos,* Pound included an excerpt from an early draft of his Browning poem, which had originally been the first, not the second, *Canto* in his epic. His poem begins with the explosive, "Hang it all, there can be but one 'Sordello'!" But in these lines Pound contemplates taking Browning's "whole bag of tricks": "Let in your quirks and tweeks, and say the thing's an art-form." He ends, however, opting for his own language: "I stand before the booth, the speech; but the truth / Is inside this discourse—this booth is full of the marrow of wisdom."[54]

Zukofsky also thought that "the truth / Is inside [his] discourse." In a letter of 7 December 1931 to Pound, Zukofsky defended the originality of his work and enumerated what he perceived to be the distinction between the two epics:

> I think structurally no one has done anything like 1–7 of "A". That is, I feel, the climaxes in each movement and as they proceed over the 7 movements are *right*.
>
> The value of "A" 's diction, linear technique—no where approaching Cantos. On the other hand, *up to now,* I think there is a different grasp of sequence, of placing & developing movement out of movement—if even in a more traditional sense—which is, granting the interest of the detail, invention. The building up by section on section, block on block, of the Sixth movement—gratifyingly from a critical standpoint the longest—has not been done otherwheres. If anything like the 7th movement exists in English I do not know it. . . .
>
> The difference between Cantos and "A" aside from diction ⟨& quality of line⟩ is the matter of musical approximation—The difference between polyphony (many voices of angels, if you will permit it) and one human voice thematically split in two—but so far the fugal principle is more obvious in the last. We both partake of the cinematic principle, you to a greater & more progressive degree, tho' it wd. be pretty hard to distinguish in either case where montage leaves off & narration begins & vice versa.[55]

Zukofsky makes a number of distinctions between the two works, including matters dealing with voice, structure, and music. We could make a quick comparison of the two works by looking at their beginnings. Of course, through such a modest comparison I do not intend to present any comprehensive overview of the two epics; rather, I wish to examine the works in the framework that Zukofsky suggests—that of voice, structure, and music. We should keep in mind that at this time Zukofsky had written seven of his movements and had read thirty of Pound's *Cantos*.

As Edward Said has observed, beginnings provide the reader with an entrance into a text and serve as a point of origin that "establishes relationships with works already existing, relationships of either continuity or antagonism or some mixture of both."[56] For two works that are noted for their difficulty and complexity, *"A"* and *The Cantos* start with relatively conventional and straightforward openings. Beginning with the heavy beat reminiscent of Anglo-Saxon poetry or a Latin translation of a Homeric epic, Pound links *Canto* 1 with the *Odyssey:*

> And then went down to the ship,
> Set keel to breakers, forth on the godly sea, and
> We set up mast and sail on that swart ship,
> Bore sheep aboard her, and our bodies also
> Heavy with weeping, and winds from sternward
>   (*Cantos,* 3)

In his use of a dramatic persona, Pound also links *Canto* 1 with Browning, with whose work Pound had, to use Said's words, a relationship of "continuity and antagonism." Of course, *Canto* 1 also demonstrates the results of Pound's antagonism, that is, his originality: his skilfull working with sound and rhythm; his ideogrammic method—the juxtaposition and interaction of particulars; and the indeterminate ending "So that." (Zukofsky, in his 1929 essay on Pound, perceives "So that" to be emblematic of Pound's method; like the connective "so that" and "and," Pound's ideograms also connect diverse ideas, people, and historical events. Zukofsky also notes that the connectives are precisely the words that are often missing in Pound's elliptical poetry.) Thus, Pound's allusion to Odysseus functions as a link to past epics as well as an indication that Pound would be commencing his own journey to the islands— fragments set adrift—of art and civilization.

Zukofsky begins *"A"* by alluding not to a literary realm (the Odyssean journey) but to a musical sphere (Bach's *Saint Matthew Passion*):

A
  Round of fiddles playing Bach,
    Come, ye daughters, share my anguish—
  Bare arms, black dresses,
    See Him! Whom?
  Bediamond the passion of our Lord,
    See Him! How?
  His legs blue, tendons bleeding,
    O Lamb of God most holy!
  Black full dress of the audience.
                    ("*A*"-1, 1)

Because I have already discussed "*A*"-1 in an earlier chapter, I will simply reiterate that Zukofsky's allusion to Bach functions both structurally and thematically: (1) Zukofsky wishes to transfer "the feeling of the contrapuntal design of the fugue" to the music of poetry; (2) he wishes to transform the superstructure of Bach's Christian myth to the linguistic structure of poetry.

Let us look at these two beginnings in light of Zukofsky's observations about voice, structure, and music. For Pound, Odysseus is one of the many voices he uses in his polyphonic chorus, what Zukofsky calls the "many voices of angels." In contrast, Zukofsky states that his poem is represented by "a human voice split in two." It is interesting to observe, in light of Zukofsky's statement, that some critics have suggested that Pound's personae seem more "human" than Zukofsky's "human voice." For example, Marjorie Perloff has noted that Zukofsky's "*A*" abandons the "speaking subject" further than Pound does in *The Cantos*—an interesting phenomenon when one considers that, in the end, "*A*" is not so much an epic about history and civilization as it is an epic about the self.[57] Zukofsky sees himself as a "human voice" insofar as he is represented in the language of the poem; inasmuch as one "hears" Bach when one listens to his music, one also hears Zukofsky when one listens to his poem. Zukofsky also perceives himself as a character in the poem; but one might say that in the poem he is not so much a "speaking subject" as he is a "speaking object." Zukofsky exists as a material word in his poem; Zukofsky realizes that even a "hero" begins as a word.

Zukofsky also feels that his poem demonstrates "the fugal principle" in a "more obvious" fashion than does Pound's. Michael André Bernstein, who regards *The Cantos* as fragmentary, has called the first thirty cantos an "astonishing poetic *tour de force*" that "give[s] the impression of a series of set-pieces, a pageant of isolated, momentary encounters."[58] And although Zukofsky, in his essay on Pound, recognizes a "oneness" in the world of Pound's *Cantos,* Zukofsky indicates in his letter that he succeeds in achieving a fugal structure in a way that Pound does not. Indeed, although Zukofsky also works with a "collage text," his first seven movements clearly work together as a sequence—one movement growing out of the next. In his sixth movement Zukofsky brings his themes and questions all together. One of his primary questions is "Can / The design / Of the fugue / Be transferred / To poetry?" As all poets do, he must ask himself, "With all this material / To what distinction"? Zukofsky believes that his answer is in the music and structure of "*A*"-7.

Both *The Cantos* and "*A*" are records of two men's search for revelation. Pound condemns the "obstructors of knowledge" and searches for the particulars of an ideal civilization. In this way, as Charles Altieri suggests, Pound raises "particulars to the level of universals whereby they come to provide models for human experience."[59] Zukofsky is looking for another possible answer, and he finds it in the poet's very material: language. Zukofsky perceives the literal materiality of one of the supreme mythic statements: "In the beginning was the word."

> Horses: who will do it? out of manes? Words
> Will do it, out of manes, out of airs, but
> They have no manes, so there are no airs, birds
> Of words, from me to them no singing gut.
> For they have no eyes, for their legs are wood,
> For their stomachs are logs with print on them;
> Blood red, red lamps hang from necks or where could
> Be necks, two legs stand A, for together M
> "Street Closed" is what print says on their stomachs;
> That cuts out everybody but the diggers;
> You're cut out, and she's cut out, and the jiggers
> Are cut out. No! we can't have such nor bucks

> As won't, tho they're not here, pass thru a hoop
> Strayed on a manhole—me? Am on a stoop.
>
> ("*A*"-7, 39)

The above sonnet is only one of seven in the canzone of Zukofsky's
seventh movement. In his own way Zukofsky has set up a predeter-
mined linguistic universe with its own set of very complicated laws.
Not only is Zukofsky following the rhyme scheme of the highly
specialized form of the canzone, but he is also conducting an intri-
cate play with words and sounds. As Kenner has observed about
these lines, Zukofsky links "manes" (Latin for ancestral spirit) with
"airs," which, in turn, is tied to both "words" ("a mouthful of air")
and "singing gut."[60] For Zukofsky, revelation is not to be found in
Bach's world of extrahuman providence; the great "I AM" must give
way to the material "A" "M" of the sawhorses. Moreover, even the
human "I" surrenders its autonomy to the words on the page ("Am
on a stoop"). Zukofsky concludes, "Spoke: words, words, we are
words, horses, manes, words." Zukofsky's canzone, however, is not
merely a linguistic exercise in sound and form, for Zukofsky realizes
that words such as "Street Closed" also have power to cut off, to
exclude. Zukofsky is aware that he lives in a society where the poor
worry about a "month's rent in arrear" and cry out, "Bother, /
Brother, we want a meal, different techniques." Both the literary and
socioeconomic world (and word) need "different techniques" to
undergo a transformation.

Zukofsky considered the seventh movement to be his revolution-
ary poem. He was especially proud of his original poetic language,
for his poem demonstrated his ability to place his many themes to
the music of the canzone—"like two or three balls juggled in the air
at once and the play got from the reflected lights in the colors of
them balls."[61] In fact, he constructed the poem in answer to an
article Pound had written for the *Dial* in which Pound suggested,
according to Zukofsky, "The sonnet occurred automatically when
some chap got stuck in effort to make a canzone." Pound perceived
the cutting away of the canzone into the sonnet to be a danger to
composition, in fact a type of "dissociation of sensibility": "It marks

an ending or at least a decline in metric invention. It marks the divorce of words and music."[62] Zukofsky was trying to marry words and music once again.

For his part, Pound only observed that "A.7 was technical O.K. Experiment." He did, however, concede that "WAAAAL. Every generation has to do something its granpap can't quite make out."[63] But essentially, for Pound, Zukofsky was losing "contact with language as language." Pound was also voicing his concern that Zukofsky was separating the word from the world. The danger always exists: if one retreats into the word, what becomes of the world? Yet Zukofsky's poetics, articulating the ways that a culture is embedded in the material lives of its people, demonstrates his desire to interweave the world and the word, the aesthetic and social demands of a literature not "based on the *abuse* of *language*" nor "on *language* as a creator of illusions" (*"A"*-8, 94). The very material of Zukofsky's epic poem is the language of the world—of history, of personal letters, of documents, of conversations, and even of printed words on sawhorses at a construction site. Moreover, Zukofsky's politically committed poetics of the 1920s and 1930s actually provide an important alternative to Pound's own ideology. Both Pound and Zukofsky were dedicated to poetry as a craft and as a means of restoring a moral order; but Zukofsky looked to Spinoza, Lenin, and a Marxist dialectic, whereas Pound opted for Confucius, Mussolini, and a Fascist vision as a means for cultural renewal.

In fact, critics such as Burton Hatlen and Edward Schelb have observed how Zukofsky developed a Marxist aesthetic in his poetry of the 1930s. Hatlen, examining the dialectic patterns between artistic and social concerns that Zukofsky establishes in the first ten sections of *"A"*, sees in these poems a trajectory of Zukofsky's own hopes for his society—moving from the political revolutionary hope of the 1930s to the despair of the war years. Especially in *"A"*-8 and the first section of *"A"*-9, Hatlen argues, Zukofsky found a means of marrying the word to the world through "an explicitly Marxist conception of labor as the distinctively human act by which we collectively transform the world and make it our own." The poet's labor— his poem—can have the potential to transform society; through a revolutionary aesthetic, the poet can realize a radical act. Facing the disillusionment of the war years, however, Zukofsky ultimately replaces labor with love as the motivating force that shapes history.[64] Schelb concurs with much of Hatlen's assessment of Zukofsky's poetry of the 1930s; however, he argues that Zukofsky's "turn toward domesticity and sentiment" in his poetry after *"A"*-8 "should be recognized as a reintegration of repressed emotions and a refusal of coercive relations toward nature, language and history" rather than a "nostalgic flight from the disorder of history."[65] Nevertheless, both critics attest to Zukofsky's effort to enact a politically committed poetics in his epic work.

For his part, Zukofsky, in a 1935 letter, writes to Lorine Niedecker that *"A"*-8 justified *"A"* 1–7: not quite, Zukofsky states, " 'all history in me,' " but rather "always coming in A 1–7 'to where I am now.' " Although both Pound and Zukofsky used their poetry as a means of exploring the nature of right and wrong action, neither poet resolved the multiple voices of his epic into a single ideological voice. In his letter to Niedecker, Zukofsky insists that *"A"*-8—with its eight voices, eight themes "pumped on the organ"—"must be music music of the statements, but not explanation ever . . . the reader will have to learn to read statement juxtaposed const[ant] as music."[66] As if to underscore this point, sixteen years later Zukofsky warns Niedecker not to make the mistake that James Laughlin made when, in writing the preface to the 1937 New Directions annual, he stated that in *"A"*-8 Zukofsky "wuz writing the proletarian epic." Instead, Zukofsky writes, Niedecker should consider "references to K. Marx etc. as history & poetry. . . . I wuz recording and making a pome [*sic*]. For the rest: the 'A'-ethics & politics is as old as Aristotle."[67] Ultimately, both Pound and Zukofsky were engaged in an Aristotelian project—searching for "different techniques" to revitalize a sociopolitical and aesthetic culture.

The late 1920s and the early 1930s marked the period of Zukofsky's and Pound's closest interactions. In 1935 Pound dedicated *Guide to Kulchur* to Basil Bunting and Zukofsky as fellow "strugglers in the desert." In time, because of their political differences, heightened by Pound's wartime anti-Semitic and Fascist speeches, their friendship would change—alternating, on Pound's part, from silence and criticism to respect for Zukofsky as a mature fellow poet. Zukofsky, although bewildered by Pound's economic and political beliefs, maintained a respect and love for his mentor. Despite the changes in their friendship, Zukofsky could always find a constant friend in Pound's poetry; for in the language of poetry, in the act of reading, friendship remains constant, "exempt from all the vicissitudes and changes and tempers that are involved in friendship."

5. Williams: A Clear Mirror

In 1928 William Carlos Williams wrote Zukofsky a letter indicating that he recognized a significant historical link between the young poet and himself:

> I did not wish to be twenty years younger and surely I did not wish to be twenty years older. I was happy to find a link between myself and another wave of it. Sometimes one thinks the thing has died down. I believe that somehow you have benefited from my work . . . that the thing moves by a direct relationship between men from generation to generation.[1]

Zukofsky and Williams had an ongoing friendship from 1928 until Williams's death in 1963. Zukofsky regarded Williams as one of the most important American writers of his generation, while Williams regarded Zukofsky as an uncompromising and original poet. And although Williams felt that Zukofsky's poetry could be unrelenting— at the expense of the reader's understanding—he also felt "the intelligent stab" of Zukofsky's poems and compared some of them to the avant-garde paintings at the 1913 Armory Show: "I begin to see the world being recreated again as it has not been since 1913."[2] In a letter dated 3 April 1941, Williams wrote to Zukofsky, "You are fast becoming the most important and neglected poet of our time and place."[3] Both Zukofsky and Williams regarded their relationship with the eyes of literary historians, imbuing their personal friendship with historical significance—as though they also were "contemporary particulars" placed within the framework of a modern literary history. And, indeed, they were right, for their relationship represents an important segue between the Modernist "revolution of the word" and the postmodernist fracturing of the word—both of which involve fundamental attitudes about the medium of language and the mediating subject.

In 1928 Pound had acted as a matchmaker to their friendship, urging both Williams and Zukofsky to contact each other. Their eventual meeting proved fruitful, and the resulting relationship gave birth to a number of projects: Zukofsky wrote several articles on Williams and edited and even published a series of Williams's poems; Williams, for his part, advised and encouraged the young poet and wrote several pieces about Zukofsky's poetry. More than with any of the other Moderns I focus on in this book, Zukofsky could identify with Williams's cultural heritage. Although Williams, who embodied many middle-class American values, was closer to the cultural authority of America than was the ghetto-born Zukofsky, Williams's own English father and Puerto Rican mother were immigrants, and he recognized the force of a culturally pluralistic America whose language was from "the mouths of Polish mothers."[4]

Despite the fact that Williams was twenty years older than Zukofsky, Williams rarely behaved as the elder teacher; in fact, if anyone, it was Zukofsky who assumed the didactic role. In the early 1930s their friendship suffered a brief rift, apparently because Williams felt that Zukofsky "represented certain critical restraints that acted as a check" on the older poet. Explaining the temporary breach, Williams would later write: "I think that in our friendship there's much more to come and I for one am in a better position to appreciate it today than I was yesterday. We were too damned close together for a while. That's no good. The most anyone can do is to be a kind of mirror for the other. And the mirror had better be a clear one, not a tinted one, just clear."[5]

It is important to stress that Zukofsky effected a reciprocal influence on Williams. Although Zukofsky's relationship with Williams demonstrates both Zukofsky's appropriation and growth out of the central tenets of Modernism, Williams's relationship with Zukofsky gives us insights into Williams's later poetry in which he was influenced by the theoretician Zukofsky. Both men recognized that, as Williams stated, they shared a "common ground which is our common inheritance of poetry": "it is the essence for us—uniting our differences."⁶ For a lifetime the two poets would share a common Objectivist struggle: how does the poet reconcile the numinous object and the numinous thought; were there "no ideas but in things"? how does the poet reconcile the thinking "I" and the recording "eye"? how does the poet reconcile the poetics of experience and the materials of history? Their joint endeavors would lead them to different solutions. Although Williams insisted that each should be a clear mirror for the other, the two men actually would see each other's work refracted through their own understanding of poetry.

Williams, of course, represents that first wave of modern American poets. Rejecting a Romantic and Symbolist sensibility, Williams bequeaths to his fellow poets a naked world, stripped of "the beautiful illusion," a world in which the self coexists with numinous objects. In *Spring and All* Williams articulates his desire to raise the individual "to some approximate co-extension with the universe"; "to refine, to clarify, to intensify that eternal moment in which we alone live"; to "escape from crude symbolism, the annihilation of strained associations, complicated ritualistic forms designed to separate work from 'reality.' "⁷ To achieve such a desired end, Williams created seemingly simple poems such as the famed "Red Wheelbarrow" and, in doing so, inaugurated what some would call a poetics of reality, others a poetics of experience, and still others a poetics of presence. Such poems are a manifestation of Williams's concepts: his rejection of symbolism, his primordial union of subject and object, his wish to purify and renew the language, his particular treatment of time and space to create an object, the poem, that dances with a life of its own.⁸ In such poems as "The Red Wheelbarrow" or "Young Sycamore," the first line urges the reader to participate in the immediacy of the poem; the lines "so much depends" and "I must tell you" demand that the reader confront the text. The objects—whether a red wheelbarrow and chickens or a tree and pavement—exist side by side, each pointing to no greater meaning than themselves. But these objects, by the invitation of the first line, call for a participation of the reader, a union of object and subject, and so much depends on that function of the poem—for the imagination to engulf and be engulfed by a purified and renewed language.

When Williams read Zukofsky's early poetry, he saw his own image reflected in the text, that link between one generation and another. But what exactly did Williams see? Certainly, Zukofsky owed much to Williams's revolutionary work *Spring and All;* here Williams not only challenged the precepts of Symbolism and traditional metric verse but also found a language and rhythm to replace those conventional poetics. In fact, Barry Ahearn, attempting to justify the appearance of four of Zukofsky's earliest poems—radical departures from the Keatsian "cream puff" verse of Zukofsky's college days—points to Williams's poems as possible models. But in his early "Poem 2," Zukofsky was already creating a poetics distinct from Williams's:

> Not much more than being,
> Thoughts of isolate, beautiful
> Being at evening, to expect
>   at a river-front:
>
> A shaft dims
> With a turning wheel;
>
> Men work on a jetty
> By a broken wagon;
>
> Leopard, glowing-spotted,
>   The summer river—
> Under: The Dragon:
>   (*CSP,* 22)

Ahearn focuses not so much on the "look" as the "sound" of the poem, noting that both Williams and Zukofsky "aim for unity of effect by incorporating complex linking sound patterns into poems whose syntax and vocabulary seem at odds." Thus, Williams's "Poem XIX" of *Spring and All*—with its repetition of *r, s,* and *z* sounds ("Out of their sweet heads / dark kisses—rough faces")—could be regarded as a model for "Poem 2"—which demonstrates Zukofsky's dexterity with *n* and *r* sounds.[9]

Ahearn's assertion is certainly a reasonable one, for Zukofsky admired Williams's "cadenced verse." But one should also note that at this time the young poet was absorbing much of the "sound and sense" of a number of his contemporaries. For example, it is just as likely that in 1924, Zukofsky was also influenced by the sound patterns and typography of E. E. Cummings, whom, at that time, Zukofsky greatly admired. In January 1922 the *Dial*, which Zukofsky read faithfully, published Cummings's "Five Poems":[10]

> of evident invisibles
> exquisite the hovering
>
> at the dark portals
>
> of hurt girl eyes
>
> sincere with wonder
>
> a poise a wounding
> a beautiful suppression
>
> the accurate boy mouth
>
> now droops the faun head
>
> now the intimate flower dreams
>
> of parted lips
> dim upon the syrinx

In his sensual poem Cummings works with a series of resonating sounds, including *d* ("dark," "droops," "dreams," "dim"), *s* ("sincere," "poise," "suppressions," "syrinx"), *w* ("wonder," "wounding," "flower"), and the short *e* and *i* ("evident invisibles / exquisite"). Simply put, Cummings is playing with various forms of intercourse: the intimate touch between girl and boy (a kiss or "dim upon the syrinx" [cervix?]); the interaction between faun and flower (fauna and flora?); the interchange between the faun and his pan-pipes ("lips / dim upon the syrinx"); the communication between poet and reader; and the sensual interlinking of sounds. Moreover, Cummings moves from the world of the "invisibles" to the world of the particulars ("accurate boy mouth") to the world of the mythical and mystical ("faun head" and "flower dreams"). In "Poem 2" Zukofsky works with similar sounds: *d* ("dims," "leopard," "dragon"), *s* ("isolate," "shaft," "dims"), *w* ("wheel," "wagon"), and the short *e* and *i* ("beautiful / Being at evening, to expect / at a river-front"). But, thematically, Zukofsky is less interested in sensual interchange than in the interchange between cognition and perception. In fact, "Poem 2" demonstrates how Zukofsky, working out of the examples of his predecessors, is searching for his own form.

In a 1968 interview L. S. Dembo asked Zukofsky if "Poem 2" demonstrated the poet's ability to see "as an Objectivist, in terms of particularities rather than wholes," in terms of things rather than abstractions.[11] Obviously, Dembo is attempting to align Zukofsky's poem with Williams's poems of numinous things, which in obedience to Pound's dicta, go "in fear of abstractions." Sidestepping Dembo's assertions, Zukofsky replied, "But the idea is particular, too. . . . This poem is an example if you deal mostly with sight and a bit of intellect." Zukofsky then explained his reading of "Poem 2":

> But it all mounts up. I suppose there's a general statement: "Not much more than being," whatever that is. The opposite would be non-being. And then I go ahead and say a little more about it; that being becomes isolate being, a beautiful being. These are all assertions. Where is this? That's the first tangible thing, a river-front; the one I saw was probably the Hudson or the East River. But the point is that the river-front becomes more solid as against the general flow of intellect in the beginning. The first part is intellective, "gaseous"; the second part would resemble the "solid" state.
>
> Now what kind of being? There is a shaft with a turning wheel; there are men on the jetty, and a broken wagon. It could have been a good wagon, but I wanted it to be broken. And above this, the sky. So actually I suppose the guy who was doing this was trying to get the whole picture, instead of saying as a "romantic" poet, "Now I'm seeing, now I'm being; I see the jetty; this wagon was once pretty."[12]

Zukofsky is interested in subverting the "romantic and symbolist sensibility" by reversing what he perceived to be the "romantic process." As Zukofsky states, the "romantic" poet would view the scene on the riverfront and say, "Now I'm seeing, now I'm being; I see the jetty; this wagon was once pretty." In his abbreviated version of the Romantic crisis ode, Zukofsky is parodying the process in which the imagination seizes hold of the object—in this case the scene—and transforms the object into an often emotive, and at times even elegiac, expression of itself. In this poem the thought coexists with the scene, or to use his words, "Now I'm being, now I'm seeing." But unlike Williams, Zukofsky is not circumventing abstract thought by seeking a radical union between the self and object. Zukofsky begins with "Thoughts of isolate, beautiful / Being" and sets these abstract thoughts next to a tangible being—a riverfront.

Whereas Zukofsky's first two sections remind one of the strophe and antistrophe—the turn and counterturn—of the Pindaric ode, the last section comes to a point of rest, suggestive of the standstill of an epode:

> Leopard, glowing-spotted,
>   The summer river—
> Under: The Dragon:
>   (*CSP*, 22)

But this epode does not end with any simple closure—say, an idyllic pastoral scene against the lazy summer river. Even though they might be the reflected lights of constellations or neon signs, the leopard and dragon seem rather ominous and enigmatic; and the colons in the last line direct us to expect a continuation, not an end to the poem. In his interview with Dembo, Zukofsky does give us a clue about his ending. About the first two stanzas of the poem, Zukofsky explains: "The first part is intellective, 'gaseous'; the second part would resemble the 'solid' state." One might reasonably surmise, then, that the third stanza seems to have dissolved into a "liquid" state—"the summer river." In "About the Gas Age" Zukofsky states, "There is a solid state, and there is liquid, and there is gas. It's the same with the materials of poetry, you make images— that's pretty solid—music, it's liquid; ultimately if something vaporizes, that's the intellect" (*Prepositions*, 169). Of course, Zukofsky is stating his own version of Pound's phanopoeia, melopoeia, and logopoeia. But here he stresses the interaction of all three, which all exist like "the composition of the atom" (*Prepositions*, 170). And in the final stanza of "Poem 2," we perceive the image of the constellation in the sky being reflected in the river; constellation, river, and image exist side by side "like the composition of the atom" and, more to the point, like the composition of a poem.

When Williams first read Zukofsky's poetry, he felt a kinship with the younger poet, but he also realized that Zukofsky was doing something different. Zukofsky has stated, "What really concerned me in these early poems was trying . . . to get away from sounding like everybody else." Apparently, Williams thought Zukofsky had succeeded. In an April 1928 letter that articulates his reaction, Williams writes, "It is a thoughtful poetry, but actual word stuff, not thoughts for thoughts. It escapes me in its analysis (thank God) and strikes me [a]s a thing (thank God). There are not so many things in the world as we commonly imagine. Plenty of debris, plenty of smudges."[13] Williams realized that Zukofsky did not "go in fear of abstractions" but had made the abstract idea a particular, the thought a thing.

The issue of "thingness" or *ding an sich* is a crucial one for Williams; and, for him, what could best convey the nature of the "thing" was the hard-edged image, a fundamental part of Williams's poetics. In fact, Williams perceived himself as a poet of the "eye," the artist who conveyed the "given-ness" of his world. Zukofsky, too, wanted to locate his poems in this world, and both Williams and Zukofsky created poems that occupied a shallow space—pointing neither outward to a symbolic other nor inward to a searching examination of the self. Yet the two men created two different open fields in which to map out their poetics. Williams's main concern, as he articulated it in *Spring and All,* was to undercut the tradition of abstract and "beautiful illusions," the transcendental impetus. Thus, Williams firmly planted the self, things, and the poem as object in this world. Zukofsky's main concern in his early poems, as he discussed them with Dembo, was a desire to subvert the "romantic" poet's desire to privilege the seeing self over the seen world. In a fine essay on Zukofsky, Burton Hatlen points out that Zukofsky recognized an implicit problem in "poems of the eye," for behind the "perceiving eye" is the "philosophical I." Quoting from Zukofsky's *Bottom,* Hatlen cites:

> *Looking* has its own logic, but (it may be inferred from Wittgenstein's *looking* logic) he who *looks* is still the philosophical *I,* the metaphysical subject, the limit—not a part of the world. To say the eye sees the whole or the wholeness of what it sees means only that the philosophical *I* has

reached the inexpressible, and this can only "show" itself: it is the mystical. As for true conceptions, they are, as Spinoza said, "of thought" until words disguise and imperil or feign them. Their wholeness is also inexpressible; it exists. But language too, like the feigning of the imagination has its own wholeness.[14]

The "philosophical I" sitting behind the Imagistic poem is just one step away from the "privileged I." For Zukofsky, the answer would lie not in the "feigning imagination" of the seeing I/eye but in the feigned wholeness of language. Yet early in his career Zukofsky would need to work out of the vocabulary of his predecessors, and the most fundamental component of that poetics was the image. But when Zukofsky depicts a scene—one that Williams could create with vitality and precision—it is quickly apparent that Zukofsky is using paints from a different palette.

Of course, Williams's poetics is not limited only to what Roy Harvey Pearce termed his "poems of seeing," poems in which the perceiving subject would make immediate and tactile contact with the perceived object. Still, for Williams the mere image represents the fundamental component of his poetics; it is his most vital "figure of contact."[15] Williams considers sight to be his greatest asset, and with an artist's intensity he portrays scenes through his medium of language. Even in a poem such as "Classic Scene," in which Williams never mentions any "I," the poet unifies the perceiving subject and perceived object. Inspired by Charles Sheeler's painting *Classic Landscape*, Williams portrays an industrial scene infused with sexual and religious power:

A power-house
in the shape of
a red brick chair
90 feet high

on the seat of which
sit the figures
of two metal
stacks—aluminum—

commanding an area
of squalid shacks

side by side—
from one of which

buff smoke
streams while under
a grey sky
the other remains

passive today—[16]

In this industrial landscape Williams brings into being Henry
Adams's dynamo, a phallic power and silent force. As the participle
"commanding" suggests, the power-house dominates the landscape.
Although the poem seems to consist of an object, not a subject, in
this case the object is the subject. The poet's sensual energy seizes the
dynamo—extending ninety feet high—and transforms the object
into an anthropomorphic image. As Dickran Tashjian suggests,
"Williams uses words that can be taken to describe the power-
house literally but that also extend a submerged conceit likening the
smokestacks to monolithic figures, ancient sculpture of the gods
on their throne perhaps."[17] Williams's simple image suggests both
the phallocentric and theocentric. Although "Classic Scene," like a
number of Williams's "descriptive phrase" poems, consists of an
incomplete sentence (in this case, an absolute construction with a
nonfinite verb), the poet's eye—in an act of penetration—presents a
coherent and complete sense of the object before us; we follow the
powerhouse as it stretches to its commanding ninety feet, and we
then focus on the balanced image of the metal stacks sitting "side by
side"—one industriously smoking, the other stack not in use. Both
the anthropomorphic images and the sibilant sounds find a resting
place in the last line: "passive today."

When he depicts his own "imagistic" poem, Zukofsky brings to
the word the attention that Williams provides for the object. When
Zukofsky constructs an American urban scene in "Poem 3" of *29
Poems,* he does not pick an image of Adams's dynamo or a red
wheelbarrow; instead, he focuses on the word "cocktails":

Cocktails
and signs of
"ads"

flashing,
light's waterfalls,

Bacchae
among electric lights

will swarm the crowds
streamers of the lighted

skyscrapers

nor tripping
over underbrush

but upon pavement
            (*CSP*, 23)

Zukofsky's poem does not provide its reader with either unity or harmony of perception. Williams's poem inevitably propels the reader from one word to the next, promising the reader a continuity of vision. But from the first word of "Poem 3," the reader looks for familiar "signs" and "signals" that mark his or her stable entry into the poem. Is the reader viewing a cocktail ad on a billboard? Or are the crowds—the Bacchae—drinking cocktails? Or does cocktail suggest a cock's tail? Or do the flashing lights look like the multi-color peacock's tail? Perspective continually shifts and dissolves throughout the poem.

Inasmuch as Sheeler's *Classic Landscape* is the inspiration for the classic lines of Williams's poem, we could just as well suggest that Zukofsky looks to the word, not the image, for his source. In fact, in the 1923 edition of *American Language*, H. L. Mencken cites the word *cocktail* as an example of American ingenuity: "In the department of conviviality the imaginativeness of Americans was shown both in the invention and in the naming of new and often highly complex beverages" in contrast to the "far more limited imagination" of the English.[18] We might say that in his poem Williams realizes precisionist clarity; and in his poem Zukofsky realizes American ingenuity, for "Poem 3" is an ingenious play with sound and meaning. Or it might be more accurate to say that Zukofsky is presenting "the image"—what he has called the basic form of the poem—but his formalistic means of rendering that image differs radically from

Williams's means of conveying the numinous object, for Zukofsky realizes that any image in a poem is first a physical word, not a numinous object.

In "Poem 3" the linguistic image is continually shifting, depending on its relationship to the words that surround it. The reader's eye is continually "cocked," tilting upward one moment to the skyscrapers and downward the next moment to the pavement. Looking up, the viewer sees "Bacchae / among electric lights" (a billboard picture of men and women holding cocktails?); looking down, the viewer sees "Bacchae / among electric lights / will swarm the crowds" (a crowd of drunken carousers?). Such continual shifts catch the reader in the tension of opposing directional forces suggested by the wordplay—exactly like "tripping / over underbrush." Moreover, in alluding to Bacchae Zukofsky is also catching the reader between opposing forces of time—past Dionysian festivities and the present moment of the carousing city dwellers. Inasmuch as Zukofsky handles visual perspective by shifts and dissolves, he handles his primary allusion—the Bacchanalia—by nullifying the past and reifying the present.

> and not with thyrsus
> shall they prick
>
> the body of their loves but
> waist to waist
>
> laugh out in gyre—
> announced then upon stairs,
>
> not upon hills,
> will be their flight
>
> when passed turnstiles,
> having dropped
>
> coins
> they've sprinted up
>
> where on the air (elevated)
> waves flash—and out—
>
> leap
> signaling—lights below
>   (*CSP*, 23)

Zukofsky suggests images of a Bacchanalia through negation: "nor tripping / over underbrush"; "not with thyrsus / shall they prick"; "not upon hills / will be their flight." At the same moment Zukofsky creates these images, he insists that they disappear, replacing the natural landscape with the urban pavement, the past with the present. The Dionysian "flight" dissolves into a flight of "stairs"; the "laugh out in gyre" dissolves into the "turnstiles." Whereas Cummings, in "Poem I" of "Five Poems," forges an erotic link between the mythic/natural world of his fauns and panpipes and the innocent/sensual world of the girl and the boy, Zukofsky, in juxtaposing absence against presence, both acknowledges and calls into question the metaphoric link. In this way the allusion does not lead, as it does in Cummings's poem, to closure but points to further ambiguity.

Interestingly, it was probably Cummings who initially mapped out this tension for Zukofsky. In "American Poetry 1920–1930" Zukofsky writes about this very tendency—to suggest an image by doubting it—in Cummings's poetry:

> Cummings is less nominalistic, more sensuously evocative, sometimes fanciful ("after all white horses are in bed") but continually interested in something like capillaries, "everything which we really are and never quite live," the sources where images begin—
>
> > if scarcely the somewhat city
> > . . . . . in considerable twilight
>
> and are known perhaps only negatively—
>
> > touch (now) with a suddenly unsaid
> > gesture lightly my eyes?
>
> His typography, illustrated by the use of the parenthesis around "now" also suggests the image, by doubting it.[19]

Zukofsky locates "the sources where images begin" not in hard-edged objects but in an unidentified yearning: "everything which we really are and never quite live." Such a statement makes images sound less numinous and more nebulous; of course, it should be clear that Zukofsky is not choosing the nebulous and evocative symbol over Williams's literal and concrete image. Rather, Zukofsky is suggesting that experience is incomplete and, by inference, that the image also is incomplete—"never quite live," never quite said. The image is caught neither between the real object and the linguistic image (the object being transformed into referential word) nor between the concrete and the abstract (image becoming meaningful symbol), but between becoming and possible being (the image suggesting possible semantic references); one discovers meaning not in the final act of realization, but in the process of understanding possible meanings. In such a poetics the unsaid can articulate the said, and one can suggest an image by doubting it.

Thus, we may surmise that Zukofsky is "getting at" the image in a way that is distinct from Williams's nominalistic method. Williams seeks an elemental contact with the object before him, an interpenetration of the subject and object. As we have seen, however, Williams's interpenetration is a poetic act akin to both religious incarnation and sexual intercourse. The "I" behind the "perceiving eye" seizes on the object in an act suggestive of both worship and rape. In this respect Williams's poem is reminiscent of other literary traditions, elements of which are antithetical to his poetics. We can well remember Donne's cry to "batter my heart, three-personed God . . . for I, / Except you enthral me, never shall be free, / Nor ever chaste, except you ravish me"; there is also the example of Yeats's "Leda and the Swan," in which both Leda and the poet are seized and overwhelmed by the power of the transcendent.[20] In Williams's case it is the conveyor of the experience, the seeing "I," who holds power as poet/creator and see-er/seer. As he writes in his autobiography, "I am extremely sexual in my desires: I carry them everywhere and at all times. I think that from that arises the drive which empowers us all."[21] Williams encounters the objects of the world with a Whitmanesque embrace, a desire for primordial union that Whitman articulates in "Crossing Brooklyn Ferry": "What is more subtle than this which ties me to the woman or man that looks / in my face? / Which fuses me into you now, and pours my meaning into you?"[22] But in these two poems, of course, Williams is not the "I" of "Crossing Brooklyn Ferry," for his intent is not to transform the world into an expression of himself. He bypasses that temptation by placing himself directly in that world, coextensive with the universe. Sensing this tension between subject and object, Harold Bloom has noted that Williams's ego seems to fuse Keats's "negative capability" with Whitman's "positive capability for conveying the positive press of himself."[23] Moreover, Williams also acknowledges that the poem is not a privileged object in that world: the powerhouse is an object and the poem about the powerhouse is an object; one does not take precedence over the other.[24] Still, within the boundaries of his text Williams remains the "empowered" mediating subject who determines what is perceived and what is spoken in the poem; it is the poet who calls the image into existence. Also, his text, though not symbolic, is clearly referential. Williams does not call into question either the mediating subject or the poem's language. Zukofsky will do both.

Although Zukofsky clearly feels he shares a "common ground" with Williams, in order to escape the metaphysical subject lurking behind the "perceiving I," he attempts to place the power in the medium rather than the mediating subject. Zukofsky desires to escape the Adamic impulse to invent the world by naming it. Whereas Williams acknowledges that he lives in a world of given objects, Zukofsky acknowledges that he lives in a world of given words—words he discovers rather than creates. As he writes in "An Objective," "One is brought back to the entirety of the single word which is in itself a relation, an implied metaphor, an arrangement, a harmony or a dissonance" (*Prepositions*, 14). When Zukofsky uses a word such as "cocktails," he realizes that the word comes to him with numerous connotations, that the word has a life of its own. No matter what the poet's "true conception" is, Zukofsky realizes that words can "disguise and imperil or feign them." The poet, in a special sense, is not a creator but a craftsman. Recognizing that the word has a number of references, Zukofsky carves the word as a craftsman would carve a piece of wood—respecting the peculiar properties of his material. In "Poem 3" we can see that Zukofsky is breaking away from a system in which language refers to meaning—that stable relationship between signifier and signified—and calling up a system in which language constitutes meaning and signifiers suggest a number of possible meanings.

Throughout "Poem 3" Zukofsky literally plays with "signs" and
"signals," regarding signifiers as dynamic forces. Zukofsky begins
his poem with "Cocktails / and signs of / 'ads.'" By putting quota-
tion marks around "ads," Zukofsky foregrounds the word, making
us think about the word, insisting that we see the word "ads" as an
opaque, not a transparent, signifier. Zukofsky concludes his poem
with his initial play with perspective: "where on the air (elevated) /
waves flash—and out— / leap / signaling—lights below." Are the
"airwaves" signaling to the lights below? Or are the lights below
signaling to the "waves flash"? Zukofsky calls into question what
we see and what we hear (airwaves are also earwaves) by destabiliz-
ing our "signals" or language markers. Moreover, in fracturing the
word and the "eye"—the image—Zukofsky also fractures the "I"—
the perceiving subject. When Zukofsky destabilizes the medium, he
also destabilizes the mediating subject.

In breaking the surface of the poem, Zukofsky chooses not to rep-
licate the Edenic wholeness of Williams's vision, that vision which
gives us back the unbroken essence of things. In an essay on Charles
Sheeler, Williams writes that for the artist "it is in the shape of the
thing that the essence lies. He must possess that really glandular
perception of their uniqueness which realizes in them an end in itself,
each piece irreplaceable by a substitute, not to be broken down to
other meaning. Not to pull out, transubstantiate, boil, unglue, ham-
mer, melt, digest and psychoanalyze, not even to distill but to see and
keep what the understanding touches intact—as grapes are round
and come in bunches."[25] In the moment of his poem, Williams
recovers a world and a language of visionary wholeness. Like Emer-
son's transparent eyeball, Williams encounters an "eternal moment"
in which the imagination revitalizes an Edenic world: "to see and
keep what the understanding touches intact." Zukofsky's poems, by
contrast, keep neither the world nor language intact. Zukofsky is
not seeking a visionary moment of integration in which "grapes are
round and come in bunches." For Zukofsky, the world and language
only feign the wholeness of the transparent eyeball; neither the eye
nor language, the seen or the said, is transparent.

Of course, such a comparison between Williams's "descriptive poems" and Zukofsky's fractured "word stuff" is only a limited sampling of their poetry. Zukofsky's work, as noted earlier, can be propositional and straightforward; likewise, some of Williams's poems, specifically a number of his poems in *Spring and All,* are characterized, to use Marjorie Perloff's words, by "Cubist mobility and indeterminacy."[26] In fact, critics such as Joseph Riddel, in *The Inverted Bell,*[27] and J. Hillis Miller, in *The Linguistic Moment,* have perceived Williams's poems through a deconstructive lens—observing that Williams "takes possession of the presence of the present . . . that is not perceptual but linguistic."[28] The debate over Williams's poetry can be quite complicated; for instance, in *The Linguistic Moment* Miller himself has revised his earlier phenomenological perspective of Williams—as suggested in his *Poets of Reality.* Other critics have challenged a deconstructive perspective of Williams's work, highlighting the importance of the material and perceptual nature of his "poetry of presence."[29]

Although I am aware of this ongoing critical debate, what interests me here is Williams's own early response to Zukofsky's work; and the older poet, seeking the "objective clarity of images," objected to Zukofsky's fractured and abstract language. In a July 1928 letter to Zukofsky, Williams wrote:

> Sometimes though I don't like your language. It probably is me and not you who should be blamed for this. You are wrestling with the antagonist under newer rules. But I can't see "all live process," "orbit-trembling," "our consciousness," "the sources of being"—what the hell? I'm not finding fault. I'm just trying to nail what troubles me. It may be that I am too literal in my search for objective clarities of image. It may be that you are completely right in forcing abstract conceptions into the sound pattern. I dunno. Anyway there you are.
>
> I will say that in this case the abstract, philosophic-jargonist language is not an obstruction. It may be that when the force of the conception is sufficiently strong it can carry this sort of thing. If the force were weaker the whole poem would fall apart. Good, perhaps. Perhaps by my picayune, imagistic mannerisms I hold together superficially what should by all means fall apart.[30]

Williams could not fully understand the "newer rules" Zukofsky was formulating; indeed, Zukofsky himself had not yet come to terms with these rules. Thus, Williams's misgivings about Zukofsky's language are understandable, for in the 1920s and 1930s Zukofsky was constructing the "new rules" of his poetics out of the "old rules" of his predecessors. Although Zukofsky was using the terms of his predecessors, he was rethinking and redefining those terms. For instance, Williams defined the "image" much more literally than did Zukofsky. Zukofsky allowed for both Williams's nominalistic image and Cummings's nebulous image in his own consideration of the term. Moreover, whereas Zukofsky was trying to "wrestle with the antagonist under [the] newer rules" of his developing poetics, Williams was also trying to come to terms with the implications of the poetics he had already developed. Would the "objective clarities of image" be enough for Williams's own poetic concerns, concerns that would eventually lead him to his epic poem *Paterson?* Williams would have to find a way to reconcile the poetics of experience with history.

Although Williams had told Zukofsky "not to take my theories too seriously," he was, as already noted, disturbed by Zukofsky's use of abstract language in lieu of the concrete image. "Poems are richer in thought as image," he wrote the young poet. But Williams would allow that Zukofsky had a "rare gift" for creating music in his poetry, and he concluded that Zukofsky was creating a poetics that emphasized sound over sight, music over image. In fact, to try to understand Zukofsky's objectives, Williams perceived two different but complementary functions in their artistic roles: Williams was the painter-poet and Zukofsky was the musician-poet. He did, however, warn Zukofsky that music could not take the place of the image, especially if that music accompanied abstract and stilted lyrics. As he wrote in a letter to Zukofsky, "But if it is the music, even that is not inventive enough to make up for images which give an overwhelming effect of triteness. . . . Eyes have always stood first in the poet's equipment. If you're mostly ear—a new rhythm must come in more strongly than has been the case so far. Yet," the elder poet conceded, "I am willing to grant—to listen."[31]

Indeed, Williams was willing to listen to much more than Zukofsky's poetry. Although he had his doubts about Zukofsky's poetic language, Williams quickly recognized and respected Zukofsky's editorial and critical skills. Very soon after the beginning of their friendship, Zukofsky was not only editing but also writing critical pieces about Williams's poetry. In fact, soon after they met, Zukofsky helped Williams edit "The Descent of Winter" for Pound's autumn 1928 *Exile*. William Schott has argued that in "The Descent of Winter" Williams, "perhaps unconsciously, was seeking to bridge over the gap" between his poems and his theoretical prose. According to Schott, "He couldn't quite do it. Chasms of logic and event intervene. But the intent of the union is clearly there."[32] It was during this time, which Schott has identified as a dark period in Williams's life, that Williams met Zukofsky. To some extent, the young Zukofsky rekindled the older poet's desire to continue to develop key issues of his poetics. In an early letter to Zukofsky, Williams wrote, "You make me want to carry out deferred designs."[33] As Reed Whittemore testifies in his biography on Williams, Zukofsky was to become "a significant force in WCW's career";[34] and as Neil Baldwin states, Zukofsky was "the hidden, unsung editor of almost all of Williams's substantial prose and poetry."[35]

During the early years of their friendship, both poets—junior and senior—were in the midst of developing their poetics. Of course, by the time that Williams met Zukofsky, he had already constructed the core of his poetics of presence and had written a number of his crucial works, including *Kora in Hell* and *Spring and All;* but Williams did not feel his contribution to American poetry had ceased. It was as though Williams, like Pound, existed in medias res, between the revolution of the past and the revolution of the present. Both Williams and Pound could discuss with Zukofsky the poetry revolution of 1913 as a historical event in which they had participated. When Zukofsky was editing the Objectivist issue of *Poetry,* Pound advised him to have a "historic section" consisting of Williams, Cummings, Eliot, and, of course, Pound himself. Williams and Pound recognized one part of themselves as historical selves, grounded in a hard-won authority—a position that the two poets would not actually achieve until decades later. They knew that they deserved to win the revolution and that such articles as those written by Zukofsky would surely help them; but they also realized that the winners of today's revolution could be tomorrow's canonical authorities, challenged by younger writers. As Williams wrote to Harriet Monroe, life at any moment was "subversive of life as it was the moment before." If verse were to be alive, it must be infused with "some tincture of disestablishment, something in the nature of an impalpable revolution."[36]

It was thus crucial for the two poets to continue to evolve; neither man intended to be frozen in a moment of time. When planning his Objectivist issue of *Poetry*, Zukofsky wrote Pound a letter indicating that the poets of 1913 were also the poets of the 1930s: "Think I'll have as good a 'movement' as that of the premiers imagistes—point is Wm. C. W. of today is not what he was in 1913, neither are you if you're willing to contribute—if I'm going to show what's *going on* today, you'll *have to*. The older generation *is not* the older generation if it's alive & up—Can't see why you shd. appear in the H & H *alive* with 3 Cantos & not show that you are the [younger] *generation* in 'Poetry.' What's age to do with verbal manifestation, what's history to do with it,—good gord lets disassociate ijees—I want *to show the poetry* that's being written today—whether the poets are of masturbating age or the fathers of *families don't matter*."[37]

For Zukofsky, his friends Pound and Williams were alive and well, still members of the younger generation. At the same time, however, Zukofsky regarded both men with the studious eye of a historian. By defining and interpreting what Williams and Pound, as well as other Modernists, had already done, Zukofsky was helping "to name," to define Modernism itself. After reading Zukofsky's article "American Poetry 1920–1930," a despondent Williams wrote Zukofsky a curious letter:

All you do (no not all, of course) is to make me sad. I cannot quite make out all that you say, I wish it were not I about whom you are writing. It seems too like a country I have always wished to live in and shall never find—not even when I am dead for I shall have to leave it behind. Hell, I feel that this sounds foul with sentimentality. Not at all.

This latest of yours is impossibly prose, it is surely the unthinkable thing, the comprehensive—more intuition than truth—I am not the person you think, I have not done the work you say I have. But it is the truth that I have wanted to say, to make, to make visible.

It is rather yourself who has imagined the scene and fitted our work, of a somewhat earlier generation, to your imaginings. But you have created something which we at least cannot let disappear.[38]

Zukofsky, like the biblical Adam, has created this far-off "country" by the sheer act of naming it.

In his critical writings of the late 1920s and early 1930s, Zukofsky was helping to place revolutionary Modernist theories in the public domain, extending the Modernist's "patent rights" to himself as well as other poets. In his articles on Williams, Zukofsky recognized the great contribution that the older poet had made to American poetics, and in "American Poetry 1920–1930" Zukofsky highlighted Williams as *the* important American poet of the 1920s. But Zukofsky did not merely play the objective scholar, recording a slice of history, for he was also a practicing poet, interested in building on his predecessors' contributions.

When Williams wrote Zukofsky that Zukofsky had "projected an excellence in my written work that only exists in my desires," Williams was not simply being modest. In any critical work, as Zukofsky noted years later in his preface to *Bottom*, the critic inescapably imposes his view on the artist's work: "Even a photographic eye—a lens—is placed by some human. . . . To say that his [Shakespeare's] focus *was this* is presumptuous."[39]

In his critical works on Williams, Zukofsky concentrates on the social as well as the linguistic content of Williams's poems. Although Zukofsky acknowledges Williams's "swift hold of art on things seen" and his ability to create an image "in the sudden completeness of the words envisioning them" as central to Williams's work, he is also interested in the historical and social perceptions suggested by Williams's images. Thus, in his 1928 article on Williams, Zukofsky focuses on *A Voyage to Pagany* and states that Williams writes "with a sense of the history and destiny of the United States." In "American Poetry 1920–1930" he begins his section on Williams by writing, "He is of rare importance in the last decade (1920–1930), for whatever he has written the direction of it has been poetry—and, in a special sense, history."[40]

Moreover, when Zukofsky cites specific poems in his article, he obviously prefers poems that move beyond the concrete image of the red wheelbarrow or the young sycamore, even if the poem—like "Botticellian Trees"—breaks with Williams's "own stylistic standards." In "American Poetry 1920–1930" Zukofsky makes a special reference to "The pure products of America go crazy" ("To Elsie"). For Zukofsky, "To Elsie" represents "history as the facts about us." These facts, these "isolate flecks," like Elsie, express "with broken brain the truth about us." The text suggests a definite social context—one that highlights the "living values" and "social determinism of American suburbs in the first thirty years of the twentieth century." Williams's social awareness is the "product of the singular creature living in society and expressing in spite of the numb terror around him the awareness which after a while cannot help be but general." Zukofsky situates Williams not in the midst of things but in the midst of society. In such a world a painter's perception must be enhanced by a writer's vision; the image is not enough for "the living creature becoming conscious of his own needs through the destruction of the various isolated around him." Through the poet's vision, others, "too, become conscious of demands unsatisfied by the routine senseless repetition of events."[41]

Zukofsky felt that Williams's things were the very materials of American history and destiny. Even when Williams simply desired to capture the moment whole, Zukofsky still wished to see history refracted from that moment. In a 1948 article on Williams, Zukofsky comments that Williams's poem "A Horse" contains "man's 'whole grasp of feeling and knowledge in the world.'" Zukofsky insisted on placing Williams's simple text—in which Williams concretely recreates the image of the horse in the same manner he depicts "Classic Scene"—in the midst of contextual echoes. For Williams, "The horse moves / independently / without reference / to his load"; but for Zukofsky this horse carries a load of historical references: "Which is to say the horse is measured by Cro-Magnon ochre, and Phidias' stone, and Picasso's design, and by the twin exhausts of a car, and the pulse of verse—among an imponderable number of other things" (*Prepositions,* 50).

Of course, Williams, the painter-poet, also saw Zukofsky through his own imagistic eye. In reviewing Zukofsky's 55 *Poems,* Williams felt that the difficulty in the "precise excellence" of Zukofsky's work might very well have "invalidated" his work for "general appreciation." Although he praised Zukofsky's poems, he found them uneven, even "a dangerous sort of writing":

> This is a dangerous sort of writing, for if it doesn't click, if it doesn't do the magic and arouse the reader or doesn't find one who is sensitive enough, trained enough and ready enough to place himself exactly in tune with it to appreciate its just observations and careful statements of facts—or if, in writing it, the poet isn't instructed by deep enough feeling (as sometimes happens here) it becomes a mere gathering and reaching. Explicit (as contrasted with this) writing at least always makes sense. Here unless the sense is instructed the writing makes too often no sense.[42]

Implicit in Williams's comments is, of course, Williams's own poetics. He is interested in poems that "click," that have "magic and arouse the reader," that are invested with "deep enough feeling," and that are "explicit." In other words, Williams is describing the synthesizing power of his own poetry, which merges the writer, the "aroused" reader, and the "explicit" text in the "magic" of the moment. He does, nonetheless, cite Zukofsky's "Poem 10" as a successful poem:

Passing tall
Who walk upon the green
So light they are not heard
If never seen;—

Willow above in spring haze,
Green sprig and pendulous;—
Wind, white lightning
In branches over us;

Sun;
All weathering changing loves,
In the high grass (kiss!)
Will not uncover us.

(CSP, 27)

Zukofsky invokes a compelling "imagistic" moment, although his images are hardly in the mode of Williams's nominalistic images. Here Zukofsky chooses to use images that are akin to Cummings's evocative "source of images," which suggests the image by doubting it. Someone or something—who is not "heard" and "never seen"—walks "upon the green." Zukofsky is rendering an image with, to use Burton Hatlen's term, a poetics of absence rather than a poetics of presence. The poem represents a series of sensory images that "will not uncover us." After reading a section of *"A"*, Williams made a comment about *"A"* that might also be appropriate for Zukofsky's "Poem 10": "It is an exciting poison. It ties up bundles not used to being together. I think it's a new state in which things wear button holes instead of clothes; what I get, then, is a feeling."[43] Although in this poem Zukofsky chooses to evoke suggestive impressions rather than nominalistic images, he nevertheless does succeed in synthesizing his "gathering and reaching" into a "magic" that "arouses the reader"; but he does so through buttonholes rather than clothes, through doubting rather than reifying the image.

Although both Williams and Zukofsky saw each other refracted through the prism of his own poetics, each poet learned much from the other. Zukofsky's tributes to Williams testify to Williams's influence on Zukofsky's poetics, and the young Zukofsky, with his acute critical eye and ear, reciprocated that influence. Not content merely to play Boswell to Williams's Johnson, Zukofsky contributed both his theories and editing skills to Williams's developing poetics.

In the early days of their friendship, Williams was intrigued by Zukofsky's theories—many of which, of course, were developed from Modernist tenets. In the late 1920s Zukofsky was especially interested in quantitative meter, the structural weight of the "little word," and the structure not of the image but of the epic. Significantly, however, when Williams adapted Zukofsky's poetics to his own works, the result was often an odd mixture of Zukofsky's theory overlaid on Williams's poem. In a letter dated 4 January 1931, Williams sent Zukofsky the following poem accompanied by a note stating, "Then there's this—thanks to you":

> To
>
> a child (a boy) bouncing
> a ball (a blue ball)
>
> He bounces it (a toy rocket
> in his hand) and runs
>
> and catches it (with his
> left hand) on a green
>
> rhomb seven floors straight
> down which is the old
>
> back yard[44]

Actually, Williams's statement as well as this poem might give any reader pause, for the poem does not appear to be easily attributable to either Williams or Zukofsky. On the one hand, the poem seems far too wordy for the concise Zukofsky; on the other hand, the poem lacks the immediacy of a Williams's poem. "To" does, however, demonstrate Williams's attempt to incorporate some of Zukofsky's ideas into his poetry. In choosing the title "To," Williams, like Zukofsky, emphasizes the importance of the little word. Whereas Williams had insisted on looking at the mundane object, it was Zukofsky who insisted on looking at the mundane word. On hearing that Zukofsky had named the Objectivist press To Publishers, Williams told Zukofsky, "I never knew *To* was a noun gosh all hemlock. I'll have to look that up. Anyway it's not a bad name for publicity—nobody can understand it or keep from thinking about it once they see it" (*Prepositions,* 47). On the one hand, Williams is referring to an inside joke, for Zukofsky named their press To Publishers as a challenge to the publishers who would not print them—in essence, raising a finger or fist at the uncooperative established presses.[45] On the other hand, Williams is also acknowledging that a little word such as *to* does have the weight of "a noun gosh all hemlock."

Williams's excitement over the word *to* seems to parallel Zukofsky's fascination with the "words *the* and *a*," both of which, Zukofsky has stated, "are weighted with as much epos and historical destiny as one man can perhaps resolve." There is, however, a significant difference between Williams's and Zukofsky's use of the little word. In his poem Williams does not foreground the word *to* in the same manner as Zukofsky foregrounds *the* or *a*. For Williams, "To" simply functions as a title and as the first word of his poem; he could very well have named his poem "To a Child," and thus his title is not really any different from the titles of his other poems such as "To Elsie" or "To an Old Jaundiced Woman." Essentially, "To" remains a transparent referent and a functional preposition. In this sense Williams incorporates ideas that bear only a surface resemblance to Zukofsky's actual ideas.

The poem "To" also reflects Williams's interest in quantitative meter, which Zukofsky, the musician-poet, cited as one of the important tenets of modern verse. Although Zukofsky was influenced by Williams's "salutary gift of quantity" in *Spring and All,* it was Zukofsky who brought the term *quantity* to Williams's attention. In a letter of 18 January 1931 to Zukofsky, Williams writes:

> I can say this for the justice of your statements concerning my work: that you have expressed precisely what I wished should be contained therein. Thus it must be that I have succeeded to some extent in doing what I set out to do.
>
> Pagany was to be a clearing of the ground preparatory to beginning. And yes, the line forms arose just out of a dissatisfaction with the looseness of vers libre.
>
> But you have contributed heavily toward the next step in bringing to my attention the word "quantity." You're quite right, that's where much if not all of the release lies. I have in my duller hours (and weeks—and years) worried over accent. But I have not thought much of quantity. Lucky for me it didn't come more to my attention earlier when it might have interfered with my practice of it![46]

We can regard "To" as Williams's conscious experiment with quantity—an experiment in which Williams counts out a number of words and syllables to each line. In the case of "To," we can probably agree with Williams that his unconscious use of quantity fared better for his poems than his conscious use of quantity. Here Williams produces a "bouncing ball" poem really worthy of neither Zukofsky nor himself—although, interestingly, both Williams and

Zukofsky decided to include the work in Pound's *Active Anthology.* Nevertheless, what this poem does demonstrate is Zukofsky's reciprocal influence on Williams quite early in their relationship; moreover, "To" also highlights the fact that Williams tended to overlay, rather than integrate, Zukofsky's theories with his poetry.

From the outset of their friendship, Williams recognized Zukofsky's gift for bringing the poetic act into the arena of the "said." In a 1932 review of Zukofsky's *An "Objectivists" Anthology,* Williams admitted that the anthology was faulty, but he defended Zukofsky as an innovator, an originator of discourse. Simply put, Williams writes, "Had *he* not said it it would not have been said."[47] But for us the important question is how exactly did Williams attempt to integrate Zukofsky's theories into his own poetics. In the late 1920s Zukofsky was constructing a poetics to meet the challenge of his epic poem *"A".* Williams, for his part, had completed a number of his revolutionary prose works and poems; but he had yet to start his final epic project, for he was still basically working out of the unity of what he called his "picayune imagistic mannerisms." In a 1930 letter to Pound, Zukofsky distinguished himself from Williams, contrasting his exigency in writing his life work *"A"* to Williams's writing of his short poems:

> I mean I don't do as Bill does—notice something and write the note down and then type it off (or write it out) and—another poem! . . . how I wish again and again that I could still be writing short poems—be excited *into* a song or something as brief and essential ⟨(!)⟩ i.e. I'd rather be the troubadours (or one of them) than Dante, Burns instead of your papa's *Ring and the Book* or *Sordello,* one of Shakes' songs than any long poem "built on a plan."[48]

Twenty years later Williams would construct his own epic poem *Paterson;* but in those intervening years Williams searched for a means that would enable him to write that epic. Williams would find in Zukofsky's poetics—especially in his emphasis on structure—a means of transforming the limitations of the imagistic mode into the possibilities of the epic.

In his *Autobiography* Williams recalls that his first meeting with Zukofsky occurred at a time when Williams was "thinking, talking, writing constantly about the poem as a way of life." Of course, soon after their meeting in the late 1920s, Zukofsky began *"A"*, which was his own poem of a lifetime or "poem as a way of life." In his *Autobiography* Williams succinctly sums up their relationship in the early 1930s by outlining their endeavor—along with such poets as Basil Bunting, Charles Reznikoff, and George Oppen—to create an Objectivist poetics. Williams recounts, "We together inaugurated, first, the Objectivist theory of the poem, and then the Objectivist Press. Three or four books were published, including my own *Collected Poems*. Then it folded." Williams seems to dismiss the project, for "nothing much happened in the end."[49] Indeed, in 1948 when Williams wrote his *Autobiography*, Zukofsky probably encouraged him to dismiss the project. Years later in an interview with L. S. Dembo, Zukofsky denied that he had inaugurated any real Objectivist movement, for, as he stated, some of us were "writing to say things simply so that they will affect us as new again." Moreover, he stated that he felt dubious about burdening any poet with "blasted terminology" or "any of those *isms*," for "you start becoming a balloon instead of a person."[50]

Nevertheless, Williams and Zukofsky certainly did not dismiss their Objectivist project in the 1930s. In a letter of 17 March 1937 to Zukofsky, Williams wrote, "We have developed, in Objectivism, an important step toward a full understanding of what modern poetry is attempting and must have attempted. It is the inevitableness of it that impresses me."[51] In fact, in the early 1930s Zukofsky was hoping to usher in a new age of Objectivist poetry; as he wrote to Pound, "Think I'll have as good a 'movement' as that of the premiers imagistes."[52] Regardless of his feelings years later, Zukofsky certainly felt at that time that he was announcing a program of ideas. In 1930, at Pound's urging, Harriet Monroe asked the young poet to edit an issue of *Poetry*. According to Zukofsky, since Harriet Monroe insisted that he have a movement and, moreover, that he give that movement a name, Zukofsky invented the term *Objectivist*. But Zukofsky did not merely initiate the Objectivist movement to appease "old Harriet"; for when Zukofsky compiled the poems for the 1931 Objectivist issue of *Poetry*, he included a theoretical explanation entitled "Program: 'Objectivists' 1931." And soon after his *Poetry* issue was published, Zukofsky published *An "Objectivists" Anthology,* which he prefaced with an article—one may say "manifesto"—citing his program. Soon after that, Williams and Zukofsky began their Objectivist press. Despite Williams's and Zukofsky's dismissal of the Objectivist project—that "nothing much happened"—their activities certainly point to the contrary. What caused both men to retreat from their initial impetus to excite poetic reform?

During this flurry of activity, Zukofsky discovered that he had not inaugurated a new age in poetry but rather had invited a whole host of challenges to his program—and the strongest criticism came from his potential supporter, Harriet Monroe. After reading Zukofsky's issue of *Poetry,* Harriet Monroe was dismayed and angered; rising to the occasion, she sent a challenge to the young whippersnapper. In the next issue she aimed a sharp rebuke entitled "The Arrogance of Youth" at Zukofsky. She scolded Zukofsky for consigning poets to "outer darkness" because they did not "fit into a theoretic scheme spun out of brain fabric by a group of empirical young rule-makers"—in other words, the Objectivists. Moreover, she questioned whether or not Zukofsky's Objectivist principles were unique only to his elect. She argued that a whole group of poets—not only the proponents of Objectivism—were concerned with the "objectively perfect" or interested in "clear and vital particulars." Furthermore, she complained that Zukofsky was simply revamping well-known literary truisms into his "gaseous definitions." "And," she asked, "what is objectification but our old friend imagination, somewhat circumscribed and specialized?"[53]

Certainly Zukofsky smarted from Harriet's well-aimed rebuke. Moreover, her criticism of his "gaseous definitions" was justified, for Zukofsky, in the midst of developing his own poetics, was still caught in the language of his predecessors. Like his predecessors, Zukofsky was interested in the clarity and precision of words; yet at the same time that he talked about the poem as an object, he also set that object in the midst of a context and an ongoing process. Rather than narrowing his definitions, Zukofsky was interested in making his definitions inclusive. When Williams, at several different times, asked Zukofsky for a further delineation of the Objectivist theory, Zukofsky became increasingly vague, finally replying that all good poets from Homer on had been Objectivists.

When in the 1930s Lorine Niedecker asked Zukofsky for a definition, however, Zukofsky gave a much more specific reply, indicating that the Objectivists, unlike their predecessors the Imagists, "suggest the direction of things which we call history" and "their own judgment on history."[54] To define the Objectivist goals essentially involved a definition of the Objectivist problem—to move beyond the Imagist dicta. In his *Autobiography* Williams writes: "The Objectivist theory was this: We had had 'Imagism' (*Amygism,* as Pound had called it), which ran quickly out. That, though it had been useful in ridding the field of verbiage, had no formal necessity implicit in it. It had already dribbled off into so called 'free verse' which, as we saw, was a misnomer. There is no such thing as free verse!"[55] Moreover, Williams asserted that the poem should be "treated and controlled" as an object—"but not as in the past." For the Objectivist, the crucial question was where would the poets go from Imagism? Williams attempted to define the Objectivist goal: "The poem being an object (like a symphony or cubist painting) it must be the purpose of the poet to make of his words a new form: to invent, that is, an object consonant with his day. This was what we wished to imply by Objectivism, an antidote, in a sense, to the bare image presented in loose verse."[56] In his letter to Niedecker, Zukofsky, however, goes further in his solution to their dilemma; he found the answer in reconciling the image with history. The epic form—shaped by linguistic rather than transcendent and psychological structures—would allow Zukofsky to incorporate the "the tendency in things which we call history" into his poetry.

Zukofsky discovered at least the hazy outlines of his poetics in the late 1920s and early 1930s. During this time, as noted earlier, he wrote a letter to Pound, distinguishing his epic imagination from Williams's lyric one. Although one can't help but hear—to use Harriet Monroe's phrase—the "arrogance of youth" in Zukofsky's tone, Zukofsky, in attempting to formulate his own critical and poetic language, needed to undergo a process of individuation. During this time Williams was struggling with his own poetics, which—as he admitted to Zukofsky in a letter—was dominated by a desire for the whole: "Perhaps by my picayune, imagistic mannerisms I hold together superficially what should by all means fall."[57]

In developing the epic form of *"A"*, Zukofsky did allow his belief in the whole to fall apart. Unlike Williams, Zukofsky found his answer not in transformation—in which the parts cohere in a whole, a functional common reality—but in repetition and free play—in which signification is realized in a field of options. Within his poetic field of options, Zukofsky created a system of words and structures that did not have to rely on a transcendent referential system.

Almost twenty years later, when Williams completed the first section of his own epic work *Paterson,* his poetics was still dominated by his desire for the whole. Nevertheless, he seemed to be looking for a critical language that would enable him to complete his epic *Paterson,* a conception he had had since the 1920s; and the language that was most pivotal to Williams's work was akin to Zukofsky's own critical language. But, as in Williams's poem "To," there can be quite a gap between Zukofsky's theory and Williams's praxis.

When he was in the process of writing *Paterson,* Williams had already adopted several of Zukofsky's key concepts. In his 1948 essay "The Poem as a Field of Action," Williams writes:

> I propose sweeping changes from top to bottom of the poetic structure. I said structure. . . . More has been done than you think about this though not yet specifically named for what it is. I believe something can be said. Perhaps all that I can do here is to call attention to it: a revolution in the conception of the poetic foot—pointing out the evidence of something that has been going on for a long time.[58]

Of course, Williams is correct when he states that the "revolution of the poetic foot" has been "going on for a long time"; to see the inception of the revolution, one need only look at Pound's imagistic verse or Williams's *Spring and All,* or one could, of course, travel further back to Whitman's pioneering free verse. But in the above passage, Williams emphasizes not only the poetic foot but also poetic structure, demonstrating that his interest in the all-encompassing vision of the eternal moment in *Spring and All* has given way to a discourse about poetic structure. Williams's language in this passage resonates with Zukofsky's own theoretical language of the early 1930s. In his "Objectivist" article the young Zukofsky emphasized the importance of "resolving of words and their ide- ation into structure" and of perceiving the "definite object" as a "personal structure of relations."[59] Of course, Zukofsky's article was in part a justification for his own epic poem *"A"*, in which he constructed a "personal structure of relations." Twenty years after Zukofsky began *"A"*, Williams would publish the first book of his epic *Paterson*. The key factor that would allow Williams to trans- form his lyric impulse into an epic one was his concept of structure. In "The Poem as a Field of Action," Williams argues, "Imagism was not structural: that was the reason for its disappearance."[60]

Attempting to monitor Zukofsky's exact influence on Williams's epic can be a rather tricky prospect. Williams corresponded with a number of poets who shared ideas with him. Moreover, Zukofsky developed his poetics from many of the concepts of his predecessors; as Zukofsky himself has said, he filtered his ideas from "what wuz in the air of a time." He learned from Williams and, in turn, Williams learned from Zukofsky. But as I have noted already, Williams re- spected Zukofsky's ability to articulate critical tenets, transforming praxis into theory, bringing the poetic act into the arena of the "said." Zukofsky's comments allowed Williams to focus anew on his own ideas about the "rhythm of a line," encouraged him to rethink his understanding of how abstract thoughts could actually be incorporated into a poem as a "thing," and influenced him to con- ceive of a poem in structural rather than imagistic terms. Zukofsky also felt that he influenced Williams's later poetics; as he wrote to Lorine Niedecker, "Bill's Paterson I re-*particular* it comes *long after* A-1, as do other notions in him that were in A. But then there's Bill's letter saying he [was] reading me—& that lots wd. come out of it for him, while working on Paterson."[61]

Moreover, as Neil Baldwin has noted, Zukofsky was instrumen- tal in helping Williams edit his 1944 collection of poems *The Wedge*, which "can be seen as a threshold work, opening the way for Williams to *Paterson* I."[62] During that time Williams wrote the work *Under the Sun*, a dialogue between an aging George Washington and his young comrade Lafayette, who encourages the weary general. Here, Baldwin argues, Williams was projecting his relationship with Zukofsky onto the two wartime comrades; Williams and Zukofsky were simply fighting their revolution on another battlefield on which the younger Zukofsky enacts the role of Lafayette counseling the elder Washington/Williams.

In his editing of Williams's *Wedge*, Zukofsky was an effective counselor, influencing Williams in both the sound and sense of his poems. He advised Williams to be restrained in both words and emotions. For instance, Zukofsky suggested that Williams eliminate the last four lines of the following draft:

> The (lang)WEDGE
> With the tip of my tongue
> I wedge you open
> My tongue!
> the wedge of my tongue
> between those lips parted
> to inflame you . . . [63]

Zukofsky felt that the last four lines were unnecessarily repetitious. Williams decided, as he did with many of Zukofsky's suggestions, to follow Zukofsky's critical eye and ear; he eliminated not only the four lines but the entire draft from his final collection. In the above poem Williams's composing and Zukofsky's editing converge in revealing ways. Obviously, "(lang)WEDGE" is metaphorically linked to a sexual act of penetration; the work is unabashedly phallocentric. The poem resonates with Whitmanesque sensuality, a sensuality that Zukofsky apparently wishes to curb, trimming Williams's Whitmanesque impulse. The intellectual, placing the self within the confines of language, restrains the bard, who wishes to thrust his tongue into the reader. In fact, the very repetition in these lines seductively calls to the reader, as Whitman, in *Crossing Brooklyn Ferry*, seductively uses language as the mediating force between himself and his audience: "Consider, you who peruse me, whether I may not in unknown / ways be looking upon you."[64]

Although Zukofsky respected Williams's work, he preferred a poetry in which the self would be realized in the interstices of language, not in the bold call of either the self or, as in *Paterson,* a symbolic structure.

Dedicating *The Wedge* to L. Z., Williams did not feel as though Zukofsky, whose editorial suggestions were always tactfully made, exercised any tyrannical force over his writing. In the end, Williams remained intrinsically Williams. Finally, even though Zukofsky and Williams shared a critical vocabulary and a central concern with language/lang(wedge), they enacted their own distinct "grammar of motives" in their poetry.

In *"A"* Zukofsky had already deployed a number of poetic strategies: perceiving ideas as things, reifying linguistic structures rather than resorting to transcendent superstructures, and recognizing that language could serve as a mediating force that not only refers to but also constitutes meaning. In *Paterson* Williams, with a number of abstract assertions sprinkled through his epic, also recognizes ideas as things even—paradoxically—when he asserts "Say it. No ideas but in things. Mr. / Paterson has gone away / to rest and write. Inside the bus one sees / his thoughts sitting and standing."[65] Considering *Paterson* to be Williams's "high point," his successful synthesis of the power of the idea with the thing, Roy Harvey Pearce asserts that in this epic Williams finally achieves the "derivation of ideas from things and the discovery of thingness in ideas."[66] One can't help but hear in Pearce's remarks an echo of Williams's 1928 letter to Zukofsky when Williams states, with an almost surprised discovery, "It is thoughtful poetry, but actual word stuff, not thoughts for thoughts. It escapes me in its analysis (thank God) and strikes against me [a]s a thing."[67]

Although Pearce sees *Paterson* as a culmination of Williams's lifework, other critics are quick to disagree. Marjorie Perloff suggests that in *Paterson* Williams fails to give his audience a revolutionary work like *Spring and All* and *Kora in Hell;* instead, Williams resorts to the "alien rhetoric of Symbolism."[68] In *Spring and All* Williams articulates his desire to "escape crude symbolism," and in an essay on Pound he asserts that the "principle move in imaginative writing today" is "that away from the world as symbol toward the world as reality." Yet, ironically, this same man who wrote of the "bastardy of the simile," writes in *Paterson:*

> A man like a city and a woman like a flower
> —who are in love. Two women. Three women.
> Innumerable women, each like a flower.[69]

Williams creates a symbolic construct that contains its own mythic hero and cosmos. Michael André Bernstein considers *Paterson* a failed poem because "*Paterson*'s symbolic structure is inadequate to its purpose, and second, the solutions Williams proposes for his town's dilemma are so abstract and general . . . that he unwittingly succeeds in making the terrible waste seem historically both inevitable and irreversible."[70] Citing James Breslin, Bernstein notes that Williams's best poems "create a literal specificity" rather than "combine into symbolic clusters"; furthermore, Bernstein finds *Paterson* most successful when Williams is caught in the fragmentation of the "delirium of solutions" and wakens from "this dream of/the whole poem." In other words, Bernstein finds Williams most successful when he is able, in some measure, to fragment the "whole." And as Williams once wrote Zukofsky, perhaps he holds "together superficially what should by all means fall apart." Here Williams was talking about his Imagist technique, but we can see that Williams transfers his desire for wholeness from his lyrics to his epic poem.

Despite Williams implementation of Cubist fragmentation, Williams ultimately wanted the fragments to cohere. When Williams saw Charles Demuth's painting of his poem "I Saw the figure 5 in Gold," he complained that the painting had lost "the completion that was once felt" and advised that the painting "would gain by a unity of treatment which would cast a unity of feeling over it all."[71] Moreover, he praised Charles Sheeler for keeping "what the understanding touches intact."[72]

Zukofsky is willing to fracture the surface of his work; Williams wishes to leave the surface whole. Both Zukofsky and Williams were searching for a renewed language, but Zukofsky discovered the richness in signifiers when he was able to sever the sign from a specific signification, whereas Williams perceived a cohesive bond between sign and meaning: language is basically referential. For Williams, not only is the word referential, but structure is also referential. I would argue that although Williams intended to implement a revolutionary concept of structure in his poem, because of his desire for the whole, his structure cohered into a symbolic unity. In "Against the Weather" Williams writes:

> We should have a revolution of some sort in America every ten years. The truth has to be redressed, re-examined, re-affirmed in a new mode. There has to be new poetry. But the thing is that the change, the greater material, the altered structure of the inevitable revolution must be *in* the poem, in it. Made of it. It must shine in the structural body of it. . . .
>
> Think of a work of art—a poem—as a structure. A form is a structure consciously adopted for an effect. How then can a man seriously speak of order when the most that he is doing is to impose a structural character taken over from the habits of the past upon his content? This is sheer bastardy.[73]

Unfortunately, Williams commits his own "sheer bastardy." Ironically, when Williams searched for an appropriate structure for *Paterson,* he found his structure in the symbolic methodology of his old nemesis: Eliot. In *Paterson* Williams suggests that he has located his myth: "And the myth / that holds up the rock, / that holds up the water thrives there— / in that cavern, that profound cleft, / a flickering green / inspiring terror, watching."[74] Zukofsky clearly states that he wishes to free himself from the superstructure of myth and make a case "for the poet giving some of his life to the use of the words *the* and *a*" (*Prepositions,* 10). Like Eliot and Pound, who glorified a mythic past, Williams also glorifies the mythic past of *Paterson.* For Zukofsky, mythic superstructures are not sufficient for a poet who believes in the "epos and destiny" of the little word.

Williams died on 4 March 1963. Zukofsky responded by intertwining a coronal—a wreath of flowers—in memory of Williams through his *"A"* 15–17. *"A"*-17, subtitled "A Coronal for Floss," is a direct tribute to the lifelong relationship between these two men of letters—a relationship that inscribed itself on Zukofsky's text. Both *"A"*-15 and *"A"*-16 resonate with Williams's presence. At the end of *"A"*-15, Zukofsky writes:

negritude no nearer or further
than the African violet
not deferred to
or if white, Job
white pods of *honesty*
satinflower

("*A*"-15, 375)

Although Zukofsky's text resonates with a number of previous texts (Langston Hughes's "A Dream Deferred," for example), he has also mined from the richness of *Spring and All:*

Black eyed susan
rich orange
round the purple core
the white daisy
is not
enough[75]

Zukofsky endows these flowers with the social and political resonances of the 1960s, transforming Williams's sensuality into an observation about race and suffering. In "*A*"-16 Zukofsky writes four words that in themselves have a beautiful simplicity and that, when placed in the context of the poem, again resonate with social consequence:

An
    inequality

            wind flower
            ("*A*"-16, 376)

Zukofsky links the social revolution of the 1960s with the literary revolution embodied in *Spring and All* in the 1920s. In *"A"*-17 Zukofsky gives Williams what he had asked for many years before: a clear mirror. *"A"*-17 is a collage of texts—composed of excerpts from Zukofsky's poetry, from Zukofsky's articles on Williams, and from Williams's writings—that attests to Williams and Zukofsky's thirty-five year relationship. Zukofsky's mirror is not a Platonic but a textual one, a mirror that reflects a life of language. As Williams once wrote in a review of Zukofsky's *Anew:* "This poem, all Z's art, that is to say, his life."[76] Zukofsky's movement does not follow the conventions of an elegy (mourning, consolation, and affirmation of immortality); rather, it witnesses a history of a relationship that achieves an immortality in the substance of the text. At one point Zukofsky offers a poem in which Williams becomes an actual text:

> reach
> C
> a cove—
> call it
> Carlos:
>
> smell W
> double U
> two W's
> ravine and
> runnel:
> (*"A"*-17, 383–84)

Zukofsky ends his movement with a copy of a Williams's signature, an inscription Williams once gave him. Williams's identity has been caught in the signature, and such a signature has become more than a mere inscription, for this very special language has inscribed itself in Zukofsky's lifework, his poetry, "that is to say, his life."

6. A Legacy: Zukofsky and the Language Poets

In the 1920s Zukofsky was an avid apprentice of the arts, desiring to learn his craft as well as to create his own poetics. By the 1930s Zukofsky had moved from apprentice to master craftsman, a shift demonstrated by his editing of the Objectivist issue of *Poetry*. Soon after the publication of that issue, Lorine Niedecker contacted Zukofsky and began a lifelong correspondence with him; in essence, she became Zukofsky's first disciple and, at that time, his only one. Zukofsky, with his epic sensibility, enjoyed aligning himself with Walt Whitman and aligning Niedecker, with her sparse lyrics, with Emily Dickinson. Throughout his lifetime Zukofsky maintained a number of correspondences with poets such as Robert Creeley, Robert Duncan, Edward Dahlberg, and Cid Corman. Creeley, who dedicated his book of poems *Pieces* to Zukofsky, has noted that Zukofsky, along with the other Objectivist poets, provided a continuity between the Modernist and later Black Mountain and Projectivist poets.[1] Zukofsky himself felt that Charles Olson's essay on Projectivist verse, or what he referred to as Olson's "Projectile," was derivative of his own critical writings. In a letter to Edward Dahlberg, Zukofsky states, "If anything [Olson's Projectivist essay] is a steal from my Objectivist issue, etc. bungled up etc."[2] Although he was known as the "poet's poet," Zukofsky never really had any substantial following; he was respected, but like Milton, to whom Basil Bunting once compared Zukofsky, his was a "fit audience, though few."[3]

Quite early in their friendship, Williams had warned Zukofsky, "Don't expect the mountain to come to you—in the form of a public demonstration."[4] But it was also Williams who would speak prophetic words of encouragement to his fellow poet. When Zukofsky

published *Anew* in 1946, Williams wrote him a letter in which he
stated that Zukofsky's work was as important to poetry "as the
1913 Armory show was to painting. In fact my own opinion that the
whole complex of the work and thought initiate a completely new
era in the making of poems. The writers will catch on, shall we say?
in 1976 (the new American Revolution!)."[5]

Zukofsky was not doomed to be barren; in time, true to Wil-
liams's prediction, he gave rise to his new American Revolution; his
legacy was appropriated by such poets as Clark Coolidge, Ron
Silliman, Robert Grenier, Barrett Watten, and Charles Bernstein,
who together loosely form part of a group known as the Language
poets. In a *Sagetrieb* interview Robert Duncan noted that the Lan-
guage poets have "made the richest use of it [Zukofsky's work] to
date."[6] A diverse group, these poets trace their lineage back to such
Black Mountain poets as Charles Olson and Robert Creeley, such
Russian Futurist poets as Velimir Khlebnikov and Vladimir Maya-
kovsky, and such Modernists as Gertrude Stein, William Carlos
Williams, and Zukofsky.[7]

We must be careful to note that the Language poets do not
necessarily constitute a formal group as such; most poets, as did
Zukofsky, balk at subsuming the identity of their work under a
group label, a "groove in" a record. Even in the mid 1970s, when
Ron Silliman collected a number of "language-centered" poets in
Alcheringa, he stressed that these poets did not form a group but
rather that they shared similar tendencies. Nevertheless, in editing
the journal $L=A=N=G=U=A=G=E$ in the late 1970s, Bruce An-
drews and Charles Bernstein were implicitly recognizing their con-
tributors as a group, and by the time Andrews and Bernstein edited
The $L=A=N=G=U=A=G=E$ Book in the 1980s, these language-
centered poets were commonly referred to as the Language poets.
Bernstein articulates the paradoxical relationship of the lone poet to
group categories, or what he calls the "conspiracy of 'us' ": "I don't
believe in group formation, I don't like group formation, but I am
constantly finding myself contending with it, living within it, seeing
through it. 'Okay, break it up boys.' "[8] In the phrase "break it up
boys," Bernstein points to, and thus foregrounds, the complex para-

dox embedded in this trite cliché. What would the boys "break up"? The phrase suggests that some group—be it social, familial, aesthetic, perhaps based on some paternalistic ("boys") hierarchy— structures collective identity. Even to challenge, or "to break," the group is to assert that the group, as a concept, exists. After all, the act of "negation is determined by the thing negated" (*LB*, 131). In 1984, when Bernstein and Andrews edited *The L=A=N= G=U=A=G=E Book,* they compiled a selection of reviews and articles that essentially constituted a manifesto, inevitably recognizing the "conspiracy of 'us.'"

I wish to mention the dilemma the concept of the group poses precisely because in this chapter I will be regarding the Language poets not as individual artists but as a composite group. I intend to work within broad generalities that will demonstrate how this group developed a number of Zukofsky's central concerns, primarily his focus on language. In their foreword Bernstein and Andrews voice their central tenet: "We have emphasized a spectrum of writing that places its attention primarily on language and ways of making meaning, that takes for granted neither vocabulary, grammar, process, shape, syntax, program, or subject matter. All of these remain at issue" (*LB*, ix). These poets have expanded on what Zukofsky discovered in *"A"*-7: "Horses: who will do it? out of manes? Words/ Will do it, out of manes, out of airs." Like Zukofsky, these poets (1) foreground language, in order to "repossess the word," (2) reject symbolism and mythic superstructures and embrace linguistic structures, (3) perceive an interrelationship between the word and the world, and (4) regard the self as a marginal presence in the text: the mediating subject disappears.

In a tribute to Louis Zukofsky, Robert Grenier, in one of the issues of *L=A=N=G=U=A=G=E,* wrote the following poem:

"THINK SUN AND SEE SHADOW"

naked sitting and lying awake
dear eyes all eyes
destined actual infinitely initial
rove into the blue initial

an earth of three trees

rendered his requiem alive
blessed ardent Celia happy
an era any time of year
an inequality wind flower
                              —(4's & 5's from) Louis Zukofsky
                                        (*LB,* 294)

Grenier's poem offers an appropriate segue between Zukofsky and
the Language poets. Here Grenier has accumulated fragments from
Zukofsky's own works and arranged these lines into a poetic and, in
essence, archaeological artifact. In his title Grenier has transposed
Zukofsky's line "see sun and think shadow" into "think sun and see
shadow," as though he were either attesting to the strength of Zu-
kofsky's conception over his perception or simply suggesting that his
own poem would mirror Zukofsky's texts (with the image trans-
posed). On the one hand, Grenier's work reflects Zukofsky's interest
in the structural quality of the line and the pattern of the poem; Gre-
nier is playing with a pattern of four or five words to each line and a
pattern of two stanzas of four lines, which, with the addition of the
middle line, could be transformed into five lines (thus "4's & 5's
from"). On the other hand, Grenier has collected several themes—
concerning perception, music, and the family—that are interwoven
through a number of Zukofsky's poems. The lyric is not predicated
on any narrative order; rather, Grenier allows the lyric to resonate
with musical and thematic echoes from Zukofsky's own text. Gre-
nier has excavated Zukofsky's poems, transforming one poet's trib-
ute to another into a linguistic link from one text to another. Lan-
guage serves as the primary "presence" in the poem; neither a
coherent, psychological "I" nor a transcendent mythic structure
forms the central matrix of the poem. Moreover, Grenier's lyric has
neither a privileged "subject" nor a privileged "object." In other
words, Grenier's poem does not at all resemble a poem such as
Pound's "A Pact," in which the poet's persona engages in a rec-
onciliation with his predecessor, Walt Whitman. Zukofsky does
not "exist" in the poem other than the fact that he exists within
his language. In killing the two authors—himself and Zukofsky—

Grenier is actually mirroring Zukofsky's poetics. In giving the text, not the "selves," a privileged position, Grenier realizes his own, as well as Zukofsky's, poetics—a most appropriate "pact" between poet and predecessor.

Essentially, Zukofsky deployed an epistemological system that is inscribed in language, and in so doing he articulates a contemporary American poetics—further developed by the Language poets—that makes distinct claims for the constitutive role of language in society. It is important to note that neither Zukofsky nor the Language poets reduce poetry to a self-referential game in which writing is simply an interplay of signs. Zukofsky grounded his poetics in both the materials of history and the materials of his story. For the Language poets, the word is inevitably intertwined with the world; they focus on both "language and the way of making meaning"—all of which remain at issue. How language as a medium is used—rhetorically, philosophically, socially, economically—is the key to understanding our world; as E. Sapir states, "The fact of the matter is that the 'real world' is to a large extent unconsciously built up on the language habits of the group" (*LB*, 121). In fact, many of the Language poets, several of whom are Marxist in political orientation, perceive the practice of their craft to be "inevitably a social and political activity as well as an aesthetic one" (*LB*, x).

The Language poets recognize Zukofsky's seminal place in American poetics. As Ron Silliman attests, Zukofsky was "the first (& for a long time the only) to read Pound & Williams with what we wld recognize as modern eye & ear" (*LB*, 290). Silliman suggests that part of Zukofsky's importance can be ascribed to Zukofsky's understanding of language as a medium and his ability to read that language; here Silliman highlights the fact that "reading" is not a passive but an active, cognitive experience. In "Code Words" Bruce Andrews distinguishes between a reading that hypnotizes the reader "by illusions of transparency" and a reading that captures both the "code-like aspects" of writing and "the yearning singularity of the phonemes bursting off page, tape, or lips." Zukofsky, of course, was a reader, as well as a writer, of the second type. He constructed writerly (scriptible) texts, urging the reader to be a producer of meanings rather than a consumer of fixed meaning. "Reading becomes the first *production,* rather than consumption—not a relay of an author's vain transcriptions of a representational content. Reading *operates* the text, is a rewriting, a new inscription" (*LB,* 55). Actively engaging in the reading process, Zukofsky inscribed himself in the text of the Modernists and wrote that text anew.

Inasmuch as Zukofsky was a reader of the traditions of the poets who preceded him, so, too, are the Language poets readers of these traditions; only, of course, in their case Zukofsky is one of their predecessors. Neither Zukofsky nor the Language poets separate the critical and inquiring intelligence from the creative act. As Stephen Fredman has noted, the Language poets are "originally critical, practicing a vigilant self-awareness that calls forth language and subjects it to an examination of its mediatory function."[9] In their own way, the Language poets, like Zukofsky, are poets of "classroom accuracies." But, of course, in the Language poets' historical framework, Zukofsky is no longer the reading subject but a text, a particular placed within the context of literary history. The Language poets celebrate Zukofsky's ability to hear the "phonemes bursting off page, tape, or lips," and as Ronald Johnson asserts, "the finest ears in the business is heading somewhere 100,000 years an hour (or so). Do you not hear them thunder?" (*LB,* 295). Silliman suggests that Zukofsky was the *first* to read with modern eye and ear: here Zukofsky represents a historical watershed. Johnson states that Zukofsky's ears are heading somewhere 100,000 years an hour: Zukofsky's poetry is still participating in an ongoing revolution. In a way, the Language poets regard Zukofsky as he regarded Pound and Williams: both as literary artifact and as a producer of texts whose influence interacts with a vital present. Zukofsky would appreciate this dual perception of himself. When Zukofsky saw Donald Allen's anthology *New American Poetry 1945–60,* he was amused to find himself categorized as "of the 'period' before" the "crowd of 'young' " poets. Relating his reactions to Lorine Niedecker, he simply asserted, "We'll show em!"[10]

For many of the Language poets, Zukofsky represents one means of anchoring their own identity in the history of American poetics.

Many of the Language poets perceive themselves as outsiders—
outsiders of academia, outsiders of the canon, outsiders of the cap-
italistic American culture. They have appropriated Zukofsky, the
outsider, in much the same way that Zukofsky attempted to appro-
priate the Modernists, who carried the "thin milk . . . from the pap"
of American culture.[11] In tracing their lineage to Zukofsky, they are
making a choice in terms of both poetics and culture. For instance,
Grenier charts the difference between Eliot and Zukofsky, and in so
doing he adumbrates the choice the Language poets make:

> Difference between Eliot & Zukofsky's use of materials: E. disappears
> into linguistic conventions, religious symbols, traditional view of the
> world via assumptives of language, swallowed up by machine he oils, he
> reenergizes with blood & verbal capacities, a sacrifice; Z. takes a linguis-
> tic structure (e.g. 5-word line in "A-22") or theme (the idea of natural
> chronology) as a situation, like a friendship, opening not only his own
> muscular display (fast-talking, action painting, wit) but equally chance
> for the realization of another in language & concomitant change in self's
> nature thereby.[12]

Grenier is outlining the differences between Eliot's Symbolist and
Zukofsky's Objectivist methods. On the one hand, Eliot constructs a
world of religious symbols in which a transcendent force is the
primary other to whom he, as the high priest, sacrifices himself;
Zukofsky, on the other hand, engages in a dialogue with language
that is his primary other, and both the self and language undergo
a "concomitant change." We may well suggest that Zukofsky's
method grows out of Eliot's own revolution of the word, but Zukof-
sky takes the Modernist credo one step further: not only is the word
a medium that is transformed, but the word *is* the transforming
medium. Zukofsky's realization of the power of linguistic structures
and the epos and destiny of the little word leads him away from the
transcendent structures and the Modernist religion of God, Culture,
or Art as the Word. In doing so, Zukofsky is making a choice for
process and history: transformation is not defined by the meeting of
the temporal with the eternal; rather, it is defined through historical
development.

    In his comparison of Eliot's and Zukofsky's methodologies, Grenier makes it clear that he, like a number of his fellow poets, has made a choice for the "realization of another in language" and the "concomitant change" in the self over the "traditional view of the world via assumptives of language." This move—from the "traditional view of the world"—entails one fundamental shift in American poetics, a shift that can be traced from the tenets of Modernism to Zukofsky's Objectivist vision to the demands of the Language poets, a shift that involves fundamental questions about the role of the self, language, and history in American poetry.

In the 1920s, when Zukofsky struggled with the problem of identity in *Poem beginning "The"*, he was grappling not only with a literary identity (the role of the poet) but with a social and economic identity. Zukofsky faced a basic dilemma concerning the concept of identity that was predicated on his actual situation. Where could he anchor the self? He was caught between his role of poet—with all its ties to an elitist literary and cultural past—and his role as a Jewish immigrant's son with familial and social ties to the ghetto. He could not fully embrace the religion or language of his parents, and at the same time he could not fully embrace the socialization of the American culture. He adopted literary Modernist fathers—like Adams and Pound—but he did so with a full awareness of his cultural place. He realized that his hope was not in a traditional past that he could not fully appropriate; rather, he saw hope in a Marxist vision of history and in the actual fact of Lenin's revolution in Russia—a revolution that would give cultural as well as political power to a ghetto dweller such as he. As Zukofsky writes in *The,* "It is your Russia that is free, mother." But Zukofsky lived in America, not Russia; he did not wish to see his homeland, America, and his parents' original homeland, Russia, set in opposition to each other. In fact, Zukofsky sustained a belief that he could marry Adams's vision of history with a Marxist hope: a marriage that might resolve the contradictions of his own identity. Zukofsky never realized that marriage of an American past with a Marxist future, and Zukofsky was never to achieve power in either the literary or the social order of things. For all his life, Zukofsky remained an intrinsically marginal character—a man who lived not in the center but on the circumference of American literary and social life.

The Language poets, for their part, are children of a post-Vietnam and post-Watergate era and inheritors of a cold war legacy. Many of them, as well, embrace a Marxist vision, but unlike the young Zukofsky of the 1920s, history has not told them, "It is your Russia that is free"; they have seen the various failings of the ambitious socialist experiments. Their Marxist vision is not so much a vehicle of hope as it is a vehicle of opposition—a means to criticize the existing conventional language used by both capitalistic and communistic societies. As such, these poets champion a marginal stance—in terms of both their language and their place in the cultural hierarchy. Jerome McGann has argued that the most crucial characteristic of the Language poets is their oppositional politics, a politics that stands in sharp contrast to the more conservative and traditional stance of the poets of accommodation such as Robert Pinsky and John Hollander. Perceiving the Language poets and the poets of accommodation as representatives of the two major divergent lines of contemporary American poetry in the 1970s and 1980s, McGann notes that the poets of accommodation write a "personal or localized verse" that is stylistically characterized by "a moderated surface urbanity" and substantively characterized by "an attempt to define 'social' and 'political' within a limited, even a personal, horizon." The ideological gap between the two groups is further polarized by the groups' respective institutional power: whereas many of the Language writers are "situated—economically and institutionally—outside the academy, their counterparts—critics and poets alike—occupy important scholastic positions."[13]

In many ways, the Language poets choose to be poets on the circumference of society; but it is important to reiterate that these poets choose to exist on the margins of not only capitalist but also communist institutions. Despite their "oppositional politics," the Language poets are just as critical of the conventional language used by the Left as they are of the transparent language used by the Right. Moreover, as dedicated to the "politics of poetry" as some of the Language poets may be, they do not stand up and cry, "Workers take off your chains," nor do they applaud the populist realism of other writers of the Left. Instead, they continually foreground language, urging the reader to be aware of the alienation existing in institutional societies rather than urging the reader to take revolutionary action against those societies. If the Language poets wish to instigate a revolution, they wish to instigate a revolution in language, offering an alternative to the conventional language of both capitalist and communist societies. They desire to deconstruct the operation of representation in order to expose the ideology that informs it. In *Content's Dream* Charles Bernstein states, "There is an instructive value in working with—reading *and* writing—texts that offer alternatives to the directional, unifunctional, hierarchialized structures that dominate both Capitalistic and Communist societies." Moreover, he urges, "We have got to understand that the failure of socialist revolutions are related to failures to break with these structures. It is not enough, as has often been said, to just switch the operators of the same state/corporate machine: the machine itself must be dismantled. But it is also not enough simply to *say* that." Bernstein suggests that society must envision alternatives beginning with a "total de/reorganization of the formal norms embraced by both realist/populist and academic writing."[14] In the transformation of language lies the seeds of social transformation.

The Zukofsky of the 1920s and the Language poets of the 1980s are separated by more than half a century of history. As a young poet Zukofsky was developing an ideology out of his experience. Looking back over the twentieth century, the Language poets are applying their ideology to experience. In *The* Zukofsky demonstrates his struggle between his social and artistic identity; the two identities did not always coalesce: "So then an egoist can never embrace / a party / Or take up with a party? / Oh, yes, only he cannot let himself / Be embraced or taken up by the party." In these early years Zukofsky felt that an artist could not retreat from the world, for he would only discover that his ivory tower was in reality the Chrysler Building. But at the same time, he did not want to subsume his identity into a political party. Zukofsky found his answer, as he suggests in *"A"*-7, in words, for language ultimately serves a mediatory function in political, social, as well as literary systems.

Language poets such as Ron Silliman also unite politics and poetry by focusing on the social implications inherent in the revolutionary word. In fact, if Silliman were to examine Zukofsky's dilemma, he would approve of the dialectic nature of Zukofsky's struggle and the fact that Zukofsky resolves his struggle in the "philosophy of practice in language." In "Disappearance of the Word, Appearance of the World," Silliman even advocates a type of program for poets:

> By recognizing itself as the *philosophy of practice in language,* poetry can work to search out the preconditions of post-referential language within the existing social fact. This requires (1) recognition of the historic nature and structure of referentiality, (2) placing the issue of language, the repressed element, at the center of the program, (3) placing the program into the context of conscious class struggle. (*LB,* 131)

Standing on the circumference of society, both Zukofsky and the Language poets place the issue of language at the center of their program—although Zukofsky emphasizes neither language as a social fact nor the poetics of politics in the programmatic manner of Silliman or Bernstein. Moreover, because they believe that language is the subject (both as substance and as the "I") of the poem, all three poets—Zukofsky, Bernstein, and Silliman—situate their own identity within the interstices of language. Although Zukofsky believed that a poet should communicate "judgment" in his poem and although the Language poets are vocal in their oppositional politics, both surrender the mediating voice of the empowered self to the medium of an empowered language. As Bruce Andrews succinctly quotes from Roland Barthes *Image-Music-Text:* "It is language which speaks, not the author" (*LB,* 54).

In the process of developing his poetics, Zukofsky buried the author in his language. Initially, Zukofsky, searching for an alternative to the poetry of the past, wished to subvert the primacy of the Romantic self. In fact, when he wrote an article on the great innovator Pound, Zukofsky applauded him for being able to escape the subjective self:

> In short, Pound has not wrapped mannerisms around his subject matter but made the subject matter his style. His archaisms vary with his subjects. Pound's objectivity and range are, therefore, his only identifications. He has not obtruded personally, never found it worth his while to discover an interesting subjective self to please people. One does

not generally deplore sincere attempts at self-discovery but notes that Pound's objectivity in the *Cantos* is an excellent way of doing it. (*Prepositions*, 82)

In this early article Zukofsky is particularly interested in how Pound, who adopted various personae to escape the subjective self, made "subject matter his style." Although Zukofsky wished to eschew the subjective self, he did not elect to use Pound's solution—the voice of the persona. He did, however, choose to make "the subject matter his style" and established a poetics in which the "style" or language became the subject matter of the poem. In the enactment of such a poetics, the self would not be the central concern of the poem but simply one of the linguistic limits in the language of the poem. In "Poem 22," for example, Zukofsky situates the "I" in the world of coexisting objects:

> To my wash-stand
> in which I wash
>   my left hand
> and my right hand
>
>   To my wash-stand
> whose base is Greek
>   whose shaft
> is marble and is fluted
>   (*CSP*, 52)

Zukofsky creates a song to his washstand—his humble version of a "Grecian Urn"—yet he realizes that his "song out of imagining" stands side by side with a "song of water from the right faucet and the left." The poet can create a song about the washstand, but the washstand can create its own sound/song. The self is not the central organizing factor in the poem; rather, it exists—as does the washstand—as a linguistic limit in the poem. Even when Zukofsky looks into the mirror above the washstand, he glimpses "half an oval," a literal image of his head. In this moment of possible self-identification, he leaves the image of his head fragmented without attempting to foster an imaginary wholeness out of his reflection in the mirror. Zukofsky does not enact what Jacques Lacan has termed the "mirror phase" of child development, in which the child sees a reflection of himself in the mirror and first imagines himself as a coherent and self-governing individual, a "specular image." Instead, Zukofsky sees his image as a fragmented object in a world of objects. Moreover, Zukofsky emphasizes the fact that a perceiving subject does not transform the objects or events that surround it into an expression of itself; for Zukofsky suggests that the washstand can designate a boundary for the self: "is my wash-stand / since its marble has completed / my getting up each morning / my washing before going to bed." The washstand, not the self, is the central actor in the poem; the washstand—a word object—defines the beginning and the end of the day. Here Zukofsky is attempting to "think with things" as they exist in the world.

In other poems Zukofsky, eliminating any intrusive "I," lets the words of the poem stand alone as tangible phonemes and morphemes. Charles Bernstein has noted that Zukofsky's "It's a gay li-ife" foregrounds the word, making language concrete and opaque:

> There's naw—thing
>   lak po—ee try
> it's a delicacy
>   for   a horse:
> Dere's na—thing
>   lak pea-   nut-brittle
> it's a delicacy
>   for   the molars.
>   (*CSP*, 43)

Such a poem becomes a "perceptual field/experience 'independent' of 'author.' " As Bernstein further states:

> So to go from 'thinking' as an activity of 'self' to a world creating/perceiving idea. *Thinking things the world.* So that in the end the poem stands as another particular being, hence object, like myself, in the world, and I beside it. And I return not to myself "as some egocentric center, but experience myself as *in* that world," that with the meaning and limits therein revealed I have also placed myself. (*CD*, 71)

Moreover, neither in his poetry nor his life does Zukofsky perceive the self as a static entity, for that self, like language, is ever-changing and interactive. In "Poetry" Zukofsky writes to his son Paul, "I do not presume that you will read 'me.' That 'me' will be lost today when he says good night on your third birthday, and not missed tomorrow when he says good morning as you begin your fourth year" (*Prepositions,* 11).

The "death of the author"—or at least the challenge to his "author-ity"—is also a fundamental departure point for many of the Language poets. When asked in an interview if his primary goals were to himself, Bernstein questioned the interviewer's underlying assumptions: "Not to myself, that's what I don't understand. What is that 'to myself.' When I'm sitting down and reading I'm not thinking 'Gee, this makes sense *to me*.' I'm not thinking about 'me.' I'm not thinking about 'you.' I'm thinking about 'it.' " Bernstein is challenging what he calls the "conduit metaphor," which suggests that one individual transmits a message to another individual (A to B): "So we think if we're not talking about communicating to 'B' we must be talking about communicating to 'A,' oneself, as if masturbation is going to be the next metaphor." Such a metaphor of communication essentially posits that communication is a unilinear exchange between two autonomous selves. Bernstein challenges the underlying assumption of such a statement: a model of communication that consists of "these preconstituted individuals who are terminal points of an enclosed channel." "That's why," Bernstein explains, "I object when you say it makes sense 'to me' as opposed to 'to you' " (*CD* 420–24). Bernstein is not interested in "a projection of 'self' as centering the language experience": "It's a mistake, I think, to posit the self as the primary organizing feature of writing. As many others have pointed out, a poem exists in a matrix of social and historical relations that are more significant to the formation of an individual text than any personal qualities of the life or voice of an author" (*CD,* 408).

Thus, the Language poets are looking for an alternative to conventional means of organizing a poem. Most of them choose to disseminate the self through language. Alluding to poststructuralist theory and specifically quoting from Roland Barthes, Bruce Andrews writes:

> Author dies, writing begins. The subject loses authority, disappears, is *unmade* into a network of relationships, stretching indefinitely. Subject is *deconstructed,* lost, "diminishing like a figurine at the far end of the

literary stage"; deconstituted as writing ranges over the surface. A *float-ing* or cutting across replaces the barriers of nomenclature and identifica-tion. Normalization gives way to *significance,* an eroticism, a multi-dimensional tissue or weave of signs by which any apparent subject is produced. Writing, as *infinite* association, explodes the definitions, en-distances origins (or Origin), rejects closure, *exempts* meaning. The vise of the signified is unhinged; simplistic notions of truth are relativized. (*LB,* 54)

Thus, we can see that in such a poem as "Larry Eigner Notes," Clark Coolidge disseminates the self, both as subject matter and voice, within the language of his poem:

> "Who wants to see himself"
>
> I see . . .
>
>> the noun states accent in air
>>
>> so much that an "on" or "hard" takes on
>> solidity of noun at line-end
>>> (*LB,* 224)

Coolidge begins his poem with a relative clause, which he fore-grounds by placing in quotations. In a conventional syntactical sequence, the reader would expect a relative clause to modify a subject—which, in this case, ostensibly focuses on a self-reflexive subject (Larry Eigner?): "who wants to see himself." Coolidge re-sponds to the clause with "I see"—a statement that suggests to the reader that there is a perceiving subject at the center of the poem. Coolidge thwarts the reader's expectations, however, as he demon-strates that what the "I" sees is not a message (a conventional poem of self-revelation or a poem commemorating his friend Eigner) but an opaque medium, filled with nouns and prepositions. Completing his poem, Coolidge writes:

> start made at a word
> everything to follow
> the word its word
> again the following
>
> I do not think of Eigner.
>> (*LB,* 227)

Coolidge is writing a poem that begins and ends with words; the poem does not represent a cognitive unveiling in which the reader discovers the author's consciousness throughout, or in a culminating point of, the text. The culminating point of the text is not a moment of closure or revelation; Coolidge's final line—"I do not think of Eigner"—points to the recalcitrant nature of the poem. The "I" *does not* think of the "subject" of the text: Eigner. Here it is the language that speaks, thinks, and acts; the "subject loses authority, disappears, is unmade into a network of relationships." Both the subjects—the "I" and the "you"—have been subsumed within the words generated within the poem.

Although the Language poets are working out of a poststructuralist framework and Zukofsky is working out of a Modernist vocabulary, both are essentially confronting an epistemological understanding of the self. Situating the self in the field of existence, they both reject the idea of an essential identity, an autonomous Cartesian self. For them, identity can be plural and discontinuous, an identity that arises out of the chaos of existence itself. The self is not an enclosed and coherent entity; rather, the self exists in and adapts to a series of cultural transactions. And most important, the self is a product of language that is at once an instrument of institutional socialization and a vehicle—by its very dynamism and productivity—to challenge that socialization: "Writing, as *infinite* associations, explodes the definitions, endistances origins (or Origin), rejects closure, *exempts* meaning" (*LB,* 54). More simply: writing is a means of definition and discovery, a means to denote and detonate meaning.

Although both the Language poets and Zukofsky are primarily interested in the self as it is manifested in a network of social and linguistic interactions, they are also interested in the sphere below the level of consciousness—free associations, parataxes, and dreams. Typically this sphere has been associated with Freud's psychoanalytic interpretations. For Freud, the individual is a product of the interplay of binary oppositions, the interaction of the conscious and unconscious that is determined by biological and cultural influences of the past. Thus, the individual's action is determined, to a certain extent, by an "other" contained in the self—in this case, the memories existing in the layers of its unconscious. For Freud, even the most arbitrary actions have meaning and are guided by an inner force that compels the conscious mind to satisfy the psychic energy of repressed, unconscious desires.

The dream narrative is especially important for Freud as a mode of interpretation, for within the context of the dream the mind enacts the dialectic interplay between the conscious and the unconscious: the mind, moved by the instinctual energy of infantile wishes, uses the "day residue" of the present to propel the repressed contents of the unconscious into the conscious domain. Traditionally, poets have long used the dream narrative to point to a transcendent framework of interpretation. Through the medium of the dream, a vehicle for the interplay of the natural and the divine realm, the individual imposes symbolic order, attesting to an ideal unity, on his or her chaotic existence. Dante of the *Inferno* and the Pilgrim of *Pilgrim's Progress* both wake to find themselves in a dream narrative; their journey leads them to heaven, their religious origin and destination. Freud uses the dream as a vehicle for psychological rather than transcendent structures of interpretation. If the self is on a journey, it is on a journey to reveal the synchronic patterns of the past, its psychological origins. Zukofsky and the Language poets, who eschew transcendent and psychological interpretations, also use dream narratives, but they posit a completely different framework for interpretation.

In "che di lor suona su nella tua vita," Zukofsky recounts a dream experience and even provides his own explanation at the end of his dream poem:

> I walked out, before
> "Break of day"
> And saw
> Four cabins in the hay.
>
> Blue sealed glasses
> Of preserves—four—
> In the window-sash
> In the yard on the bay.

Further:
The waters
At the ramp
Running away.
    (*CSP*, 77)

Zukofsky uses images that seem slightly skewed and surreal. Although Zukofsky presents a miniature journey ("I walked") and a scene (the juxtaposition of a long-range view of four cabins against a close-up of four glasses of preserves), the reader ingests not an orderly narrative but a series of sensations.

A psychoanalytic critic would surely attempt to ascribe significance and even a particular signification to Zukofsky's images; such an interpretation would focus on how unconscious memories and desires are manifesting themselves on Zukofsky's present dream landscape: the present becomes the function of the past. But Zukofsky appends his own interpretation to his dream poem—an interpretation that focuses not on the self but on language:

> The comma in line 1 of this poem is meant as a pause in the expectancy of the dream. Perhaps the capital B of "Break," after the opening quotes of line 2, gives the feeling of some unexpected person taking part in one's expected activity: I was aware in the dream that I was writing a poem and also aware of verses by others.
>
> The word "bay" is what I could reconstruct later from the feeling of the action in the dream, as I moved from place to place, and should convey something of all the meanings of the word "bay": red-brown, the laurel, the laurel wreath, a bay horse, a deep bark or cry, a window-bay.
> (*CSP*, 102–3)

Barrett Watten begins his impromptu talk with Coolidge with a query about dreams: "There's something definite on my mind about language and dream, like literally knowing where your perceptions lie from the language expression of dreams, after the fact, and then the self that watches the dream, like what it sees, how you see a dream unfold" (*Stations*, 11). Actually, Watten, like Zukofsky, is aligning the dream experience with the writing experience: "Let's start from while you're dreaming, watching, there's a situation which has potential but no definition, or there's feeling. Then there are definite points at which the complex is defined and therefore altered. Whatever is perceiving in the dream is also part of the picture show, or the sense that something's there" (*Stations,* 11). The self/author of the dream is not so much the creator of the dream as the discoverer of the dream. The author, surrendering his "authority," has been transformed into a perceiver of events: "the self that watches the dream, like what it sees, how you see a dream unfold."

For Watten, a dream is like a language problem: "where does one word end and another begin, or what is a relation of a thought to a sentence?" Watten is interested in the dream as a linguistic process, one that seems to unfold before the individual's eyes. When Watten asks, "What is a dream?" Coolidge is quick to answer, "Well, language." Both poets perceive language as interacting between the conscious and unconscious levels; as Coolidge states, "I've had a feeling there's a translation from what's going on behind into the conscious, where language operates. What's going on behind is either electrical impulse or some system of images or just some sort of motion. That is then defined into use by words or whatever we think with." Watten responds, "So that's being a dream configuration and making a shift, and that's a discrimination. You have this forward motion, and what gets you on to articulation is energy, that you want to."

The dream experience and the writing process both are dialectic configurations that can never be fully defined. Commenting on Coolidge's *The Maintains,* Watten writes that the work is a "dream of structure—endless contained architectures—mirrors phenomena, 'language breeding itself,' play." This time, when Watten asks himself what is a dream, he answers, "Language is discrimination. The entire reactive mess is forced into a new structure. Another world. What a combination" (*Stations,* 8). Watten's answer demonstrates how he has collapsed the terms *dream* and *language.* In the dream state, repressed desires are propelled into the conscious domain; in writing, "the entire reactive mess is forced into a new structure": combinations of phonemes and morphemes constitute language, which in turn constitutes a world. Watten merges the synchronic layers of the unconscious with the structure of language: an interchange that manifests itself not in any images decorating a surrealistic dream narrative but in a linguistic process revealing the "inscape" of language.

Entitling his collection of essays *Content's Dream,* Bernstein also connects the dream experience with his act of writing:

> I want in my writing a texture of wordness opaque and alone
> separate untouched   of particularity and presentness
>   intended and specific   unadulterated and so made
> whole   complete   of stillness
>   from a sense that my most particular/private/unique
>   insistence, way of seeing, aesthetic sense, dream
>   is the most completely
>   collective—public—knowable
>   that when language is at the threshold of its
>   coming to mean   at the border of
>   sense and
>   sound
>   we find a scripture
>   open to
>   (CD, 50–51)

Bernstein wishes to connect his private dream sphere with the collective experience. To do so he will not look to "finite interpretations" but to the "play with possibilities":

> figuring it out
> or letting it come of itself
> ways of
>   (never known prior, always coming out
>   in the com(op)posing,
>   it going on).
>   (CD, 51)

The self—whether writer, reader, or the subject in the text—does not transcend but is caught in the flux of the writing experience. The poem, like the dream text, is not fully knowable: it exists at the "border of sense and sound," like Zukofsky's limbo. And for both the writer and reader, the act of composing (which is aligned to the act of reading) is an interplay of "figuring it out / or letting it come of itself." The self participates in the flux of immanent experience—responding and reacting to the energies (repressed and exploded) of language. Language becomes that means for the self to confront a multitude of "unknowable others"—ontological others such as God and Death; psychological others such as the unconscious—the self realizing that these "others" exist in the primary other which is language.

For Zukofsky and the Language poets, what is perhaps most fundamental about language is that it functions as a primary other. As suggested in *The,* Zukofsky embarked on his career in language at a point of alienation; he vowed to take the tools of socialization and execute the "villainy they teach me." Zukofsky discovered that he could "execute" (achieve and destroy) the process of socialization through language, turning his own turmoil into a syntactic turmoil. Using the Modernist credo—the "revolution of the word"—as his departure point, Zukofsky recognized the doubleness inherent in language: he recognized a word both as a tangible artifact as well as a referential sign, both as an object and an object existing in a context (its descriptive and gestural function), both as music and speech. Thus, Zukofsky could be fascinated with the power of the comma in the following line of text:

> A dog that runs never lies down—and of the dog who if not mythical has rhetorical distinction, having been stopped by commas—
> A dog, *that* runs, never lies down. (*Prepositions,* 10)

He is not interested in identifying whether the dog is a mythical or actual dog; whatever the dog's identity, the "dog" is a linguistic construct and commas can still "stop" him.

Zukofsky also recognized that language is a forum for a number of dialectic exchanges—between perception and conception, things and ideas, the real and the ideal, the conscious and the unconscious. Although Zukofsky's poetry does not reach outward to the heavens nor inward to the psyche, Zukofsky does not ignore the fact that transcendent and psychological structures are immanent in language. Thus, one of the central tenets of his poetry—the "desire for what is objectively perfect"—incorporates both the concepts of "desire" and "perfection," language typically associated with the psyche and the absolute: the desire of the ego to transcend chaos and disorder in a transcendent sphere (i.e., *eros, thanatos,* heaven). Ironically, Zukofsky's desire for perfection can be realized only in a medium that is itself characterized by flux and change.

The Language poets also recognize the interactive and dialectic nature of language. In fact, as Bernstein suggests, every act of composition is an act of opposition: "never known prior, always coming out / in the com(op)posing, / it going on." In this sense every act of writing and every act of reading becomes part of a network of reaction and choice; but language itself contains a complex series of oppositions. Like Zukofsky, the Language poets recognize both the materiality and referentiality of language, both its descriptive and gestural function. Moreover, they recognize the dialectic interplay in language; in fact, alienation, suggesting unresolved dialectics, often acts as a catalyst for their poetry:

> We imagine there is a gap between the world of our private phantasies & the possibilities of meaningful action. & so it becomes easy to talk & talk on what is lacking, to discourse on end, & yet feel impotent. "What's to do." But this gap is the measure not so much of our desires or depression or impotence but of our*selves.* It has been the continual failure of Marxist aesthetics to insist that this gap is simply another illusory part of our commodity lives. It is at the root of our collectivity. (*CD,* 31)

Alienation, the divisive gap between desire and action, is actually the "root of our collectivity"—what we all share. Poetry can be a means to enact the dialectic of alienation; it can also be the means to momentarily resolve that dialectic: the world of private fantasies and collective experience. For Bernstein as well as other Language poets, the power of poetry provides the momentary "bridge to this gap." Silliman writes that "art provides him or her with experiences of that dialectical consciousness in which subject and object, self and other, individual and group, unite" (*LB,* 130). In essence, like Zukofsky, the Language poets also finally find the ideal (the inclusive possibilities) in language. Bernstein, Silliman, Coolidge, Watten—all invest language with pantheistic power: a transference of power from the world of natural objects to the linguistic sphere. In "Thought's Measure," Bernstein speaks of language as an almost ontological force:

> As persons, we are born into language and world; they exist before us and after us. Our learning language is learning the terms by which a world gets seen. Language is the means of our socialization, our means of initiation into a (our) culture. I do not suggest that there is nothing beyond, or outside of, human language, but that there is meaning only in terms of language, that the givenness of language is the givenness of the world. (*CD*, 62)

Bernstein suggests that language provides us with origin, destiny, and meaning. Moreover, Silliman refers to the "utopian content" of language. Apparently, the Language poets inevitably suggest that if an ideal exists, it exists in the transformative power of language.

The belief in language espoused by Zukofsky and especially the Language poets has interesting ramifications for their political sympathies. In asserting a Marxist critique of capitalistic ideology, both Zukofsky and the Language poets are affirming a belief in the transformative power of history. But finally even history is subsumed in language. Although Zukofsky believes it is important to recover the materials of his history in his poetry, he often subverts historical (if we understand history to be akin to narrative process) time—juxtaposing past and present events. Neither Zukofsky nor the Language poets believe in the necessity of adhering to linear, narrative time. For the Language poets, such a concept of time may simply be a means to reinforce illusions fostered by a repressive capitalistic society. Of course, the Language poets' Marxist views and their own art often seem to clash. In *The Age of Huts* Silliman recounts how a friend of his, a member of the Old Left, challenged his aesthetics: "It is a more crucial lesson, I argue, to learn how to experience language directly, to tune one's senses to it, than to use it as a mere means to an end. Such use, I point out, is, in bourgeois life, common to all things, even the way we 'use' our friends."[15] Proponents of the Old Left, however, tend to support a social realist aesthetic, often depicting a decadent capitalistic society as well as the hope provided by the socialist state. Silliman's debate with his friend actually mirrors several classic Marxist debates—from Georg Lukacs and Bertolt

Brecht to Jean-Paul Sartre and Roland Barthes. Lukacs and Sartre, at different times, have argued that the writer has an ethical obligation to educate, to communicate, even to liberate the class consciousness of the proletariat; both writers have thus criticized the formalist preoccupation, the private, obscure, and angst-ridden nature of works by such avant-garde Modernists as James Joyce and Franz Kafka. Both Brecht and Barthes, however, have countered that, paradoxically, the artistic norms of social realism arise out of the conventional mode of writing most associated with the bourgeois. Rather than replicate the illusions of realism, writers should strip that illusion, unmasking the false disguises of capitalistic society. As Brecht states, "Reality changes; in order to represent it, modes of representation must change."[16]

The Language poets' aesthetics clash with the ideology of the Old Left in two other ways. In focusing on the word and its mode of production, they do not necessarily focus on the inevitable movement of a dialectic history; language is not intrinsically historical: that is, a word can exist just in the "stillness of the moment," and it can resonate with references that can link it to multiple contexts. In foregrounding the materiality of language, the Language poets are often setting language in space rather than time. Moreover, in their poetry the Language poets eschew any "finite interpretation," any singular myth. In fact, the process of interpretation may be far more important than any one particular interpretation. Bernstein writes:

> So for instance I may not agree with a particular political opinion in a poem, it may be false from my point of view. But it is the anxiety of indetermination that is of interest. The political dimension is not the opinion of any isolated sentence, but the experience of *hearing* the possibilities of truth and lies and in-between, and, as readers, *choosing*. Because to read is to choose; I just want to bring that process to the fore. (*CD,* 456)

In some ways, the Language poets—in their faith in the "literal" word, in their faith in individual perception and revelation—adhere to Protestant rather than Marxist models of "salvation." After all, they believe that the individual, interacting with the "sacred" text, will come to a moment of revelation and choice. The Language poet, however, is attempting to convert the reader to a religion of "disbelief"—an exfoliation of illusions. A reader who believes in process, in multiple and ever-changing interpretations, in plural and discontinuous identities, may very well choose not to believe in the social myth of Marxism.

Both the Language poets and Zukofsky have carved out a poetics that has specific ramifications for our understanding of the self, language, and history. The Language poets have an acute understanding of Zukofsky's praxis; in one specific way the Language poets read Zukofsky with greater sympathy than he read himself. In his critical works Zukofsky often berates himself for being born into the "gas age"—the age of thought—rather than the "solid age." Zukofsky states that perception is more valuable than conception; he valued the eye over the "erring brain." Yet, as Bernstein notes, Zukofsky's "works present some of the most realized alternatives to the poetry of sight in modern American writing" (*CD*, 151). One suspects that Zukofsky never fully separated himself from his literary Modernist fathers—as though he could never fully free himself from a Modernist critical vocabulary, although his poetry spoke eloquently of his liberation. The Language poets, however, easily integrate Zukofsky's alternate poetics. In *Progress* Barrett Watten writes, "The idea / Is the thing."[17] The point of Zukofsky's struggle becomes the Language poet's point of acceptance.

Notes

Introduction:
Among American Friends

1. Harry Gilonis, ed., *Louis Zukofsky, or whoever someone else thought he was: a collection of responses to the work of Louis Zukofsky* (Twickenham and Wakefield, Eng.: North and South, 1988), 3.

2. See Roland Barthes, *S/Z*, trans. R. Miller (New York: Hill and Wang, 1974), 10.

3. Louis Zukofsky, *Poem beginning "The"*, in his *Complete Short Poetry* (Baltimore: Johns Hopkins University Press, 1991), 18. Further references to this edition will be cited in text as *CSP*.

4. The term *postmodernism* is, of course, controversial. Linda Hutcheon, *The Politics of Postmodernism* (London and New York: Routledge, 1989), offers a valuable discussion of the term with its various meanings. Hutcheon points to the paradoxical nature of postmodernism, which "at once inscribes and subverts the conventions and ideologies of the dominant culture and social forces of the twentieth-century western world" (11). She nevertheless argues that "the postmodern's initial concern is to denaturalize some of the dominant features of our way of life; to point out that those entities that we unthinkingly experience as 'natural' (they might even include capitalism, patriarchy, liberal humanism) are in fact 'cultural'; made by us, not given to us" (2). Moreover, in a collection of essays—*Postmodern Genres* (Norman: University of Oklahoma Press, 1989)—Marjorie Perloff has noted that in challenge to a "pure" Modernism that emphasizes such terms as "*purity, autonomy,* and *objecthood,*" postmodernism emphasizes such words as "*violation, disruption, dislocation, decentering, contradiction, confrontation, multiplicity* and *indeterminacy*" (7–8). Zukofsky, with his search for what is "objectively perfect," anchors himself in a Modernist tradition; at the same time, in experimenting with the medium of language and subverting the conventions and ideologies of the dominant culture, he links himself with a decentered and indeterminate postmodernist sensibility.

5. Cary Nelson, *Repression and Recovery: Modern American Poetry*

and the Politics of Cultural Memory 1910–1945 (Madison: University of Wisconsin Press, 1989), 11.

6. David Perkins, *A History of Modern Poetry: Modernism and After* (Cambridge: Belknap Press, Harvard University Press, 1987), 320.

7. Barry Ahearn, "Two Conversations with Celia Zukofsky," *Sagetrieb* 2, no. 1 (Spring 1983): 118.

8. Hugh Kenner, *A Homemade World: The American Modernist Writers* (New York: William Morrow, 1975), 193.

9. Marcus Klein, *Foreigners: The Making of American Literature 1900–1940* (Chicago: University of Chicago Press, 1981), 288.

10. Barry Ahearn, *Zukofsky's "A": An Introduction* (Berkeley and Los Angeles: University of California Press, 1983).

11. See Marjorie Perloff, "The Contemporary of Our Grandchildren: Pound's Influence," in *Ezra Pound: Among the Poets,* ed. George Bornstein (Chicago: University of Chicago Press, 1985), 195–229; and Laszlo Géfin, *Ideogram: History of a Poetic Method* (Austin: University of Texas Press, 1982).

12. See Burton Hatlen, "Art and/as Labor: Some Dialectical Patterns in *'A'*-1 through *'A'*-10," *Contemporary Literature* 25, no. 2 (Summer 1984): 205–34; and Edward Schelb, "The Exaction of Song: Louis Zukofsky and the Ideology of Form," *Contemporary Literature* 31, no. 3 (Fall 1990): 335–53.

13. Gerald Graff, "American Criticism Left and Right," in *Ideology and Classic American Literature,* ed. Sacvan Bercovitch and Myra Jehlen (Cambridge: Cambridge University Press, 1986), 109.

14. See Eric Homberger, *American Writers and Radical Politics, 1900–39* (London: Macmillan, 1986), Ralph F. Bogardus and Fred Hobson, eds., *Literature at the Barricades* (University: University of Alabama Press, 1982); and Norman Finkelstein, *The Utopian Moment in Contemporary American Poetry* (London and Toronto: Associated University Presses, 1988). Homberger regards Zukofsky as a Marxist poet who identified with the proletariat; yet the American Left, espousing a social realist form, criticized Zukofsky's work as a "nihilistic protest against the poet's isolation in a capitalistic and materialistic society" (172). Although Hugh Kenner, in his article "Oppen, Zukofsky, and the Poem as Lens" (in *Literature at the Barricades*), asserts that Zukofsky respected Marx's intellect and envisioned a "social and material world of the dialectic," he argues that the poet was ultimately a philosophical rather than a political poet (170). Finkelstein explores the Objectivist's "aesthetic ideology" which uses such "utopian tropes" as Zukofsky's "totality of perfect rest" to reconcile the "immediate particulars of the world" with historical process (31).

15. Michele J. Leggott, *Reading Zukofsky's* 80 Flowers (Baltimore: Johns Hopkins University Press, 1989).

16. Celia Zukofsky, ed., *American Friends* (New York: C. Z. Publications, 1979).

17. Louis Zukofsky, *Prepositions* (Berkeley and Los Angeles: University of California Press, 1981), 24. Further references to this edition will be cited in text.

18. Bruce Andrews and Charles Bernstein, eds., *The L=A=N=G=U=A=G=E Book* (Carbondale: Southern Illinois University Press, 1984), 290.

19. See Peter Quartermain, " 'Only is order othered. Nought is nulled': *Finnegans Wake* and Middle and Late Zukofsky," *ELH* 54 (Winter 1987): 957–78; and Alan Golding, "The 'Community of Elements' in Wallace Stevens and Louis Zukofsky," in *Wallace Stevens: The Poetics of Modernism*, ed. Albert Gelpi (Cambridge: Cambridge University Press, 1985), 121–40.

20. Letter circa 1953 from Zukofsky to Lorine Niedecker. This letter (which Niedecker cut up in fragments, as she did the other letters she contributed to the collection) is in the Zukofsky Collection at the Humanities Research Center of the University of Texas at Austin (subsequently cited as HRC).

21. See Charles Norman, *Ezra Pound* (New York: Funk and Wagnalls, 1969), 318–19.

1. Zukofsky and the Act of Reading

1. Louis Zukofsky, *Collected Fiction* (Elmwood Park, Ill.: Dalkey Archive Press, 1990), 119–20.

2. William Carlos Williams, afterword to *"A" 1–12*, by Louis Zukofsky (Kyoto: Origin Press, 1959), 291. In this essay Williams also admits, "I was looking for the wrong things. The poems whatever else they are are grammatical units intent on making a meaning *unrelated* to a mere pictorial image."

3. J. Hillis Miller, "Introduction to William Carlos Williams" in *Issues in Contemporary Literary Criticism,* ed. Gregory T. Polletta (Boston: Little, Brown, 1973), 129.

4. For an extended analysis of the role of interpretive communities, see Stanley Fish, *Is There a Text in This Class?* (Cambridge: Harvard University Press, 1980).

5. See Thomas F. Sharp, " 'Objectivists' 1929–1934: A Critical History of the Work and Association of Louis Zukofsky, William Carlos Williams,

Charles Reznikoff, Carl Rakosi, Ezra Pound, George Oppen," diss., Stanford University, 1982; and Michael Heller, *Conviction's Net of Branches: Essays on the Objectivist Poets and Poetry* (Carbondale: Southern Illinois University Press, 1985).

6. L. S. Dembo, "Sincerity and Objectification," *Louis Zukofsky: Man and Poet,* ed. Carroll F. Terrell (Orono, Maine: National Poetry Foundation, 1979), 265–66.

7. Basil Bunting, "Open Letter to Louis Zukofsky," *Current Mare* (1932). A copy of "Open Letter" is in the Zukofsky Collection, HRC.

8. Bunting, "Open Letter," 3.

9. Letter circa 1937 from Zukofsky to Lorine Niedecker, HRC.

10. Dembo, "Sincerity and Objectification," 272.

11. Charles Altieri, "The Objectivist Tradition," *Chicago Review* 30, no. 3 (Winter 1979): 5–22.

12. Louis Zukofsky, *"A"* (Berkeley and Los Angeles: University of California Press, 1978). Further references to this edition will be cited in text as *"A".*

13. Ahearn, *Zukofsky's "A",* 68.

2. Zukofsky and Adams: Appropriating an American Tradition

1. Here (*Prepositions,* 169), Zukofsky states his appreciation of Adams's "thermodynamic" view of history.

2. Alfred Kazin, *On Native Grounds: An Interpretation of Modern American Prose Literature,* 2d ed. (1942; rpt. New York and London: Harcourt, 1970), 194.

3. Letter dated 9 Nov. 1959 from Cid Corman to Zukofsky, HRC.

4. Letter dated 3 Mar. 1938 from Zukofsky to Lorine Niedecker, HRC.

5. Burton Hatlen, "Art and/as Labor," 225.

6. Louis Zukofsky, "Henry Adams: A Criticism in Autobiography," *Hound & Horn* 4, no. 1 (Oct.–Dec. 1930): 70.

7. Henry Adams, *The Education of Henry Adams* (Boston: Houghton Mifflin, 1961), 3. Further references to this edition will be cited in text as *Education.*

8. Louis Zukofsky, *Autobiography* (New York: Grossman, 1970), 13.

9. Henry James, *The American Scene* (New York: Scribner's, 1946), 131.

10. James, *American Scene,* 139.

11. Matthew Arnold, "Stanzas from the Grande Chartreuse," in *The Poems of Matthew Arnold,* ed. Miriam Allott, 2d ed. (New York: Longman, 1979), 302–11.

12. Celia Zukofsky, *American Friends*, 52.

13. Klein, *Foreigners*, 18–38.

14. Terrell, "Louis Zukofsky: An Eccentric Profile," *Louis Zukofsky*, 35.

15. Letter dated 14 Nov. 1959 from Zukofsky to Cid Corman, HRC.

16. Zukofsky, *Autobiography*, 33.

17. Letter circa 1937 from Zukofsky to Lorine Niedecker, HRC.

18. Letter dated 26 Mar. 1953 from Zukofsky to Lorine Niedecker, HRC.

19. Louis Zukofsky, ed., "Notes and Books Received," *Poetry: A Magazine of Verse* 37, no. 5 (Feb. 1931): 294.

20. Wilfrid Mellers, *Bach and the Dance of God* (New York: Oxford University Press, 1981), 304. Fred Hamel was the first to recognize the cross in Bach's musical signature. (In the European system—unlike the American system—H is part of the notational scale.)

21. Letter dated 9 Nov. 1935 from Zukofsky to Lorine Niedecker, HRC.

22. Ralph Waldo Emerson, "History," in *The Complete Works of Ralph Waldo Emerson*, ed. Edward Emerson, Centenary Edition, 12 vols. (Boston: Houghton Mifflin, 1903–4), 2:10.

23. Henry Adams, *The Letters of Henry Adams (1858–1891)*, ed. Worthington Chauncey Ford, 2 vols. (Boston: Houghton Mifflin, 1930–1938), 1:468.

24. See Barry Ahearn, "The Adams Connection," *Paideuma* 7, no. 3 (Winter 1978): 479–93. Ahearn, noting the dialectic nature of Adams's critique of history, observes that both Zukofsky's and Adams's works are filled with antinomies.

25. Ahearn, *Zukofsky's "A"*, 77.

3. Wut Wuz in the Air of a Time: Eliot, Pound, Williams

1. Barry Ahearn, ed., *Pound/Zukofsky: Selected Letters of Ezra Pound and Louis Zukofsky* (New York: New Directions, 1987), 85.

2. Letter dated 26 Mar. 1953 from Zukofsky to Lorine Niedecker, HRC.

3. T. S. Eliot, introduction to *Selected Poems*, by Ezra Pound (1928; rpt. London: Faber and Faber, 1961).

4. Edward W. Said, *The World, the Text, and the Critic* (Cambridge: Harvard University Press, 1983), 48.

5. Raymond Williams, *Marxism and Literature* (1977; rpt. Oxford and New York: Oxford University Press, 1989), 115.

6. Conrad Aiken, "An Anatomy of Melancholy," in *T. S. Eliot: The Man and His Work*, ed. Allen Tate (New York: Delacorte Press, 1966), 194.

7. Elinor Wylie, review of *The Waste Land,* by T. S. Eliot, *Literary Review,* 20 Jan. 1923, 396.

8. F. L. Lucas, review of *The Waste Land,* by T. S. Eliot, *New Statesman,* 3 Nov. 1923, 116.

9. William Carlos Williams, *The Autobiography of William Carlos Williams* (New York: New Directions, 1967), 146, 174.

10. Kenneth Burke, "Heaven's First Law," *Dial* 72 (Feb. 1922): 197–200.

11. See Ahearn, Zukofsky's *"A",* 33–37; Harold Schimmel, "Zuk. Yehoash David Rex," in *Louis Zukofsky,* ed. Terrell, 235.

12. Letter dated 15 Aug. 1925 from James Joyce to Harriet Shaw Weaver, in *Selected Letters of James Joyce,* ed. Richard Ellman (New York: Viking, 1975), 309.

13. See Peter Ackroyd, *T. S. Eliot: A Life* (New York: Simon and Schuster, 1984), 128.

14. Louis Zukofsky, "American Poetry 1920–1930," *Symposium* 2, no. 1 (Jan. 1931): 65. See also Zukofsky's letter to Pound in Ahearn, *Pound/Zukofsky,* 78–79.

15. See Stephen Spender, "Remembering Eliot," in *T. S. Eliot,* ed. Tate, 46.

16. See *The Waste Land Facsimiles,* ed. Valerie Eliot (London: Faber and Faber, 1971), 1; Grover Smith, *The Waste Land* (London: George Allen and Unwin, 1983). Eliot later explained that when he published *The Waste Land* as a book, the poem was considered too short. Thus, he added the notes. Arnold Bennett reports, however, that when he asked Eliot if his notes were serious or not, Eliot replied that they were.

17. Dembo, "Sincerity and Objectification," 280–81.

18. Letter dated Dec. 1934 from Basil Bunting to Zukofsky, HRC.

19. Louis Zukofsky, "Program: 'Objectivists' 1931," *Poetry: A Magazine of Verse* 38, no. 5 (Jan. 1931): 268.

20. T. S. Eliot, "Tradition and the Individual Talent," in *The Sacred Wood* (London: Methuen, 1960), 50.

21. F. O. Matthiessen, *The Achievement of T. S. Eliot* (New York: Oxford University Press, 1958), 49.

22. T. S. Eliot, "Ulysses, Order, and Myth," rpt. in *The Modern Tradition,* ed. Richard Ellmann and Charles Feidelson (New York: Oxford University Press, 1965), 681.

23. Joseph Frank, *The Widening Gyre* (New Brunswick: Rutgers University Press, 1963), 60.

24. Louis Zukofsky, "Preface," *Exile* 3 (1927): 8.

25. Ezra Pound, *Hugh Selwyn Mauberley,* in *Selected Poems* (New York: New Directions, 1957), 61–62.

26. John Tomas, "Portrait of the Artist as a Young Jew: Zukofsky's *Poem Beginning 'The'* in Context," *Sagetrieb* 9, nos. 1–2 (Spring–Fall 1990): 43–64.

27. Ahearn, *Zukofsky's "A"*, 36.

28. Eliot, *Sacred Wood*, 52–53.

4. Pound: The Vicissitudes of Friendship

1. Terrell, "An Eccentric Profile," *Louis Zukofsky*, 74. Paul Zukofsky has explained that his father pronounced "Louis" in the French fashion, and the family never referred to him by a nickname such as "Louie." When Terrell transcribed his interview with Celia Zukofsky, he misspelled Zukofsky's first name.

2. Ahearn, *Pound/Zukofsky*, 208.

3. Ezra Pound, *Literary Essays of Ezra Pound* (New York: New Directions, 1935), 23.

4. Letter circa 1937 from Zukofsky to Lorine Niedecker, HRC.

5. Letter circa 1941 from Zukofsky to Lorine Niedecker, HRC.

6. Pound, *Literary Essays*, 193–94.

7. Ahearn, *Pound/Zukofsky*, 76.

8. Norman, *Ezra Pound*, 181.

9. Ezra Pound, *Cathay* (London: E. Mathews, 1915), 32.

10. Norman, *Ezra Pound*, 292.

11. Letter dated 7 June 1937 from Zukofsky to Lorine Niedecker, HRC.

12. Ezra Pound, ed., *Exile* 1 (1927): 89.

13. Ezra Pound, ed., *Exile* 3 (1928): 117.

14. Peter Nicholls, *Ezra Pound, Politics, Economics and Writing: A Study of* The Cantos (London: Macmillan, 1984), 48.

15. Burton Hatlen, "Ezra Pound and Fascism," in *Ezra Pound and History*, ed. Marianne Korn (Orono, Maine: National Poetry Foundation, 1985), 145.

16. Michael André Bernstein, "History and Textuality in Ezra Pound's *Cantos*," in *Ezra Pound and History*, ed. Korn, 22.

17. Dembo, "Sincerity and Objectification," 280–81.

18. William Chace, *The Political Identities of Ezra Pound and T. S. Eliot* (Stanford: Stanford University Press, 1973), 36.

19. Pound, *Exile* 1:91.

20. T. S. Eliot, "Ezra Pound," in *Ezra Pound: A Collection of Essays*, ed. Peter Russell (New York: Peter Nevill, 1950), 26.

21. Ezra Pound, *The Letters of Ezra Pound 1907–1941*, ed. D. D. Paige, (New York: Harcourt, 1950), 9.

22. Eliot, "Ezra Pound," 35.

23. Pound, *Exile* 1:92.

24. Norman, *Ezra Pound*, 306.

25. Ahearn, *Pound/Zukofsky*, 11.

26. Norman, *Ezra Pound*, 318.

27. Terrell, "An Eccentric Profile," 65.

28. Letter dated 31 Oct. 1929 from Ezra Pound to Zukofsky, HRC.

29. *Ta Hio, The Great Learning,* trans. Ezra Pound (Seattle: University of Washington Book Store, 1928). For a discussion of the *Ta Hio* see Hugh Kenner, "Ching Ming," in *The Poetry of Ezra Pound* (1951; rpt. Lincoln: University of Nebraska Press, 1985), 37–38.

30. Jean-Michel Rabaté, *Language, Sexuality, and Ideology in Ezra Pound's* Cantos (Albany: State University of New York Press, 1986), 12.

31. See T. S. Eliot, "Metaphysical Poets," in *Selected Essays* (New York: Harcourt, 1950).

32. Zukofsky, "American Poetry 1920–1930," 60.

33. Zukofsky, "American Poetry 1920–1930," 61.

34. Ezra Pound, ed., *Active Anthology* (London: Faber and Faber, 1933), 253–54.

35. Ezra Pound, "Old Zuk," *The European* 12, no. 5 (Jan. 1959): 284.

36. Ahearn, *Pound/Zukofsky*, 163.

37. Ezra Pound, "In a Station of the Metro," in *Selected Poems*, 35.

38. Ezra Pound, *A Memoir of Gaudier-Brzeska* (New York: New Directions, 1970), 83.

39. Pound, *Gaudier-Brzeska*, 89.

40. Pound, *Gaudier-Brzeska*, 92.

41. Norman, *Ezra Pound*, 319.

42. Paul Zukofsky has noted that the phrase "The (no?)" also imitates Tibor Serly's manner of speech—as though the Hungarian-born Serly were asking, "Is it not so?" Conversation with Paul Zukofsky, 4 Sept. 1992.

43. Charles Sanders Peirce, "How to Make Our Ideas Clear," in *The Enduring Questions,* ed. Melvin Rader (New York: Holt, 1969), 98.

44. Ahearn, *Pound/Zukofsky*, 79.

45. Ahearn, *Pound/Zukofsky*, 81.

46. Ahearn, *Pound/Zukofsky*, 84.

47. Ahearn, *Pound/Zukofsky*, 79.

48. Andrews and Bernstein, *L=A=N=G=U=A=G=E Book*, 290.

49. Ahearn, *Pound/Zukofsky*, 42.

50. Ahearn, *Pound/Zukofsky*, 75.

51. Zukofsky, "Notes and Books Received," 294.

52. William Butler Yeats, *A Vision* (New York: Macmillan, 1956), 4.

53. Pound, *Letters*, 321.

54. Ezra Pound, *Selected Cantos* (New York: New Directions, 1970), 1. Further references to this work will be cited in text as *Cantos*.

55. Ahearn, *Pound/Zukofsky*, 111–12.

56. Edward Said, *Beginnings: Intention and Method* (New York: Basic, 1975), 3.

57. Marjorie Perloff, "The Contemporary of Our Grandchildren," in *Ezra Pound*, ed. Bornstein, 215.

58. Michael André Bernstein, *The Tale of the Tribe* (Princeton: Princeton University Press, 1980), 177.

59. Charles Altieri, "From Symbolist Thought to Immanence: The Ground of Postmodern American Poetics," *Boundary* 2, no. 1 (Spring 1973): 611.

60. Hugh Kenner, "Two Pieces on 'A'," in *Louis Zukofsky*, ed. Terrell, 190.

61. Ahearn, *Pound/Zukofsky*, 80.

62. Ezra Pound, "The Other Dimension," *Dial* 35 (July 1928): 17.

63. Ahearn, *Pound/Zukofsky*, 123.

64. Hatlen, "Art and/as Labor."

65. Schelb, "Exaction of Song," 336.

66. Letter dated 9 Nov. 1935 from Zukofsky to Lorine Niedecker, HRC.

67. Letter circa 1953 from Zukofsky to Lorine Niedecker, HRC.

5. Williams: A Clear Mirror

1. Letter dated Easter 1928 from Williams to Zukofsky, HRC.

2. Letter dated 2 Feb. 1931 from Williams to Zukofsky, HRC. On the one hand, in a letter dated 29 Apr. 1931, Williams warns Zukofsky that his poems' themes are so difficult that he doesn't "allow the reader to get started." On the other hand, in a letter dated 15 Oct. 1930, Williams congratulates Zukofsky for his refusal to compromise: "Certainly you have not compromised, it is precisely because you have not that it succeeds."

3. Letter dated 3 Apr. 1941 from Williams to Zukofsky, HRC.

4. Williams, *Autobiography*, 311. Pound, who saw himself and Eliot infested with the "blood poison" of an old American stock, once wrote to Williams, "You have the advantage of arriving in the milieu with a fresh flood of Europe in your veins, Spanish, French, English, Danish. You had not the thin milk of New York and New England from the pap; and you can therefore keep the environment outside you, and decently objective" (Pound, *Letters*, 158). Pound's words were more prophetic than he realized, for both Williams and Zukofsky inherited the outsiders' desire to be "decently objective," both in cultural and poetic terms.

5. Letter dated 22 Oct. 1935 from Williams to Zukofsky, HRC.

6. Letter dated 26 Jan. 1947 from Williams to Zukofsky, HRC.

7. William Carlos Williams, *The Collected Poems of William Carlos Williams*, vol. 1, 1909–1939, ed. A. Walton Litz and Christopher J. Mac-Gowan (New York: New Directions, 1986), 189.

8. See, for example, J. Hillis Miller, *Poets of Reality: Six Twentieth-Century Writers* (Cambridge: Harvard University Press, 1965); and Bram Dijkstra, *The Hieroglyphics of a New Speech: Cubism, Stieglitz, and the Early Poetry of William Carlos Williams* (Princeton: Princeton University Press, 1969); and Charles Altieri, *Enlarging the Temple* (Lewisburg, Penn.: Bucknell University Press, 1979).

9. Ahearn, *Zukofsky's "A"*, 17.

10. E. E. Cummings, "Five Poems," *Dial* 72 (Jan. 1922): 43; reprinted as "of evident invisibles" in *Complete Poems, 1904–1962*, ed. George James Firmage (New York: Liveright, 1991), 75.

11. Dembo, "Sincerity and Objectification," 272.

12. Dembo, "Sincerity and Objectification," 272–73.

13. Letter dated 2 Apr. 1928 from Williams to Zukofsky, HRC.

14. Louis Zukofsky, *Bottom: On Shakespeare* (Berkeley and Los Angeles: University of California Press, 1987), 89. See Burton Hatlen, "Zukofsky, Wittgenstein, and the Poetics of Absence," *Sagetrieb* 1, no. 1 (Spring 1982): 63–93.

15. Thomas R. Whitaker, *William Carlos Williams* (New York: Twayne, 1968), 19.

16. Williams, "The Classic Scene," in *Collected Poems*, 444–45.

17. Dickran Tashjian, *William Carlos Williams and the American Scene, 1920–1940* (Berkeley and Los Angeles: University of California Press, 1978), 85.

18. H. L. Mencken, *The American Language* (New York: Knopf, 1926), 102.

19. Zukofsky, "American Poetry, 1920–1930," 73–74.

20. See John Donne, "Holy Sonnet 14," in *John Donne: The Complete English Poems*, ed. A. J. Smith (London: Penguin, 1974), 314–15; and W. B. Yeats, "Leda and the Swan," in *W. B. Yeats: Selected Poetry*, ed. Timothy Webb (New York: Penguin, 1991), 149–50.

21. Williams, *Autobiography*, xi.

22. See Walt Whitman, "Crossing Brooklyn Ferry," in *Leaves of Grass*, ed. Sculley Bradley and Harold W. Blodgett (New York: Norton, 1973), 159–65.

23. Harold Bloom, introduction to *William Carlos Williams*, ed. Bloom (New York: Chelsea House, 1986), 2.

24. Such a supposition is a little tricky: on the one hand, Williams has stated that he emphasizes a catholic acceptance in which the individual is

raised "to some approximate co-extension with the universe"; on the other hand, he has also proclaimed the bardic role of the poet who, like Adam, creates the world through his language.

25. William Carlos Williams, *Selected Essays* (New York: Random House, 1945), 233.

26. See Marjorie Perloff, *The Poetics of Indeterminacy: Rimbaud to Cage* (Princeton: Princeton University Press, 1981), 129.

27. Joseph Riddel, *The Inverted Bell: Modernism and the Counterpoetics of William Carlos Williams* (Baton Rouge: Louisiana State University Press, 1974).

28. J. Hillis Miller, *The Linguistic Moment; From Wordsworth to Stevens* (Princeton: Princeton University Press, 1985), 381.

29. See, for instance, Terence Diggory, *William Carlos Williams and the Ethics of Painting* (Princeton: Princeton University Press, 1991).

30. William Carlos Williams, *Selected Letters,* ed. John C. Thirwall (New York: McDowell, 1957), 102–3.

31. Williams, *Selected Letters,* 101–2.

32. William Carlos Williams, *Imaginations,* ed. Webster Schott (New York: New Directions, 1970), 231.

33. Letter dated 2 Apr. 1928 from Williams to Zukofsky, HRC.

34. Reed Whittemore, *William Carlos Williams: Poet from Jersey* (Boston: Houghton Mifflin, 1975), 240.

35. Neil Baldwin, "The Letters of William Carlos Williams to Louis Zukofsky: A Chronicle of Trust and Difficulty," in *WCW & Others,* ed. Dave Oliphant and Thomas Zigal (Austin: Harry Ransom Humanities Research Center, University of Texas, 1985), 116.

36. Williams, *Selected Letters,* 24.

37. Ahearn, *Pound/Zukofsky,* 67.

38. Letter dated 2 July 1930 from Williams to Zukofsky, HRC.

39. Zukofsky, *Bottom,* 10.

40. Zukofsky, "American Poetry 1920–1930," 79–80.

41. Zukofsky, "American Poetry 1920–1930," 84.

42. William Carlos Williams, "An Extraordinary Sensitivity," *Poetry* 60, no. 6 (Sept. 1942): 338–40.

43. Williams, "Extraordinary Sensitivity," 340.

44. Letter dated 4 Jan. 1931 from Williams to Zukofsky, HRC.

45. Conversation with Paul Zukofsky, 4 Sept. 1992.

46. Letter dated 18 Jan. 1931 from Williams to Zukofsky, HRC.

47. William Carlos Williams, review of *An "Objectivists" Anthology,* ed. Louis Zukofsky, *Symposium* 4, no. 1 (Jan. 1933): 114.

48. Ahearn, *Pound/Zukofsky,* 78.

49. Williams, *Autobiography,* 265.

50. Dembo, "Sincerity and Objectification," 265–66.

51. Letter dated 17 Mar. 1937 from Williams to Zukofsky, HRC.

52. Ahearn, *Pound/Zukofsky*, 67.

53. Harriet Monroe, "The Arrogance of Youth," *Poetry* 37, no. 6 (Mar. 1931): 331.

54. Letter circa 1937 from Zukofsky to Lorine Niedecker, HRC.

55. Williams, *Autobiography*, 264.

56. Williams, *Autobiography*, 265.

57. Williams, *Selected Letters*, 103.

58. Williams, *Selected Essays*, 281.

59. In his article (*Prepositions*, 13) Zukofsky highlights the basic tenets of his own poetry. Although his language is often vague, the young poet is hewing out his own understanding of poetry—distinguishing himself from his predecessors.

60. Williams, *Selected Essays*, 281.

61. Letter circa 1953 from Zukofsky to Lorine Niedecker, HRC.

62. Neil Baldwin, "Zukofsky, Williams and *The Wedge:* Toward a Dynamic Convergence," in *Louis Zukofsky*, ed. Terrell, 141.

63. Baldwin, "Zukofsky, Williams, and *The Wedge*," 135.

64. Whitman, "Crossing Brooklyn Ferry," 164.

65. Williams Carlos Williams, *Paterson*, ed. Christopher MacGowan (New York: New Directions, 1992), 9.

66. Roy Harvey Pearce, *The Continuity of American Poetry* (Princeton: Princeton University Press, 1961), 112.

67. Letter dated 2 Apr. 1928 from William Carlos Williams to Zukofsky, HRC.

68. Williams, *Collected Poems*, 189.

69. Williams, *Paterson*, 7.

70. Bernstein, *Tale of the Tribe*, 210.

71. Williams, *Selected Letters*, 258.

72. Williams, *Selected Essays*, 233.

73. Williams, *Selected Essays*, 217.

74. Williams, *Paterson*, 39.

75. Williams, *Collected Poems*, 236.

76. William Carlos Williams, "A New Line Is a New Measure," *New Quarterly of Poetry* 2, no. 2 (Winter 1947–48): 14.

6. A Legacy:
Zukofsky and the Language Poets

1. See Robert Creeley, *Pieces* (New York: Scribner's, 1969), and "Robert Creeley in Conversation with Charles Tomlinson," in *Contexts of Po-*

etry: Interviews 1961–1971, ed. Donald Allen (Bolinas, Calif.: Four Seasons Foundation, 1973), 14.

2. Letter dated 11 July 1951 from Zukofsky to Edward Dahlberg, HRC.

3. Letter dated 3 Feb. 1951 from Basil Bunting to Zukofsky, HRC.

4. Letter dated 25 Feb. 1937 from William Carlos Williams to Zukofsky, HRC.

5. Letter dated 21 June 1946 from Williams to Zukofsky, HRC.

6. Michael André Bernstein and Burton Hatlen, "Interview with Robert Duncan," *Sagetrieb,* 4, nos. 2–3 (Fall–Winter 1985): 87–135.

7. See George Hartley, *Textual Politics and the Language Poets* (Bloomington: Indiana University Press, 1989). Hartley focuses on the complex issues involved in attempting to define the Language poets—in terms of both their aesthetics and politics.

8. Andrews and Bernstein, *The L=A=N=G=U=A=G=E Book,* 185. Further references to this edition will be cited in text as *LB.*

9. Stephen Fredman, *Poet's Prose: The Crisis in American Verse* (Cambridge: Cambridge University Press, 1983), 134.

10. Letter circa 1960 from Zukofsky to Lorine Niedecker, HRC.

11. See Pound, *Letters,* 158.

12. Robert Grenier, "Notes on Coolidge, Objective, Zukofsky, Romanticism, and &," *Stations* no. 5 (Winter 1978): 16. Further references to this edition will be cited in text as *Stations.*

13. Jerome J. McGann, "Contemporary Poetry, Alternate Routes," *Critical Inquiry* 13, no. 3 (Spring 1987): 627.

14. Charles Bernstein, *Content's Dream* (Los Angeles: Sun & Moon Press, 1986), 422. Further references to this edition will be cited in text as *CD.*

15. Ron Silliman, *The Age of Huts* (New York: Segue Foundation, 1986), 63.

16. For a discussion of the Language poets and the Lukacs-Brecht debate, see Hartley, *Textual Politics and the Language Poets,* 54–57. For a discussion of the Sartre-Barthes controversy, see Roland Barthes, *Writing Degree Zero* (New York: Hill and Wang, 1968).

17. Barrett Watten, *Progress* (New York: Segue Foundation, 1985), 1.

Bibliography

Primary Works

Adams, Henry. *The Education of Henry Adams*. Boston: Houghton Mifflin, 1961.

————. *The Letters of Henry Adams*. Ed. Worthington Chauncey Ford. 2 vols. Boston: Houghton Mifflin, 1930–1938.

Andrews, Bruce, and Charles Bernstein, eds. *The L=A=N=G=U=A=G=E Book*. Carbondale: Southern Illinois University Press, 1984.

Arnold, Matthew. "Stanzas from the Grande Chartreuse." In *The Poems of Matthew Arnold*, ed. Miriam Allott, 302–11. 2d ed. New York: Longman, 1979.

Bernstein, Charles. *Content's Dream*. Los Angeles: Sun & Moon Press, 1986.

Creeley, Robert. *Pieces*. New York: Scribner's, 1969.

Cummings, E. E. "Five Poems." *Dial* 72 (Jan. 1922): 43. Rpt. as "of evident invisibles" in *Complete Poems, 1904–1962*, ed. George James Firmage, 75. New York: Liveright, 1991.

Donne, John. "Holy Sonnet 14." In *John Donne: The Complete English Poems*, ed. A. J. Smith, 314–15. London: Penguin, 1974.

Eliot, T. S. "Ezra Pound." In *Ezra Pound: A Collection of Essays*, ed. Peter Russell, 25–36. New York: Peter Nevill, 1950.

————. Introduction to *Selected Poems*, by Ezra Pound. 1928. Rpt. London: Faber and Faber, 1961.

————. *The Sacred Wood*. London: Methuen, 1960.

————. "Ulysses, Order, and Myth." Rpt. in *The Modern Tradition*, ed. Richard Ellmann and Charles Feidelson, 679–81. New York: Oxford University Press, 1965.

————. *The Use of Poetry and the Use of Criticism*. London: Faber and Faber, 1933.

————. *The Waste Land Facsimiles*. Ed. Valerie Eliot. London: Faber and Faber, 1971.

Emerson, Ralph Waldo. "History." In *The Complete Works of Ralph Waldo Emerson*, ed. Edward Emerson, 2:3–41. Centenary Edition. 12 vols. Boston: Houghton Mifflin, 1903–4.

James, Henry. *The American Scene*. New York: Scribner's, 1946.

Joyce, James. *Selected Letters of James Joyce*. Ed. Richard Ellman. New York: Viking, 1975.

Pound, Ezra. *ABC of Reading*. 1934. New York: New Directions, 1960.

———. *Cathay*. London: E. Mathews, 1915.

———. *Guide to Kulchur*. 1938. Reprinted New York: New Directions, 1961.

———. *The Letters of Ezra Pound 1907–1941*. Ed. D. D. Paige. New York: Harcourt, 1950.

———. *Literary Essays of Ezra Pound*. New York: New Directions, 1935.

———. *A Memoir of Gaudier Brzeska*. New York: New Directions, 1970.

———. "Old Zuk." *The European* 12, no. 5 (Jan. 1959): 284.

———. *Selected Cantos*. New York: New Directions, 1970.

———. *Selected Poems*. New York: New Directions, 1957.

———, ed. *Active Anthology*. London: Faber and Faber, 1933.

———, trans. *Ta Hio: The Great Learning*. Seattle: University of Washington Book Store, 1928.

Silliman, Ron. *The Age of Huts*. New York: Segue Foundation, 1986.

Watten, Barrett. *Progress*. New York: Segue Foundation, 1985.

Whitman, Walter. "Crossing Brooklyn Ferry." In *Leaves of Grass*, ed. Sculley Bradley and Harold W. Blodgett, 159–65. New York: Norton, 1973.

Williams, William Carlos. *The Autobiography of William Carlos Williams*. New York: New Directions, 1967.

———. *The Collected Poems of William Carlos Williams*. Vol. 1, 1909–1939, ed. A. Walton Litz and Christopher J. MacGowan. New York: New Directions, 1986.

———. *Imaginations*. Ed. Webster Schott. New York: New Directions, 1970.

———. "A New Line Is a New Measure." *New Quarterly of Poetry* 2, no. 2 (Winter 1947–48): 8–16.

———. *Paterson*. Ed. Christopher MacGowan. New York: New Directions, 1992.

———. Review of *An "Objectivists" Anthology*, ed. Louis Zukofsky. *Symposium* 4, no. 1 (Jan. 1933): 114–17.

———. *Selected Essays*. New York: Random House, 1954.

———. *Selected Letters*. Ed. John C. Thirwall. New York: McDowell, 1957.

Yeats, William Butler. "Leda and the Swan." In *W. B. Yeats: Selected Poetry*, ed. Timothy Webb, 149–50. New York: Penguin, 1991.

———. *A Vision*. New York: Macmillan, 1956.

Zukofsky, Celia, comp. *American Friends*. New York: C. Z. Publications, 1979.

Zukofsky, Louis. *"A"*. Berkeley and Los Angeles: University of California Press, 1978.

——. *"A" 1–12*. Kyoto: Origin Press, 1959.

——. "American Poetry 1920–1930." *Symposium* 2, no. 1 (Jan. 1931): 60–84.

——. *Autobiography*. New York: Grossman, 1970.

——. *Bottom: on Shakespeare*. Berkeley and Los Angeles: University of California Press, 1987.

——. *Collected Fiction*. Elmwood Park, Ill.: Dalkey Archives Press, 1990.

——. *Complete Short Poetry*. Baltimore: Johns Hopkins University Press, 1991.

——. "Henry Adams: A Criticism in Autobiography." *Hound & Horn* 4, no. 1 (Oct.–Dec. 1930): 46–70.

——. "Preface." *Exile* 3 (1927): 8.

——. "Program 'Objectivists' 1931." *Poetry: A Magazine of Verse* 37, no. 5 (Feb. 1931): 268–72.

——. *Prepositions*. Berkeley and Los Angeles: University of California Press, 1981.

——, ed. "Notes and Books Received." *Poetry: A Magazine of Verse* 37, no. 5 (Feb. 1931): 294–96.

——, ed. *An "Objectivists" Anthology*. Bar, France, and New York: Le Beausset, 1932.

——, ed. *Poetry: A Magazine of Verse* 37, no. 5 (Feb. 1931).

Zukofsky Collection. Harry Ransom Humanities Research Center. University of Texas, Austin.

Secondary Works

Ackroyd, Peter. *T. S. Eliot: A Life*. New York: Simon and Schuster, 1984.

Ahearn, Barry. "The Adams Connection." *Paideuma* 7, no. 3 (Winter 1978): 479–93.

——. "Origins of 'A': Zukofsky's Material for Collage." *ELH* 45, no. 1 (Spring 1978): 152–76.

——. "Two Conversations with Celia Zukofsky." *Sagetrieb* 2, no. 1 (Spring 1983): 113–31.

——. *Zukofsky's "A": An Introduction*. Berkeley and Los Angeles: University of California Press, 1983.

——, ed. *Pound/Zukofsky: Selected Letters of Ezra Pound and Louis Zukofsky*. New York: New Directions, 1987.

Aiken, Conrad. "An Anatomy of Melancholy." In *T. S. Eliot: The Man and His Work*, ed. Allen Tate, 194. New York: Delacorte, 1966.

Allen, Donald M., ed. *The New American Poetry.* New York: Grove, 1960.

Altieri, Charles. *Enlarging the Temple.* Lewisburg, Penn.: Bucknell University Press, 1979.

———. "From Symbolist Thought to Immanence: The Ground of Postmodern American Poetics." *Boundary* 2, no. 1 (Spring 1973): 605–41.

———. "The Objectivist Tradition." *Chicago Review* 30, no. 3 (Winter 1979): 5–22.

Barthes, Roland. *S/Z.* Trans. R. Miller. New York: Hill and Wang, 1974.

———. *Writing Degree Zero.* New York: Hill and Wang, 1968.

Bernstein, Michael André. *The Tale of the Tribe: Ezra Pound and the Modern Verse Epic.* Princeton: Princeton University Press, 1980.

———, ed. *William Carlos Williams.* New York, New Haven, and Philadelphia: Chelsea House, 1986.

Bernstein, Michael André, and Burton Hatlen. "Interview with Robert Duncan." *Sagetrieb* 4, nos. 2–3 (Fall–Winter 1985): 87–135.

Bogardus, Ralph F., and Fred Hobson, eds. *Literature at the Barricades.* University: University of Alabama Press, 1982.

Bornstein, George, ed. *Ezra Pound: Among the Poets.* Chicago: University of Chicago Press, 1985.

Burke, Kenneth. "Heaven's First Law." *Dial* 72 (Feb. 1922): 197–200.

Chace, William. *The Political Identities of Ezra Pound and T. S. Eliot.* Stanford: Stanford University Press, 1973.

Diggory, Terence. *William Carlos Williams and the Ethics of Painting.* Princeton: Princeton University Press, 1991.

Dijkstra, Bram. *The Hieroglyphics of a New Speech: Cubism, Stieglitz, and the Early Poetry of William Carlos Williams.* Princeton: Princeton University Press, 1969.

Ellman, Richard, and Charles Feidelson, eds. *The Modern Tradition.* New York: Oxford, 1965.

Finkelstein, Norman. *The Utopian Moment in Contemporary American Poetry.* London and Toronto: Associated University Presses, 1988.

Fish, Stanley. *Is There a Text in This Class?* Cambridge: Harvard University Press, 1980.

Frank, Joseph. *The Widening Gyre.* New Brunswick: Rutgers University Press, 1963.

Fredman, Stephen. *Poet's Prose: The Crisis in American Verse.* Cambridge: Cambridge University Press, 1983.

Géfin, Laszlo. *Ideogram: History of a Poetic Method.* Austin: University of Texas Press, 1982.

Gilonis, Harry, ed. *Louis Zukofsky, or whoever someone else thought he was: a collection of responses to the work of Louis Zukofsky.* Twickenham and Wakefield, Eng.: North and South, 1988.

Golding, Alan. "The 'Community of Elements' in Wallace Stevens and Louis Zukofsky." In *Wallace Stevens: Poetics of Modernism,* ed. Albert Gelpi, 121–40. Cambridge: Cambridge University Press, 1985.

Graff, Gerald. "American Criticism Left and Right." In *Ideology and Classic American Literature,* ed. Sacvan Bercovitch and Myra Jehlen, 91–121. Cambridge: Cambridge University Press, 1986.

Grenier, Robert. "Notes on Coolidge, Objective, Zukofsky, Romanticism, and &." *Stations* no. 5 (Winter 1978): 16.

Hartley, George. *Textual Politics and the Language Poets.* Bloomington: Indiana University Press, 1989.

Hatlen, Burton. "Art and/as Labor: Some Dialectical Patterns in 'A'-1 through 'A'-10." *Contemporary Literature* 25, no. 2 (Summer 1984): 205–34.

———. "Zukofsky, Wittgenstein, and the Poetics of Absence." *Sagetrieb* 1, no. 1 (Spring 1982): 63–93.

Heller, Michael. *Conviction's Net of Branches: Essays on the Objectivist Poets and Poetry.* Carbondale: Southern Illinois University Press, 1985.

Homberger, Eric. *American Writers and Radical Politics, 1900–39.* London: Macmillan, 1986.

Hutcheon, Linda. *The Politics of Postmodernism.* London and New York: Routledge, 1989.

Kazin, Alfred. *On Native Grounds: An Interpretation of Modern American Prose Literature.* 2d ed. 1942. Rpt. New York and London: Harcourt, 1970.

Kenner, Hugh. *A Homemade World: The American Modernist Writers.* New York: William Morrow, 1975.

———. *The Pound Era.* Berkeley and Los Angeles: University of California Press, 1971.

Klein, Marcus. *Foreigners: The Making of American Literature 1900–1940.* Chicago: University of Chicago Press, 1981.

Korn, Marianne, ed. *Ezra Pound and History.* Orono, Maine: National Poetry Foundation, 1985.

Leggott, Michele J. *Reading Zukofsky's* 80 Flowers. Baltimore: Johns Hopkins University Press, 1989.

Lucas, F. L. Review of *The Waste Land,* by T. S. Eliot. *New Statesman,* 3 Nov. 1923, 116.

McGann, Jerome J. "Contemporary Poetry, Alternate Routes." *Critical Inquiry* 13 (Spring 1987): 624–47.

Matthiessen, F. O. *The Achievement of T. S. Eliot.* New York: Oxford University Press, 1958.

Mellers, Wilfrid. *Bach and the Dance of God.* New York: Oxford University Press, 1981.

Miller, J. Hillis. "Introduction to William Carlos Williams." In *Issues in Contemporary Literary Criticism,* ed. Gregory T. Polletta, 128–40. Boston: Little, Brown, 1973.

———. *The Linguistic Moment: From Wordsworth to Stevens.* Princeton: Princeton University Press, 1985.

———. *Poets of Reality: Six Twentieth-Century Writers.* Cambridge: Harvard University Press, 1965.

Mottram, Eric. "1924–1951: Politics and Form in Zukofsky." *MAPS* 5 (1973): 76–103.

Nelson, Cary. *Repression and Recovery: Modern American Poetry and the Politics of Cultural Memory 1910–1945.* Madison: University of Wisconsin Press, 1989.

Nicholls, Peter. *Ezra Pound, Politics, Economics and Writing: A Study of The Cantos.* London: Macmillan, 1984.

Norman, Charles. *Ezra Pound.* New York: Funk and Wagnalls, 1969.

Oliphant, Dave, and Thomas Zigal, eds. *WCW & Others.* Austin: Harry Ransom Humanities Research Center, University of Texas, 1985.

Pearce, Roy Harvey. *The Continuity of American Poetry.* Princeton: Princeton University Press, 1961.

Peirce, Charles Sanders. "How to Make Our Ideas Clear." In *The Enduring Questions,* ed. Melvin Rader, 98–110. New York: Holt, 1969.

Perkins, David. *A History of Modern Poetry: Modernism and After.* Cambridge: Belknap Press, Harvard University Press, 1987.

Perloff, Marjorie. *The Poetics of Indeterminacy: Rimbaud to Cage.* Princeton: Princeton University Press, 1981.

———. *Postmodern Genres.* Norman: University of Oklahoma Press, 1989.

Quartermain, Peter. " 'Only is order othered. Nought is nulled': *Finnegans Wake* and Middle and Late Zukofsky." *ELH* 54 (Winter 1987): 957–78.

Rabaté, Jean-Michel. *Language, Sexuality, and Ideology in Ezra Pound's Cantos.* Albany: State University of New York Press, 1986.

Riddel, Joseph. *The Inverted Bell: Modernism and the Counterpoetics of William Carlos Williams.* Baton Rouge: Louisiana State University Press, 1974.

Said, Edward W. *Beginnings: Intention and Method.* New York: Basic, 1975.

———. *The World, the Text, and the Critic.* Cambridge: Harvard University Press, 1983.

Schelb, Edward. "The Exaction of Song: Louis Zukofsky and the Ideology of Form." *Contemporary Literature* 31, no. 3 (Fall 1990): 335–53.

Sharp, Thomas F. " 'Objectivists' 1929–1934: A Critical History of the Work and Association of Louis Zukofsky, William Carlos Williams, Charles Reznikoff, Carl Rakosi, Ezra Pound, George Oppen." Diss. Stanford University, 1982.

Tashjian, Dickran. *William Carlos Williams and the American Scene, 1920–1940*. Berkeley and Los Angeles: University of California Press, 1978.

Terrell, Carroll F. *Louis Zukofsky: Man and Poet*. Orono, Maine: National Poetry Foundation, 1979.

Tomas, John. "Portrait of the Artist as a Young Jew: Zukofsky's *Poem Beginning 'The'* in Context." *Sagetrieb* 9, nos. 1–2 (Spring–Fall 1990): 43–64.

Whitaker, Thomas R. *William Carlos Williams*. New York: Twayne, 1968.

Whittemore, Reed. *William Carlos Williams: Poet from Jersey*. Boston: Houghton Mifflin, 1975.

Williams, Raymond. *Marxism and Literature*. 1977. Rpt. Oxford and New York: Oxford University Press, 1989.

Witemeyer, Hugh. *The Poetry of Ezra Pound: Forms and Renewal 1908–1920*. Berkeley and Los Angeles: University of California Press, 1969.

Wylie, Elinor. Review of *The Waste Land*, by T. S. Eliot. *Literary Review*, 20 Jan. 1923, 396.

Index

Compositor: Keystone Typesetting, Inc.
Text: 10/13 Sabon
Display: Sabon
Printer and Binder: Thomson-Shore, Inc.